Realizing Peace

An Introduction to Peace Studies

Realizing Peace

An Introduction to Peace Studies

THOMAS KEEFE • RON E. ROBERTS

Iowa State University Press / Ames

THOMAS KEEFE is Professor, Department of Social Work, University of Northern Iowa, Cedar Falls.
RON E. ROBERTS is Professor, Department of Sociology and Anthropology, University of Northern Iowa, Cedar Falls.

©1991 Iowa State University Press, Ames, Iowa 50010

Manufactured in the United States of America
⊛ This book is printed on acid-free paper.

First edition, 1991

International Standard Book Number: 0-8138-1562-2

Library of Congress Cataloging-in-Publication Data

Keefe, Thomas
    Realizing peace: an introduction to peace studies / Thomas Keefe, Ron E. Roberts. —
1st ed.
        p.   cm.
    Includes bibliographical references and index.
    ISBN 0-8138-1562-2
    1. Peace—Study and teaching. I. Roberts, Ron E. II. Title.
JX1904.5.K44 1991
303.6'6—dc20   90-25720

This book is dedicated to all children

and to Dr. Alvin Sunseri for his devotion

to realizing peace in their world.

Contents

Preface

The study of peace is an old and honorable endeavor. It does not, however, have as long a history as the execution of war. In modern times the study of peace is at once a fascinating investigation of the nature of human society and a necessary component of human survival.

Peace is the dream of humanity. But this leads us immediately to ask just what we mean by this pleasant notion. The first step in a scientific approach is to define our terms so we may establish a common sense of what we are discussing (in other words, a common universe of discourse). Chapter 1 will show the common and the not so common social science concepts that guide our studies through the topics of war and peace. Parts I and II stress the philosophical and scientific aspects of the problem. They provide us with the tools to understand the nuances of our behavior involved in peaceful or destructive choices in human history. Part III provides beginning peacemaking skills for many situations. The concluding chapter examines the technical and social trends that affect prospects for peace.

Our textbook on peace is not a call to action or activism (although we would like to believe that our readers will have the good sense and the sensibilities to act in their own interests). Rather, we have created a format for thinking about the nature of peace and its alter ego, war. If this were a religious book, we might call it a "meditation" on peace, which would mean a long and serious study of the nature of war and peace. We agree with Hannah Arendt when she tells us: "Thinking is the urgent work of a species that has responsibility for its survival" (Arendt 1970, 279).

One of the most difficult tasks in writing a book such as this one is that the logic of war and peace issues makes us wish to turn to more cheerful topics. The reality here is that conventional wars have the very real possibility of becoming nuclear holocausts, and they in turn carry the possibility of ending life on planet Earth. Some college students in the 1960s were conscious of this when they said, "our work is guided by the sense that we may be the last generation in the experiment with living." The possibilities in that statement are always lurking somewhere close to the surface of our minds.

Because those thoughts are so devastating, it is tempting to put them out of your mind completely. While that may be a satisfactory psychological trick, it does nothing to solve the larger and less immediate problem of how to prevent mass human destruction in warfare. It is primarily an act of faith that we have time to solve the problem and live our lives "as if" we were not going to be destroyed in some unplanned nuclear spasm (or "wargasm" as one wit labeled it). Writing about "Realizing Peace" requires planning and years of work and, in that sense it too, is an "act of faith". We believe that the possibility of nuclear war is not yet inevitable. There is time to learn and to change the violent course of human history, but our time is limited and there is much to learn and do.

This book proposes that we maintain an optimism of the will combined with a pessimism of the intellect—another way of saying that a turn toward the better needs a full look at the worst. We will not ignore the ruthless and self-destructive tendencies evident in human affairs. One example of why this attitude is necessary can be found in the 1984 Amnesty International organization report entitled *Torture in the Eighties*. This research documents what many people suspect, namely, that many governments of all political persuasions torture and maim political prisoners. It is without doubt a thoroughly unpleasant book to read. Yet the knowledge contained in this report has enabled people from all over the world to express their active outrage at the mistreatment of men and women in the world's prisons. Amnesty International has literally thousands of success stories involving the release of torture victims after government officials have been deluged with bad publicity. All this reinforces our point that the first step in solving the problem of human violence is a clear understanding of its extent and cause.

How do we get such an understanding? We have many tools already at hand for such work. The first tool, and one of the most powerful to use, is science. Science is neutral. It can be used to build new weapons to kill great masses of people or it can be used to find cures for diseases that have plagued humanity for centuries. The logic involved is the same.

The physical sciences gain new evidence about how warfare has unintended consequences. Recent computer models developed to predict weather have come to startling conclusions about the consequences of nuclear war including the concept of nuclear winter. They also provide real hope for improving the lot of humankind in such areas as artificial intelligence and biotechnology.

Advances in the study of the chemistry of the brain give us clues as to what happens to the brain when a person acts aggressively. Psychologists continue to provide insights on how violence is learned. Anthropologists compare peaceful societies with their warlike neighbors and ask why the differences persist between people. Sociologists examine modern military bureaucracies and their functions. Political scientists analyze the decisions-making tendencies in government leaders that promote either war or peace. Economists look at the effects of military spending on the marketplace and on employment. Social work policy analysts examine the effect of social policies on the general welfare. Linguists help us to understand how words are used to shape our consciousness about war and peace.

Of course, the scientific study of war and peace is not the only way we can approach an understanding of the issues. Philosophy helps clarify the relationship between human freedom and war and peace studies. Only history can show what Barbara Tuchman calls *The Pursuit of Folly* (1984), relating the plunges humanity sometimes takes into senseless bouts of warfare.

We also know that it would be impossible to study warfare and the making of peace without considering the religious dimension of the human condition. Religious values have paved the way to both holy wars and absolute pacifism. We ignore this side of human beings at our own peril.

These then are the tools at hand for the study of war and peace and we will draw from them constantly.

When we come across the complex definitions of peace and the many variations of those definitions, we choose to define the concept in a simple way. We ask the question, "How much can we simplify the concept of peace while maintaining its meaning?" In scientific studies when we ask such a question, we come up with what is called a *primitive term*—a simplification of reality that cannot be broken down further and make sense. Our primitive term for peace is *nondestructive human interaction*—as simple a definition as we can devise.

Having simplified the concept of peace in this way, we must listen to the warning of the philosopher Alfred North Whitehead who advises us to "simplify everything and to distrust our simplifications." What does he mean by this? Only that it is important to simplify concepts so that we can discuss them rationally. If one person believes that peace is an inner feeling and the other sees it as social justice, they can have no meaningful dialogue.

Hidden in simple concepts are complex relationships. If we say that peace is nondestructive human interaction, we must first ask the question "What does it mean to be nondestructive"? Does it mean an end to violence, oppression, and war? It is clear that shooting a person in the head is destructive in a powerful way. What does it mean to vote against food aid for the poor? Are there ways to destroy people that are not physical? Is it destructive to dominate another person? The implications are clear. The same question could be applied to "human interaction." What does it mean to be human? Is watching television real "interaction?" Thus we distrust our simplifications.

In Part I we will examine psychosocial elements and issues. Part II draws on societal and historical realities to enrich our perspective and analyzes the complexities in the concept of peace and its mirror concept, war. Part III surveys attitudes and skills that bring the practice of peace into the reality of our personal lives. Finally, we will provide in Chapter 15 a synopsis of technology, change, and prospects. We close our Introduction by quoting the Welsh writer, Gwyn Thomas (1976), who combines the pessimism of the intellect and the optimism of the will that guide our text.

> Life has been and still is in a state of fever. The germs of fear, greed, frustration, still burn in its blood. The fever will pass. The body will grow cool. The mind will become normal and will address itself to the task of living with the affectionate brotherly humility which we expect from ourselves. Always think of mankind, as one body, with limbs that move jerkily, ridiculously now, but to be treated with the same love and patience as you would give to a crippled person of your near acquaintance. . . . if it falls, never snarl at it for clumsiness. Smile at it, lift it to its feet, tell it its legs are getting stronger, its directions surer.

Acknowledgments

We wish to thank Pat Woelber for her cheerful and willing typing and proofing of the manuscript through its various stages and Vinnie Faherty whose administrative acumen provided encouragement for this work.

Part I

Psychosocial Perspectives

In Part I we examine psychosocial perspectives and issues. Chapter 1 begins with a caution to remain objective concerning our hopes for peace and to base our actions on reality rather than on overly optimistic assumptions. In Chapter 2 we plunge into the complex issues and evidence about the nature of aggression and, by extension, the nature of humankind. Part of what is seen as natural in humankind is the product of our psychosocial dynamics, which we take up along with the necessary examination of the origins of antipathy in Chapter 3 and competition and cooperation in Chapter 4. Finally, in the last two chapters we will examine the deformities of language and communication as they affect the affairs of individuals and nations.

Chapter 1

Is There Intelligent Hope on the Planet?

Resignation and Hope. There is an apocryphal story of a ship floundering about at sea that makes radio contact with another ship. "Are you in trouble?" radios the second ship to the first. "Situation hopeless but not desperate," replies the second vessel. In a strange way this story reveals a psychological reality about human beings. It is this. Being completely without hope can be a comfort because it requires no struggle. If nothing can be done to remedy the situation you need only wait for the inevitable.

The word for this attitude is *resignation*. Entire philosophical traditions rest on the ideal of resignation. Stoicism is one of the traditions stressing this approach to life. "What will be, will be" expresses this concept in many languages and cultures.

"Resignation is of two sorts, one rooted in despair, the other in unconquerable hope," says Bertrand Russell (1930, 236). When a person is defeated in some personal or political struggle, there is always the option of giving up and giving in to despair. When this happens individuals sometimes become passive and useless to other people. We tend to look up to individuals who transcend defeat because in a large sense they symbolize the hope a community needs to survive. Whether they be peacemakers or warmongers they stimulate others to follow their path and, in doing so, they energize the entire society. They are the heroes and heroines of myth and story. The greater the hardship they have overcome, the greater the honor given them.

The Ancient Greek Homer's immortal poem, *The Odyssey,* records the home voyage of Ulysses from Troy. Ulysses overcomes horrific monsters, natural catastrophe, and magic to return to his home a hero. Many writings from different cultures praise the heroic journey of an individual who overcomes the temptation to despair and defeat. Most of these tales, of course, stress distinctly unpeaceful activities. Nevertheless, the heroic warrior and peacemaker have this in common: They both overcome great obstacles to their work, and in doing so they transform their own despair into an abiding hope.

As Eric Fromm explains: "The cure of despair is not achieved by encouraging thoughts, not even by feeling part of the despair; it is overcome only if it has been fully experienced" (1966, 164). This means we can only become hopeful after we have taken a full look at the worst that could happen to humanity. When we consider *all* the possible scenarios for the end of life on Earth through nuclear war, the effect is to focus the mind wonderfully on the terrors of a nuclear holocaust. It is at this point that we earn the "right" to hope because we have taken the problem seriously. We have focused on evil possibilities to give ourselves the possibilities of finding a solution.

Having peered at the nightmare of the end of life on the planet, we can take two different paths to confront that possibility. First, there is the comfortable resignation of disengagement, which goes something like "What if they do drop the bomb, that will be the end of it. The human experiment just didn't work. Other species have come and gone, perhaps it is our turn to become extinct." This may be comforting; what is not comforting is the idea that such a passive attitude may encourage nuclear war by producing a "self-fulfilling prophecy." If we accept something as inevitable or natural, we may hasten its happening. If, for example, a couple marries with the attitude that all marriages fail or go stale eventually, their expectations work toward that end. Is it not possible that this works to some degree in world history as well? This should give some discomfort to the comfortably resigned.

Still, if we take seriously Eric Fromm's idea that despair can breed hope as well as passivity, we understand that is because total despair helps us to focus on the importance of the problem. To use an analogue, the program of Alcoholics Anonymous stresses that people can achieve sobriety only after confessing that they as individuals are helpless to change their drinking problems. That is simply another way of saying people can only be helped when they have reached the abyss of despair. Then it is possible to focus on the problem and with the aid of others and "a higher power," a solution to the drinking problem may be reached.

If we return to Bertrand Russell's concept of resignation, we remember that it may come out of despair or out of "unconquerable hope." This latter category refers to the tranquility an individual may feel with the attitude that ultimately everything will come out all right in the world. "Hope which is unconquerable must be large and impersonal" (1930, 236). What Russell means here is that personal failure and ultimately death are inevitable. Yet when we connect our hope to the fate of large human endeavors, we may be sure that we leave people to carry on the struggle. For example, a scientist finds that he or she must end the search for knowledge due to old age or poor health. If that scientist's work is not simply a function of personal aggrandizement or egoism, the scientist will take comfort in the idea that the work will continue. Scientific progress does not usually stop when the career of one scientist ends.

As a case in point, Lord Russell himself was participating in antinuclear bomb rallies in his mideighties. It was eminently clear that he was not working to prolong his own life. Russell had connected to something larger than his own impressive biography— the future of humankind.

Varieties of Bad Faith and Misplaced Hope. If hope and
hopelessness are matched against each other, most people (including your authors) will opt for the former. This is especially true in issues of war and peace. It seems likely that many people are apprehensive about hoping for too much in these sorts of contests because it is so easy to be discouraged. Having said that, however, it is still true that hope springs eternal in the human mind and heart. The question we must ask at this point is: "What sort of hope are we

promoting?" False hopes do exist. Misplaced hopes may comfort the individual for a time—perhaps a long time. Yet in the long term they do not advance the cause of peace or human justice. The better part of wisdom is to draw up a set of rules for evaluating hope and ways to decide if it is based on reality. If hope is to be useful to human survival, it must be intelligent and not simply based on a kind of mindless need for security.

"Thinkology." Our first rule for guiding intelligent hope is that *we should place little faith in solutions to human problems that exclude scientific knowledge.* It is not necessary that our hope for peace be based exclusively on scientific evidence. Indeed, that would be impossible. What is important is to embrace a hope that does not contradict or contravene scientific knowledge.

Here is an example of what we mean. Teachers of transcendental meditation claim many benefits for their techniques for individual meditators. Among these attributes are rest and relaxation (Wallace 1970). About this there is no significant dispute. However, supporters of this technique take their claims significantly beyond individual relaxation. They claim the ability to levitate via meditation and, more to our interests, the ability to establish world peace simply by increasing the number of meditators around the world.

The advocates of this idea claim that 1 percent of a population (or less if the population is large) can bring about peace in an area simply by meditation. Blurring their mystical notions with science, they refer to this technique as "a unified field of pure consciousness." Aron and Aron (1986), two advocates of the technique, quote a multitude of highly selected statistics to show that the social well-being of a city, the nation, or even the world increase by the number of meditators meditating. The required number seems to fluctuate as do the statistical proofs they use as evidence of their effectiveness.

In one study cited by the authors, meditators in Rhode Island (representing .04 percent of the population) are said to have caused the following changes in the summer of 1978: lower suicide rates for the summer, lower homicide rates, a decrease in divorce rates, and so forth. Since the authors do not give a complete data base for comparing their statistics throughout the years, social scientists are necessarily skeptical of their claims.

Also from time to time they seem to stretch the data to fit their conclusions. "There was an increase in reported rapes," the authors tell us, "However, interviews with personnel at rape counseling centers indicated that they thought the incidence was actually down. . . ." (Aron and Aron, 63). Further, we learn that cigarette sales were up in August and down in July in the state. Ozone pollution was down in the summer as well. Does this mean anything at all? Only that you can use random statistics to "prove" anything. James Randi (1982, 101) has shown that automobile fatalities went up 18 percent in Iowa two years after a colony of transcendental meditators were established there. Nevertheless, the transcendental meditators consider pure meditation as the means by which their "world peace project" will be effected.

The scientific approach accepts the idea that we must change our consciousness or way of thinking to prevent conflicts, violence, and war. What this means is that we change our way of thinking about problems leading to changes in our behavior toward each other and toward nature. We can follow the consequences of such changes through a scientific approach.

Transcendental meditation and other mystical forms of hope short-circuit this connection by eliminating human activity. In this form of thought—"thinkology"—mere thinking can change the physical universe without any "visible means of support." Somehow collective thinking changes even the level of ozone about a city. This is not scientific thought; rather, it is a magical prescientific form of thinking. Yet it obviously appeals to many people. How can this be?

"Thinkology" as a solution to problems of war and peace holds two psychologically attractive aspects for believers. First, it requires no activity on the part of the believer. Shirley MacLaine's best-seller *It's All in the Playing* (1987) involves a form of what we call "thinkology" to an incredible extreme. Ultimately she concludes that everything that happens comes from individual thought. The idea that only my consciousness determines reality is called *solipsism*. It leads to the conclusion that all victims of war, violence, and disease bring down misfortune upon their own heads. This totally excludes our knowledge of causality in the physical world and puts victims of rape, bombing, or other human-made disaster on a moral plane with those who have injured them.

The second attraction of *mystical or pseudoscience solutions* is that the future is guaranteed. Failure is impossible. Again, this is a very attractive sort of hope. The reality, however, is that we live in a world of possibilities and probabilities. When a life-threatening disease occurs we see a physician and we ask the ultimate question, "Will I live?" The physician speaks only in terms of odds or probabilities. That is not very satisfying and explains why some desperate people seek out mystics, quacks, or pseudoscientists who guarantee "wellness." The threat of war is a life-threatening "illness" as well, and it is no accident that many of us seek solutions with guarantees about issues of peace and war.

More Mystical Mythology About Peace. In a charming book on nuclear disarmament entitled *The Hundredth Monkey* (1982), Ken Keyes describes a curious phenomenon. It seems that in the late 1950s monkeys (Macaques) on several Japanese islands learned to wash in the ocean the sweet potatoes and wheat that had been given to them. Monkeys taught each other to do the washing and before long the practice spread to the surrounding islands. Keyes's book makes these modest points about this happening: (1) we learn from each other, and (2) we all can make a difference in learning from each other about peace. These are points few people could take issue with.

Lyle Watson does go much further than this in his book *Lifetide* (1979, 127), which leaps to the conclusion that at some point in the process of monkeys' teaching and learning from each other a quantum leap occurred with the addition of the hundredth or thereabouts monkey learning the technique. "[It] apparently carried the number across some sort of threshold, pushing it through a kind of critical mass because by that evening everyone was doing it. Not only that, but the habit seems to have jumped natural barriers and to have appeared spontaneously like glycerine crystals in sealed laboratory jars in colonies on other islands."

Ron Amundson (1985) has criticized Watson's mystical concept of a sort of group mind among the monkeys. Amundson shows that there was no great breaking point with regard to the monkeys learning. Furthermore, he points out that monkeys on different islands could have learned to wash their food independently. It is also true that monkeys were known to swim from one island to another. So, another alleged miracle thereby slips away. The idea that "you may be the hundredth monkey whose contribution to collective consciousness saves the world from holocaust" is attractive, but it has no firm basis in reality.

This should teach us that hope based on inflated claims and miracles is not well founded, even when we hope for something as just and good as world peace. Mystical forms of hope often dissuade us from looking at the structural causes of war. These factors include our own psychology, the material interests of groups in a society, the polarization of those groups, arms races, and failures of diplomacy.

"Technofix" and Human Hope.

In a sense, faith in technology seems to be the direct opposite of faith in mystical or pseudoscientific nostrums. That is true, but only in a sense. In some ways we worship technology with the same reverence that our ancestors worshiped wood spirits. Technology *does* seem magical. Often, we have no idea how it works. It simply does. The technological sophistication of our twentieth century life-style is amazing and to some, awe inspiring.

The question that follows this is simply How can technology lead us from war to peace? Can it do this at all? How much faith should we put in it?

Sometimes we speak of finding "the magic bullet" that will destroy a variety of cancer cells. This reminds us, too, of the attempts by our medieval ancestors to turn lead into gold through the magic of alchemy. If we find a cure for cancer, it will rightly be seen as magical.

It is, however, important to put limits on our expectations that technology will solve human problems, especially those of war and peace. One reason for stressing those limitations is technology's inability by itself to solve human problems that involve relationships between human beings. Moreover, technological solutions cannot solve problems rooted in our psychological makeup. For example, during the nineteenth century many Americans, especially women, used various patent medicine "cures" to solve health problems as well as those relating to loneliness and anxiety. Many of these medicines contained a tincture of opium as their base, and addiction to that form of opium became very frequent indeed.

Dr. Bayer, who invented aspirin, came up with a cure for opium addiction. It was called heroin (Drayer 1977). Heroin addiction has since become commonplace and a chemical "cure" for it was developed during World War II. The cure, methadone, was a synthetic drug that parallels the effects of heroin. The addict is now addicted to methadone. There are certain beneficial effects to being addicted to a legal rather than illegal drug. For one thing, it reduces the crime rate (Ray 1983). Having said that, we must admit that the addict is still addicted.

This is the essence of the technofix solution. Technology seems to be the answer to our problems. Yet in a different form, the problems remain. In this sense the addiction to opium, heroin, and methadone parallel the arms race. Each new weapons system is seen as a cure for the previous one.

Another example of the technofix in action has to do with food shortages around the world. Technological breakthroughs have created seeds of corn, wheat, and rice that have the potential to produce more grain than native varieties of the plants. With these new seeds a "technological euphoria" gripped many in the scientific community. Hunger could be cured by the new strains of seeds. Yet worldwide hunger has not ended. The new strains required irrigation, fertilizer, storage, and other costly inputs. This meant that the poorest farmers in the world could not use the new grains to their advantage. Wealthier farmers who had no hunger problems in the first place were able to plant the new varieties of seed and were able to increase their profits. As we know, hunger was not eliminated by the technofix efforts of the green revolution (Harrington 1977, 163).

Our last example of the technofix solution concerns the arms race itself. Hope for the technofix solution to world peace was articulated in its purest and most naive form by Alfred Nobel (1833–1896), the Swedish industrialist and inventor of dynamite, who claimed: "My dynamite will sooner lead to peace than a thousand world conventions. As soon as men will find that in one instant whole armies can be utterly destroyed, they will surely abide by golden peace" (Evlanoff 1943, 29).

In our own time the extension of the arms race to space seems to run on now-familiar arguments for the technofix. In 1983 President

Ronald Reagan called on the scientific community "who gave us nuclear weapons, to turn their great talent now to the cause of mankind and world peace, to give us the means of rendering these nuclear weapons impotent and obsolete" (*New York Times* March 23, 1983). Since that time, several realities have emerged about his Strategic Defense Initiative (SDI). First, it could not be used to defend the population of the United States; it is designed to retaliate against nuclear attack. Second, parts of the program could be used for offensive as well as defensive purposes. Finally, the Excaliber X-ray laser, part of the SDI program, would actually involve putting nuclear weapons in space (Herken 1987).

While we argue that the technofix hope leads to dangerous misunderstandings, we do not see technological creation as useless or without application. *Technology does play an important role in achieving peace, but it does this only when combined with changes in social relationships.* That is true for solving problems of drug addiction and world hunger as well. More often than not, new technologies are created simply for profit or to increase the domination of one group over another. As with drugs, technology cannot solve the problem of addiction. With the establishment of trust and cooperation, technology can solve many problems. Without these factors it seems that we must run as fast as possible to stay in place.

When the World Health Organization decided to eliminate smallpox from the earth, several ideas fell into place. A vaccine against the disease had been developed, which was the first vaccine successfully used by science. A massive program of inoculation was developed that eventually required the cooperation of every nation on earth. Resources were gathered and an organized attack on the disease was launched. By the early 1970s the disease, as far as anyone could tell, had been practically exterminated. This remains a remarkable example of intelligent hope acted upon in an intelligent way.

Toward Healthful Hope. Hope keeps us going. It may be an evolutionary force in humankind promoting the survival of the species when times get difficult as they are wont to do. Misplaced hope leads us away from solutions that could save our human skins.

Hopefulness about issues of war and peace is especially useful in getting us out of our self-imposed mess of increasing violence and war. It becomes necessary that our hopes about peace are based on reason and reality rather than our own simple psychological needs.

Intelligent hope about the establishment of peace must recognize that wars in the twentieth century have been the most numerous, bloody, and deadly in human history. That knowledge is a source of despair; yet oddly enough, it is the starting point to intelligent hope. "In a dark time, the eye begins to see," said the poet Theodore Roethke (1966, 23). Despair can cause us to focus merely on the problem at hand if we do not choose to accept it as inevitable.

It appears that the hope for peace cannot be based on quick and easy solutions. In this, the cause of peace, seems to be like other worthwhile causes in our lives. It takes work, not magic. We may be wrong in the tactics we choose and furthermore we may fail in our efforts.

Still, we see fragments of success in peacemaking throughout human history. As we learn more about the psychology and sociology of conflict, we can devise new and better informed tactics in our work toward peace. We cannot put our hope into the technology of magic or the magic of technology. The most healthful approach involves changing our ways of thinking as we attempt to restructure the social relations causing hatred rather than love to dominate our communities and our planet.

In Chapter 2 we examine bases for intelligent hope. Namely, we will survey the findings and theories of the biological and behavioral sciences that elucidate our understanding of aggression and violence—fundamental concerns in the study of peace.

Chapter 2

Aggression, Violence, and Empathy

To study and nurture peace we must uncover the roots of its disruption. Ironically, aggression and violence may help to maintain certain temporary conditions of peace, yet they are seldom defined as peaceful. What exactly is aggression? Does aggression among animals and human individuals spring from the same sources? Is collective violence related to these forms of aggression? Those concerned with peace must eventually grapple with these and related questions.

A variety of answers to these questions will be proposed. First, however, we need to address some of the problems of defining aggression and violence. Next, we will survey the prevailing theoretical perspectives on aggression, followed by a model of human aggression that is intended to bring some clarity to the understanding of peace and its disruption. Finally, the importance and positive role of empathy as an antidote to human aggression and violence will be discussed.

What Are Aggression and Violence? Violence and aggression are paradoxical. They are simple to recognize, yet they are enormously complex. We know when we experience or see aggression or violence but actually defining them is not so easy. Even scholarly and insightful discussions of aggression and violence sometimes do not attempt to define these concepts in a formal way (Goldstein 1986).

Here are two simple and standard definitions of our terms. *"Aggression* is the initiation of hostile action" (Webster's 1984). *"Violence* is physical force employed so as to damage or injure" (Webster's 1984). Given these definitions, violence might well be seen as a subcategory of aggression—aggression with physical force. Much of the ensuing analysis will focus primarily on the larger concept of aggression in its many forms.

"The initiation of hostile action," like "doing good" or "committing a sin," requires judgment from a particular perspective. A few questions will illustrate this point. On what do we base the notion of aggression? The harmful effects on the victim? Would this include physical damage, psychological damage, or inconvenience? Does the initiator have to be experiencing anger or physiological arousal? Is a fish or bird defending its territory hostile and therefore aggressive? Do we call the snarling vigorous encounter between two wolves in a struggle for dominance aggression and the ritual display of feathers and colors among other species for the same purpose something else? Are the ends of the behavior important in defining aggression while the means are something separate? Do we consider whether or not the aggressive human being intends to do harm? Does this mean that animals or severely retarded, injured, or unknowing individuals who do the same things are not to be considered violent? Finally, is it still aggression when the victim requests or seeks punishment?

The answers depend upon understanding the perspective of those defining the aggression. Some clarity can be achieved if we examine the perspectives of those who have studied aggressive and aggressivelike behavior. Their insights depend upon the level of analysis at which they are examining the phenomena, that is, the size of the system studied. Small or microsystems are individuals or small groups. Large or macrosystems are organizations, populations, or political entities. We will look first, very briefly, at aggression in small systems.

Microsystem Perspectives. Is human aggression—the initiation of hostile action—learned or innate? This question is central to the debate among exponents of a variety of perspectives on aggression. Beneath the social conditioning of our societies and cultures, do we have inborn predispositions to aggression and violence that propel our aggressive social behaviors?

Certainly other species have instinctual behaviors that include aggression. The applicability of these patterns to human beings is still largely in question. There are those who would see in these findings some of the basic sources of human aggression (Lorenz 1966; Morris 1967; Wilson 1975). Others would see such patterns as effaced or overridden by human learning, social modeling, or socialization (Bandura 1973; Goldstein 1986). But aside from the issue of our ability to generalize from these findings on human aggression, they should be examined for what they can tell us about aggression and violence in and of themselves. We should examine, too, the origins of human aggression. We will attempt to discern whether they are rooted in the genes or in the social milieu of which each human psyche is a part. What follows then is an examination of microsystem perspectives that would strip away—artificially— the influence of human social life and bare the possible primitive components of violence and aggression.

Lessons of Ethology. Ethology is the scientific study of animal behavior in its natural setting. One of the foremost students and popularizers of the field is Konrad Lorenz. Lorenz (1966) provided particular understandings about aggression from ethology studies. He saw aggression as occurring only between members of the same species. The function of such aggression is to gain for each individual sufficient space and food for its survival.

VARIETIES OF AGGRESSION. Ethologists have identified a variety of aggressivelike behaviors. These behaviors help to gain or preserve territory, play a role in mating, or help to generate and maintain dominance. Such behaviors facilitate survival of a species as they help insure a food supply, insure the selection of the stronger or more fit individuals, or help to order feeding behaviors. Less common is aggressive behavior of a member of one species toward a member of another. Maternal aggression in defense of offspring and extreme pain induced aggression (Gleitman 1981) are examples.

Predatory behavior seems to derive from different genetic or neurological bases than other interspecies aggressions. Observers of wolves and other predators note that hunting and bringing down prey is not accompanied by the usual angry signals that would accompany altercations with their own species (Lorenz 1966). Instead, the predator is responding to hunger and the predatory behavior some have observed has many aspects of play—for the hunter, of course.

FIXED-ACTION PATTERNS. The various patterns of behavior that could be seen as aggressive among subhuman species depend upon environmental cues for their release (Tinbergin 1952). Tinbergin (1951, 1952) observed that the concept "instinct" is insufficient to describe the complex behavioral patterns elicited by environmental cues from organisms in a state of readiness. *Fixed-action pattern* is another term that implies genetic control of complex behaviors.

Yet despite their complexity, these animal instincts and fixed-action patterns seem insufficient to explain all animal aggressive behavior and most human aggression. Other factors must play a part. Indeed, such factors have been identified by ethologists and others studying aggression with an eye toward developing comprehensive theories to explain it.

Basic Motivation and Learning Theories of Aggression. First among these theories is the famous *frustration-aggression hypothesis* (Dollard et al. 1939; Miller 1941). This view simply stated, is that aggression is one product of frustration. When an organism is blocked in its pursuit of a goal, it experiences frustration. Frustration can increase physiological arousal and elicit a variety of behaviors including increased motion, vocalization, and aggression.

The hypothesis does not answer questions as to whether aggression is innate or learned in human beings. Obviously, humans can learn to be aggressive or nonaggressive in particular frustrating situations. The originators of the hypothesis saw the possibility for innate aggressive responses to frustration in humans, yet our capacity to learn responses that mask others does not permit clear support for this possibility.

EXCITATION TRANSFER. In the complexity of human aggression such factors as what we have learned, what causes us to become aroused, and how we interpret both the situation and our arousal come into the picture. These factors are components of what is called the *excitation-transfer theory* of aggression (Zillmann 1979). When an organism is excited, the excitation can be transferred to another situation and help to elicit aggressive behavior. Hence we see fans at a soccer game, excited by the game, as more predisposed to fights than they would be when in a more relaxed setting. But what of the influence of the crowd? By now we see that the question of human aggression becomes more nettlesome as we consider its social components.

SOCIAL LEARNING OR MODELING BEHAVIOR. Primates, including humans, learn much of what they do through observational learning or *social modeling* (see review by Dueax and Wrightman 1984). An aggressive adult serves as a model for children who observe him or her. They may copy the aggressive behavior in later life when in a similar situation. Modeling behavior can be very intricate. It may be the primary means for learning the concrete behavioral manifestations of attitudes, norms, and values of the society or identity groups within society. We can extend the potential for modeling aggressive behavior over a wide range from interpersonal violence to the mimicking of drill instructors by soldiers as they progress up the ranks or move to the battlefield. Yet as ubiquitous as modeling behavior is, it too has its limitations as a universal explanation of aggressive behavior in humans.

Freudian Theory of Human Aggression. For Sigmund Freud the concept *identification* was similar to the later concept of modeling behavior (Freud 1920). In order to deal with primitive fears and hostilities the young children were seen by Freud as identifying with the like-sexed parent and incorporating aspects of the parent's personality into their own developing personality. But the process was seen by Freud as part of the human effort to contain and control an innate potential and drive for aggression. Freud saw the mature adult ego as needing to defend itself against the primitive instinctual urges of the species that lurks in each of us. Freud was theorizing before the development of ethology and its findings about the positive selective value of aggression and fixed-action patterns of behavior in other species. Freud saw a death instinct, *Thanatos,* as an extension of the disorderly forces of the universe that propelled toward randomness and chaos. Thanatos was the energy source of human aggression.

DEATH INSTINCT. In this view, it becomes the task of the *ego,* the conscious thinking and acting part of the personality, to defend itself by repression, suppression, sublimation, and other means against the encroachment of Thanatos that could burst forth as hostility and aggression. Each individual has therefore the potential for violence. And the innate energy of Thanatos must find its expression that is to be discharged in socially acceptable ways or it will be discharged in socially destructive ways. Humans beings, by extension, have the potential for mass violence—the ultimate manifestation of which is warfare (Freud 1920, 1975).

In the Freudian system then, the individual must learn control and ways of directing or channeling the aggression instinct—as well as the life instinct, *Eros*—that lies at the core of each individual psyche. This control is learned in part by children from adults *modeling* (identifying and incorporating) socially appropriate ways of dealing with situations that have potential for releasing aggression.

In a society in which authoritarian family structures predominate, the population may be predisposed to follow and obey the dictates of an authoritarian patriarch. His call to aggression or warfare would be heeded as an appropriate outlet for aggression. The objects of his animosity would become the targets of his followers. Freud's theories have been challenged by later thinkers who attempted to understand the psychological causes of Hitler's and of Germany's actions leading to World War II.

Neo-Freudians and the Demise of the Death Instinct. Freud's ideas have been applied in many ways since his death. One group of theorists based in Frankfort, Germany, escaped to the United States during World War II. Several of these prominent scholars attempted to account for the horrifying results of Nazism in Germany by combining Freud's ideas with an analysis of capitalism.

Theodore Adorno, one of the Frankfort scholars, saw the uncontrolled changes in capitalism as undercutting the traditional role of the father in the patriarchical family. The father was the all-powerful figure in society, but with the rise of capitalism the patriarchical structure of the family changed drastically. "The actual weakness of the father within society, which indicates the shrinkage of competition and free enterprise extends to the cells of the psychic household; the child can no longer identify with the father. . . ." (Adorno et al. 1972, 141). When the male figure can no longer get a sense of identity from the patriarchal father, he is drawn to totalitarian political figures such as Hitler. The results of this warped identification process are, of course, destructive and tragic.

Freud has been revived in other ways as well. Theorists such as Wilhelm Reich (Edwards 1967), Eric Fromm (1955), and Alfred Adler (1969) took a radically different view of humankind from Freud, despite drawing upon many of his ideas. This powerful critique asserts that there is no dark Thanatos, at least not at the core of each personality. Instead, human beings are either innately social, nurturing, and loving, or at worst a neutral blank slate upon which society inscribes what the individual is to become. This notion is a more benevolent view of the species and is an idea of central importance to the study of the psychosocial sources of peace and war.

If the core of the personality is a naturally loving, social being or at least a neutral potentiality, then from where does aggression and ultimately mass aggression arise? The general answer of the neo-Freudians is that society through familial and mass conditioning, regimentation, sexual and economic oppression, and exploitation frustrates the natural loving, social self of most individuals. The results of this frustration, especially sexual frustration, is a neurotic and conflicted personality which is predisposed to aggression. This predisposition is manipulated into competition and into individual and collective violence. Manipulating these conditions, the despot identifies certain people or kinds of people as the source of economic and social unrest. He then suggests war as a means of regaining self-respect or proving sexual potency or "true" masculinity.

Instead of each individual having a "fortress ego," which defends
civilization against the aggressions of Thanatos as Freud envisioned,
each individual is first frustrated in his or her natural loving, social,
and sexual pursuits and is then misled into collective violence. The
postulation of this basic deceit, then, finds the source of human
aggression in the social environment that frustrates and perverts
the natural personality. What is important here is the social
environment, not our supposed instincts shaping our consciousness.

SURPLUS REPRESSION. From the perspective of the Freudian
critics, the central mechanism in social conditioning of the individual
psyche is *repression*. Freud discovered that conscious recall of early
childhood psychological trauma in his patients was blocked and
became accessible only through extraordinary routes such as dream
interpretation, hypnosis, or free association (1920). This blocking
out of memories of early trauma and the associated feelings of lust,
anger, and fear seemed to protect the adult ego, allowing it to
continue to function with attention to daily coping. For Freud the
blocked or repressed memories seemed to center around universal
themes of sexuality. Every person was seen to have some repression
operating in his or her personality. The critical view extends this
analysis by seeing the dominant economic conditions of society as
generating repression in people beyond what is needed to hold
society together. This is *surplus repression* (Marcuse 1955).

Surplus repression results from the demands placed upon workers
in an economy that must continually expand. The demand for profits
in capitalist economies—or for increasing quotas in state run
economies—extracts a toll on the workers' psychic life. Industrial,
service, and clerical wage workers are increasingly regimented.
Their jobs are routinized for efficiency of production. Longer hours,
less socializing in the workplace, use of only a small portion of each
worker's mental talents and physical abilities, hazardous working
conditions, and a general lack of worker control over the nature or
destiny of the product generate a work environment that requires
individual repression of sexual, social, and creative aspects of their
selves. This surplus repression has its consequences.

Needs not met in the workplace in the long hours of work must
be met in off hours. The individual who must be disciplined and
repressed during work hours must then be able to shift gears and

become suddenly sociable, perform openly and spontaneously in sexual relationships, and uncover creative talents during the period of rest and recuperation. In economies dominated by transnational corporations and in mixed, competitive economies, it is important that significant portions of the work force also consume the products of their labor.

The mass media encourages consumption through advertising. The advertising often pairs products with symbols representing or eliciting responses tied to basic needs, such as sex or belonging. Needs frustrated in the workplace are thereby exploited in the interest of consumption.

These contradictory social messages, "Be disciplined and repressed at work; be self-indulgent in consumption," create difficulties in people's lives. Surplus repression becomes a magnified frustration. To the extent that aggression is tied to frustration, the potential for individual and mass aggression is amplified. Hence, in the view of the critical Freudians, surplus repression generates a reservoir of frustration from which interpersonal violence and mass warfare draw some sustenance. The person split in two by societal demands and psychological needs that are not met may become a recruit for a message of scapegoating and hatred.

Stress-coping Paradigm. Physiologists and students of both animal and human behavior have contributed to a large, growing contemporary body of research and theory that can be called the *stress-coping paradigm*. Some of the major aspects of this paradigm contribute to our understanding of human aggression, particularly interpersonal violence.

GENERAL ADAPTATION SYNDROME. The foundation of the stress-coping view is the work of Selye (1956/1978). Selye postulated that commonly occurring responses to disease were the effects of stress. Some endocrine changes in animals occurred across many diseases and could be induced by artificially subjecting animals to stressful situations. He called this response the *general adaptation syndrome*. This initial insight was extended by the work of Cannon (1953) who helped to identify the role of endocrine and neurological systems in the stress response. Selye and Cannon's contributions helped to map the territory between perception of a stressful event and the physical response.

COGNITIVE APPRAISAL. Mason (1971) has demonstrated that cognitive processes shape the endocrine responses to stress. Later, Lazarus (1977) pointed to the role of individual appraisal of stimuli in determining its stressfulness and the individual's response. In essence, stress occurs when the demands of a situation exceed the person's previous adaptation. When stressed, the individual usually experiences physiological arousal that prepares the body to fight or to flee. Through endocrine and neurological pathways, the brain stimulates those bodily processes useful to fighting or running. It suppresses those bodily processes that are not useful to fighting or fleeing. In the modern social world fighting and fleeing are usually not appropriate or adequate responses to situations that the individual appraises as stressful. Consequently, the individual must substitute more complex, cognitively directed behaviors than those the body is preparing to provide.

Stressful situations may vary from mild intermittent annoyances to acute and severe life events such as death of a loved one or divorce. The individual's appraisal of the stressor, his or her level of arousal, and his or her coping repertoire will determine the coping response.

In this paradigm, interpersonal violence is but one coping response among many. The human individual is seen in this view as having the physiological readiness for violence but also as having the capacity to respond with a wide variety of other responses that may or may not draw upon the body's preparations. In light of this idea then, *interpersonal violence* is an attempt to cope with a stressful situation. Whether this coping option is "successful" from the stressed individual's perspective may well determine its possibility of being chosen again. Whether violence is the "best" choice becomes a matter of social consequences, social mores, and law.

The existential philosopher and therapist, Rolo May (1972), observed, "Violence arises not out of superfluity of power but out of powerlessness." When an individual has no coping responses but violence in a stressful situation he or she is in a position of relative powerlessness. He or she has few choices. *Empowerment* consists of providing the individual with other coping options such as more information, permission to leave the scene and not loose face, a capacity to assert personal views, or more financial resources.

SOCIAL SUPPORT. One form of empowerment is *social support*. As identified in the stress-coping paradigm, social support has both subjective and objective aspects. Subjectively, it is the feeling of belonging to a group of people who hold you in esteem (Caplan 1979). Objectively, it is the provision of resources and information. Both subjective and objective aspects help a person who is in a stressful situation seek effective alternatives to violence as a method of coping.

Because individuals usually cope through their relationships with others, social support is a very important factor in maintaining one's composure or sanity. Those persons to whom we feel close are often the ones who will provide us with ideas, emotional support, information, resources, and assistance in coping. In stressful times, persons who see themselves as lacking social support tend to have more health problems than persons who perceive themselves as being supported (Gore 1978).

Support networks can also perpetuate violent means of coping. Some subcultures sanction corporal punishment of children and wives. Military social conditioning helps soldiers accept violence during war. But more often social support networks help people find responses that effectively substitute for violence. Within these networks people often see nonviolent responses modeled. When they choose nonviolent options, they may be praised or sense approval. Formal support groups for abusing parents or spouses can provide options and emotional support similar to that provided by natural networks.

We can summarize the stress-coping view of human aggression as follows:

1. Stress is a condition in which perceived demands exceed previous adaptation.
2. Violence is usually one coping response elicited by stress among many options.
3. Violence may be repeated when it in some way reduces the situational discomfort.
4. Nonviolent behaviors that cope with the stressful situation and relieve discomfort can be substituted to prevent or

eliminate interpersonal violence.

5. Social support networks provide models, resources, and
    rewards for a much wider variety of responses than would be
    available to an individual coping alone. Many of these
    options are likely to be nonviolent.

Several of the ideas from the stress-coping paradigm are relevant
to understanding human aggression. They, together with social
identity, also help to elucidate particular forms of interpersonal
violence.

Social Perspectives on Interpersonal Aggression. Family
violence, sexual aggression, rape, mugging, and homicide each
have a multiplicity of causes.

Deindividuation and Dehumanization. Stanley Milgram's famous
studies on authority disclosed that subjects will cause apparent
pain in other human beings when under the influence and behest of
authority figures (1974). In these classic studies and in other
experiments, the degree of social closeness to the other (e.g., seeing
their face as opposed to their face being covered, etc.) was also
discovered to be a factor in the willingness to inflict pain or to be
aggressive against another person (Milgram 1964). The process of
deindividuation, or removing the self as a possible source of evaluation
in aggressive actions (Zimbardo 1970), can apply to the aggressor,
e.g., "I won't be seen or judged," or to the victim, "That is an
anonymous entity, not a person I know." Such a process seems to
hold for interpersonal aggression and to be similar to the manipulative
propaganda that encourages a dehumanized perception of the enemy
during war.

Role Socialization. Stereotypes are perpetuated through role models
in families, in mass media, and in other forms of socialization.
Stereotypic role models can include expectations of aggressive

responses and attitudes in a variety of situations. For example, some subcultures encourage the use of violent punishment for children or violent control of spouses. Persons who experience violence as children are more likely to favor violence as a means of achieving their goals as adults (Owens and Straus 1975). In addition, logic suggests that when other means of coping with a situation are not available, those socialized to behave aggressively are more likely to do so.

Goldstein (1986) has suggested that the occurrence of violence is a product of long-term and situational factors tending to elicit aggression or nonaggression. Long-term factors include *socialization* and *social norms* and *locations* such as a bar versus a church. Situational factors fostering aggressive behavior would include *alcohol, emotional arousal, presence of a weapon,* and *anonymity.* Situational factors eliciting nonaggression might include the *presence of a police officer, strong sense of self,* or *presence of a parent* (Goldstein 1986). While the intensity of these factors may be arguable and may vary from person to person, they illustrate the complex and social nature of human aggression.

Differential Social Dispersion of Aggressive Behavior. Different cultures, subcultures, and social classes have different degrees of violence. For example, families living below the poverty line have a greater incidence of spouse abuse than families with higher income (Straus et al. 1980).

We hold that social factors play a dominant role in human aggression. This role must be sufficiently dominant to override genetically determined patterns if they are present in human beings. Otherwise there would not be this *differential social dispersion*—as we would call it—of aggressive behavior.

If aggressive behavior toward other members of the species were a firmly fixed instinct or *fixed-action pattern,* we would expect incidents of interpersonal and group violence to be more uniformly dispersed across cultures, subcultures, social classes, and income levels. Yet much of the aggression that does occur has elements in common with the forms identified by ethologists and motivational theorists. What this may suggest is that the presence of inborn patterns of aggressive behavior together with our physical configuration may impart the potential for aggressive violence toward others. How then can we integrate the variety of microsystem perspectives on human aggression? Before we take up the subjects of collective violence and war, we propose a simple model.

Model of Human Interpersonal Aggression. There are four major parts to our model of violent interpersonal aggression. Each is a necessary but not sufficient cause of aggression.

1. *Potential.* We postulate the presence of potential and capacity to behave aggressively. This is not an energizing instinct or inborn universal force but rather the simple neurological, endocrine, and musculoskeletal system that allows frustration, arousal, and aggression to occur when environmental conditions elicit them.
2. *Model.* A role or identity model for aggressive behavior must be present that has been observed or described in sufficient detail to allow copying. This may come from observation of parents, visual media, training instructors, and elsewhere.
3. *Cues.* There are two types of cues that may permit aggressive violence.
    Internal Cues. The individual's particular sensation of bodily arousal (such as increased heart rate, increased respiration) or pain associated with past or expected aggressive behavior. Each individual has unique areas and levels of awareness of bodily cues.
    External cues. The means, weapons, and target for aggression must be present. This may be mediated by social status and dominance factors.
4. *Context.* A sufficient degree of stress must be present in an interpersonal situation. Simultaneously, an absence of coping responses other than aggression would impel the person toward violence.

We do not see the "intent" of the violent person or that of victim as a part of the model. We believe that if other factors are held constant, individuals can learn nonaggressive or passive responses to replace the aggressive responses if the new responses cope with the situation effectively. Consequently we have rejected some of the theories we have reviewed that rely upon instinct theory for humans and genetic explanations that may work for some species but may not work for human beings.

Seville Statement. In 1986 a group of social, behavioral, and natural scientists gathered in Seville, Spain, to discuss the scientific evidence for aggression as an innate part of human nature. Among other positions, the conferees asserted that it is scientifically *incorrect* to maintain that there is an inherited tendency to make war, that human evolution has selected aggressive behavior more than cooperative behavior, that humans have a "violent brain," and that war is caused by instinct or other single motivation. They concluded that violence is neither in our evolutionary legacy nor in our genes and that the species inventing war is capable of inventing peace (Kohn 1988). The *Seville Statement* is a refutation of the widely held view of the biological inevitability of aggression in human experience. It is a statement of considerable importance that can help the world begin to look for the sources of individual and collective violence, including war, in the social environment and the political and economic arenas.

Our model of aggression does not address collective violence. Much of human aggression occurs not as a result of an individual acting alone in an interpersonal situation with one or two others, but as a result of collective behavior. We see the myriad forms of collective violence as having roots in the variables identified thus far but having wholly different factors as major determinants.

Collective Violence. The traditional cowboy movie in which the wily sheriff defuses the lynch mob in front of the jail by calling out the names of individuals in the crowd and shaming them for their behavior is not without its element of real-life truth. The deindividuation and identity with the group in a crowd may help to account for violent behavior of crowds which no particular individual acting alone (and detectably) would commit. The level of arousal, elevated temperatures, and widespread dissatisfaction with the calls of a referee no doubt contribute to the violence of sports audiences. Furthermore, no one individual takes responsibility for his or her violent acts.

If we add the ingredients of racial hatred, threats to economic and social status, the dehumanization of the victims, the anonymity of costume, or the cover of night, we have some of the conditions for organized mass violence.

Violence Not Seen as Such. Perhaps more curious and even more massively destructive and enduring is the "violence which is not seen as such." This refers to violence borne of bureaucratic functionalism or oppressive social policy. Here a violent act toward an individual or group is set aside as necessary social control. It does, after all, keep the victim in his or her place.

The violence toward other species and ecocide usually involves attitudes of dominance and exploitation coupled with greed or shortsighted bureaucratic procedure. From the near extinction of the American bison to the stripping of the Amazon jungles, our aggression toward other species and their habitats is usually viewed only by ecological-minded individuals as violence.

MASS MURDER. The systematic enslavement and extermination of members of our own species has rested heavily on similar factors of intentional oppression. Such oppression is initiated through political and social policy. Often it is tolerated by a fearful and obedient majority. It is usually carried out through mindless bureaucratic functioning by many individuals who perform only one small operation in the system.

The most telling historical example was the systematic extermination of Jewish and other peoples by the Nazis and their functionaries. One individual informs his or her neighbors, another rounds them up, another loads them on trains, another assigns work or death, yet another makes the lethal gas, and another sorts clothes or guards a concentration camp. Each individual in the vast network that carries out the homicide of fellow human beings is only responsible for his or her small function. Someone else at the top is responsible for the policy. The person at the top, of course, may be mad.

These factors in collective violence may seem remote from our current perspective. We might examine the design, manufacture, and dispersion of delivery systems for nuclear warheads. Most individuals in American and Soviet societies are aware from a very young age of the danger and potential for mass extinction from the nuclear arms race (Escalona 1982; Schwebel 1982; Yudkin 1984). Thousands of people who would dread and fear a nuclear war nevertheless participate in the manufacture of the bombs and their delivery systems in well-paid, technically demanding jobs. Participation in this potential holocaust is rationalized by individual financial need, belief in the necessity of the weapons for deterrence (a point passed long ago), and a trust in a succession of leaders at the top not to use the weapons by reason of madness or accident.

SOCIAL AND ECONOMIC DEPRIVATION. Another form of "violence not seen as such" is the deprivation of the necessities of life for sectors of the population of the country (or the world). Adequate income or means of sustenance to meet common human needs are often denied people through their oppression or exploitation in the economic or political interest of a ruling or dominant class. Examples of deprivation and oppression include slavery, forced labor, economic oppression, and homelessness. The retaliation or organized violence of a victimized group or class against an oppressing or exploiting government or elite is seen by some as a unique form of violence morally separate from the initial violence perpetrated upon them (Sorel 1908).

Empathy: An Antidote to Aggressive Violence. It is clear
that both interpersonal and collective violence derive from a variety of causes. The perceptual, emotional, cognitive, and social factors that make up situations of aggressive violence are also components of other behaviors, even skills, that we learn and use each day. Clearly it would be too simple to propose that there is but one alternative to aggression. Yet one common human skill seems conspicuously absent in the presence of most aggressive violence. That skill is empathy.

Empathy is the sensing of another's feelings and social role or situation based upon what you see in the situation and in your communications about the experience of yourself. This sensing and accurate communication of the experience to another are behaviors that can be perfected and taken together are a skill. Nearly all people must develop some empathy skill in order to function with others. Moreover, there is evidence that persons with high levels of empathy skill have more profound physiological responses to other individuals' plights, suggesting a higher level of emotional response as a component of their empathy (Gellen 1970). Aggression seems to occur when good development of these cognitive and emotional aspects of empathy are not present or fail.

Would we strike another person if we perceived that their injury and terror were as strong as our rage? Would we tolerate political policies and governments that create the economic conditions of homelessness if we fully sensed the fear, discomfort, dejection, and hopelessness of homeless people we see? These are not simply academic questions. We will explore empathy in more detail in Chapter 13.

Compassion. Of course, empathy with others who suffer may cause us pain. We may then avoid the suffering as a way of avoiding pain. More often empathy causes us to act in a way to reduce the suffering of other people. We may decide on the basis of imaginatively putting ourselves in other peoples' positions, that no one should have to endure what they are enduring. This may cause us to desist from our aggression toward them. Or this may cause us to act to reduce the violence being done to them by others or by impersonal social forces. When we recognize the separateness of another person, yet sense and understand them as another expression of consciousness and human experience like ourselves, empathy becomes compassion. *Compassion* is a mode of life, a value that guides action both day to day and in extreme situations.

Compassion or even highly developed empathy would generally be dysfunctional to violent organized or institutional processes. Dehumanization of a potential or actual enemy is often part of the process of preparing people to engage in violence. Rigid authoritarian or totalitarian bureaucracy, military training and indoctrination, political propaganda, and ethnic and racial stereotyping strip away potential empathy individuals may have with the targets of planned or ongoing institutionalized violence. This is accomplished by endowing the victims with nefarious qualities or less than human, moral, intellectual, or physical capacities and motives. This is also accomplished by strong expectations of aggressive actions as a condition for identity with or successful membership in the aggressing institution or group. We can see that attempts to destroy empathy are preludes to aggressive violence.

Empathy by itself may be insufficient to overcome the directions of authority, the deindividuation of a crowd or bureaucracy, or the situational distance from victims of violence. In situations similar to the Milgram studies, institutionalized mass violence and war, a strong sense of self, independent identity, and strong personal values may be necessary to act empathetically rather than aggressively. In addition, as we will see (Part III, Skills for the Practice of Peace), empathy is a skill that can be imparted. Empathy can facilitate effective and constructive alternatives to violent and aggressive coping.

Some individuals and groups have resisted participation in the ultimate mass violence—war—on the basis of religious or personal conviction that includes elements of compassion. But empathy and compassion may well be insufficient by themselves to prevent war because it arises from many forces and enlists many values and feelings. War is a special case of aggressive violence. We will briefly examine war, its causes, and social and historical trends affecting its occurrence later. But first, we will examine the genesis of attitudes of affinity and anticipation that underlie human relations including war.

Chapter 3

The Psychology of Antipathy and Solidarity

It may not always be appropriate to look to human emotions for the sources of war and peace. As we shall point out later, war often happens due to random events or accidents. It is just as likely to take place due to failed political strategies or diplomatic errors.

Nevertheless an understanding of why we feel hatred or antipathy toward our fellow humans goes a long way to understanding why wars are supported and justified by the masses of the earth's population. On the other hand, it is important to appreciate those factors in our makeup that cause us to show sympathy, affection, and other bonds with people we may or may not know.

Emotional Textures. Any human emotion serves some sort of need for self-preservation. For example, fear of strangers, heights, wild animals, and the like keeps our guard up against being careless around danger. When fear becomes something other than that moment of protective self-consciousness, it can produce human misery as well as a way of avoiding it. This happens when fear becomes a way of life or a project in a person's life. When fear dominates an individual, we can call it an *aversion*. Individuals who have experienced fear through personal experience of a rather dramatic sort may hold on to such fears in ways that injure others as well as themselves. A woman who has been the victim of sexual abuse by a male friend or relative has a justifiable reason for fearing male members of the species. Her wariness could save her the pain of being in a situation where she would be attacked again. As a victim of another person's rage against women, a woman would likely maintain some element of anxiety about men throughout her life. However, if this fear becomes a lifelong aversion to men, the victim becomes victimized yet again, this time by her own fears, for she will be constantly calculating her behavior to avoid men—all men.

The roots of most of our fears are reasonable. Victims of oppression in Eastern Europe may fear communism with good reason. Some Eastern European emigrés have spent their entire lives in anticommunist endeavors. This aversion to communism can lead to unfortunate consequences when it becomes an obsession. Some "professional" anticommunists use all manner of undemocratic and unsavory means to rid the world of their focus of fear. In many parts of the world, this means forming an alliance with a right-wing or fascist version of anticommunism. Nazism in the 1930s was in part an aversion to communism.

We know that many blacks growing up in America have developed an aversion to white people through racist actions and attitudes they have experienced. Retreating from oppression is understandable. However, it does not promote understanding. When fear dominates human relationships, the subtleties of our interaction fade; we see each other not as individuals but as part of a large and simplified category. A white person becomes more a *white* than a person in this situation. In the history of slavery and later racism in America, many laws and customs were designed to negate the personality and individuality of blacks. Various stories, jokes, and news items ridiculed them and endowed the black image with a terrible simplicity, reinforcing the view that *"they are all alike."* These attitudes perpetuated the "Sambo" image with its inference of white supremacy and black inferiority.

Well into the 1960s many Southern states had on their books "Jim Crow" laws prohibiting the mingling of black and white on a social basis. The purpose of these laws was to promote white supremacy as well as racial aversion. That is exactly what they did. It was difficult if not impossible for whites and blacks to feel comfortable with each other in a social situation. A mutual aversion had been created between whites and blacks. Yet the aversion was never complete because white society needed black labor and services, and blacks needed the employment whites could provide. Whites needed blacks but were taught to fear and despise them. Those contradictory feelings and relationships shaped racial conflicts in the United States for many years.

Anger. Anger is a distinctly unpeaceful feeling. Flashes of anger often end in violent activities such as murder. Yet anger, like fear, is useful to human beings as they attempt to survive all of life's problems and dangers. Anger is a way of promoting self-preservation. It most often appears when individual goals are blocked or when the self-image of the person is threatened.

Anger is also related to issues of control. We must not forget that fear is often the underside of anger. Males and sometimes females are able to get their way in situations by threatening, "Now don't make me mad, I can't be responsible for my behavior." Often anger works in controlling others if it is put forth by a dominant individual. Among children we call this "bullying." Among nations it has been called "gunboat diplomacy," "power politics," and the like.

What is odd about this emotional and physical expression is that anger can be turned inward toward oneself. When we express anger towards ourselves, we tacitly admit that we as individuals have split personalities. This insight is very important because if your consciousness or personality is split, you may be at war with yourself. That, of course, is another nonpeaceful feeling.

How does anger work when you are at war with yourself? It may work like this. In a classic study of anti-Semitic college girls, Else Frenkel-Brunswik and her partner found that individuals who invested much anger toward Jews expressed both contempt and envy for their supposed sexuality. "An important tendency of the girls high on anti-Semitism is thus to keep one's basic needs repressed, to keep oneself pure and reputable, primitive needs are rendered ego alien and projected onto an alien group" (Frenkel-Brunswik and Sanford 1949, 281).

This process of transferring anger from yourself to another individual or group is called *projection*. It is a method of dealing with your own inadequacies without having much self-insight. Here ignorance of self turns anger toward others. Aristotle may be right that evil in the world is based upon ignorance. We would add that a great deal of energy is used in maintaining our self-deceptions and ignorance.

There are other things we can do with the anger that comes from a split personality. *Displacement* is a possibility. This occurs when we exhibit aggression toward the individual who has the misfortune of being closest to us when we are angry. Yet another dishonest thing we can do with our anger is called *reaction-formation* by Freudians. This happens when we repress motives or ideas that are incompatible with our self-concept or image and then act in a way so that conscious feelings and behavior are in complete opposition to these repressed ideas.

Jules Masserman, a psychiatrist, cites a textbook example of reaction formation in a letter received by a medical researcher. The researcher had been using cats for medical research. Protesting this action, a letter written by a young woman argued that it was inhumane to do the research and put forth these opinions: "I'm glad I am just a human being without letters after my name. I'd rather be just myself with a clear conscience, knowing I had not hurt any living creature, and can sleep without seeing frightened, terrified dying cats. . . . No punishment is too great for you and I hope I live to read about your mangled body and long suffering before you finally die—and I'll laugh loud and long" (Masserman 1961, 38).

Here the humane concern for the well-being of a cat is distorted by tremendous hostility and sadism. The amazing things humans do with anger keeps psychiatrists in business. Unfortunately, both individuals and the populations of great nations fall into these psychological errors.

There is another aspect of anger we must deal with to put it into the nexus of war and peace. Anger is sometimes compared to a storm cloud that appears on the horizon, vents its fury, and moves on. That is sometimes the way it works in humans, but not always. Anger can be made to last a lifetime, and it can be the focus of a person's

existence. If this does happen, anger has become something else—
hatred or *antipathy*.

Hatred requires energy and often the intense focus of a lifetime.
Herman Melville's *Moby Dick* tells the story of a man's obsessive
hatred of the white whale. Captain Ahab's family, friends, and work
are ruined by his forty-year pursuit of Moby Dick. Once in a rare
moment of lucidity Ahab cries out, "All my means are well thought,
it is only my ends are mad" (1851, 549).

Hatred magnifies and maintains that anger over the years. It is
often manifested in family conflicts, racial prejudice, or class conflicts.
Hatred, like fear, can be manipulated to promote the ends of
governments, social classes, or religious groups. It is also true that
hatred amplifies the differences between the hater and the object of
the hatred. What we are saying here is that hatred often contains
strong helpings of self-delusional modes of thought such as projection,
displacement, and reaction formation.

The modern world provides us legions of examples of the
propaganda of hatred. In 1984 the Soviet journal *Military Knowledge*
described the behavior of American troops in battle in this way:

> One can boldly and without exaggerations call these cutthroats in
> the U.S. uniform monsters. And what, in fact, is human in these
> frenzied, teeth-baring physiognomies, in these eyes, the eyes of
> killers and rapists.... They will not be moved by pity on seeing the
> tears of a child, the desperate cry of a dying woman, their hands will
> not falter in killing a defenseless old man.

The language of hatred assures us of several things about our
enemies. They lie, they torture, their behavior is uncivilized, but
most important, *they are not like us*. The bonds of humanity are
severed in hatred-ridden thought. To admit that *they* and *we* share
the same motives in some oblique way is to lessen the power of
hatred.

Fear, Hatred, and War. When we talk about such volatile
emotions as fear or anger, it would seem we are laying the
groundwork for understanding the causes of war. Actually, we are

not. We must realize that many people go to their graves fearing or hating others without acting violently toward them. Also, people often work up a healthy (or unhealthy) hatred for their enemies only after war has begun. Even in the modern world many millions of people are only vaguely aware of the existence of people in foreign lands. This is true even if those foreigners have been defined as enemies of one's own country.

It is not the case that war follows a democratic vote after hatred for the other side reaches a fever pitch. The hatred of one political leader for another has often prompted wars in the past. More relevant to modern situations are motives of leaders such as greed, fear of losing face, geopolitical considerations, or simple miscalculations. Although hatred and fear are the emotional dynamos keeping the population willing to sacrifice blood and treasure, they do not start wars. Nor can they of themselves keep them going. A case in point involves Iraq's leader Saddam Hussein, who in 1980 saw Iran weakened and vulnerable under the leadership of the Ayatollah. Hussein invaded and after eight years of fighting both sides agreed to a United Nations sponsored cease-fire. During that time, 1 million troops and civilians were killed, 1.7 million were wounded, and 1.5 million refugees were created. Surely this was one of the great human tragedies of modern times.

News cameras of the world often focused on crowds of the two nations who were incited to hatred of each other. Each accused the other side of practicing an impure form of Islam. Nevertheless, the eight-year slaughter could not have maintained itself on shouts of heresy alone. Some 16 billion dollars of military aid was sold or given to Iraq. About 9 billion worth of deadly weapons were sold or given to Iran. Iraq was sold weapons by Jordan, Egypt, Poland, Czechoslovakia, and Chile (which sent cluster bombs). Libya, Israel, Syria, and Argentina fortified Iran.

More to the point, the United States, the Soviet Union, China, France, Italy, East Germany, Switzerland, North Korea, and Brazil sold weapons to both sides (Cockburn 1988). The significance of these actions cannot be overstated. What is implied is that the profit motive for both capitalist and communist was a vital reason for the length and viciousness of the war.

This does not mean that we should lose sight of the psychological factors in war making, but only that they are incomplete ways of understanding warfare and its causes. The real reasons for dealing with our fears and anger in a reasonable way is that we have no chance of a satisfying life if we cling to these patterns. Moreover, family life, where we develop many of our emotional problems, cannot be a peaceful association if we do not handle our emotions wisely.

Healthful and Peaceful Psychological Possibilities. Only recently we have begun to think about the psychological factors leading to more a peaceful interpersonal life-style. It is clear that the creation of peaceful ways of life must begin with the family.

The family is the cradle of conflicts and how those conflicts are dealt with at this level is of great importance. Family counselors have learned that family members can improve their relationships by following a fairly simple rule—that is, reward people for what you want them to do. Do not punish them for what they do wrong; reward them for what they do right. "Once partners know these principles, they can reverse the vicious cycle by reinforcing the friendly helpful gestures that they have previously ignored. What this requires is that one partner is willing to make the first move toward reconciliation, to begin to relinquish vengeance and attack, and to start rewarding the other" (Walsh 1984, 61). As we will show later, the ability to recognize and reward positive gestures by others is a skill that can be learned. Insofar as peace is defined as human beings living in harmonious and nonhurtful ways with each other, the idea of rewarding positive exchange between people or nations has considerable merit.

There are personality attributes that positively relate to the harmonious relationships we seek as ideal. Traits such as generosity, tolerance, as well as the ability to perceive and forgive human weakness are surely important to that ideal. Charles Hampden-Turner (1971) has reviewed many studies of tolerant and generous people. He finds, not surprisingly, that individuals showing these qualities tend to have a higher degree of individual self-esteem and security than the general population. How do we develop these qualities? That is a question not easily disposed of by a simple answer, but we repeat that this may involve our early experiences with families.

Uncertainty about one's livelihood, great poverty, chaos, and teenage parentage do not contribute to the self-esteem with which we are concerned. But these factors are characteristic of much of the world's poor today. It is clear the improvement of life among the poor is not only needed for humanitarian reasons, but also for future human connections that promote social harmony.

Irwin Staub (1979) has shown that children tend to exhibit greater altruism when they are given tasks in the family that stress responsibility for the care of brothers, sisters, or pets. Again, as we will show later, empathy toward others is learned. As it turns out, it usually is learned fairly early in a child's development.

A peaceful world not only demands that we produce individuals with a higher level of tolerance and altruism, it requires an entirely different combination of traits as well. This is what Staub calls *critical loyalty,* "the capacity and willingness to express their disagreement with and to work to counteract destructive actions by the groups they are in" (1988). Whenever large-scale acts of human destruction take place, it is because individuals have assented to it. Every war crime in the twentieth century has been justified by individuals who say, "I was just following orders." Saying no to the inhumane demands of your nation or bureaucracy must be seen as a positive virtue. The refusal by individuals in the 1950s and 1960s to participate in racial segregation, civil defense drills for atomic war, or war in Southeast Asia was justified on precisely these moral grounds. This does not imply that saying no is always the morally or strategically correct choice. It is not. Nevertheless, teaching children that it is correct to stand for humane principles means that they will sometimes be required to say no. Saying no to preparation for nuclear annihilation has been called "the great refusal."

There is at least one other psychological skill that is useful in preparing an individual for peaceful activities in life. Elise Boulding (1988) argues that workshops for creating images about peace will motivate and focus the individual on the relationship of peace to their own lives. Boulding argues that imagining a world without nuclear weapons can give individuals the stimulus to work for utopian goals. She has developed techniques to structure the imagination of individuals so they may visualize the possibilities of a world without nuclear weapons.

Thus we come to stress another psychological skill while working for peace—the imagination. This may seem a flimsy concept to apply, and yet it may be that the lack of utopian ideals in the twentieth century is part of the problem. Imagining a utopian society without nuclear weapons may seem farfetched. Indeed the word utopian is often given the definition of a farfetched figment of the imagination. Nevertheless, fragments of utopian thought have been integrated into industrialized societies. Even when utopias fail, they are often useful. Thus utopian thinking is not without justification. It may sound farfetched to dream of a nuclear weapon–free world. Having said that, we must also agree that it must be thought equally improbable to believe the nations of the world can continue manufacturing nuclear weapons at the rate of three to five per day and not end the arms race in nuclear war.

There is at least one other healthy psychological process that has great implications for a more peaceful attitude prevailing in the world. In one sense, it is the very opposite of reaction formation. This is the kind of honesty that comes from *self-criticism*. When self-criticism is honest and unforced, it can become a psychological base for lowering the level of rancor and hatred toward "the other." The most recent example of such self-criticism has been taking place in the Soviet Union while this book is being written. The spirit of openness (*glasnost*) has enabled Soviet citizens to read for the first time detailed information about the repression of the Brezhnev era as well as the massive scale of terrorism practiced by Stalin. The English language *Moscow News* (October 1989) tells us:

> Stalin's terror reached its peak in the 1930s. But it began much earlier at the end of the twenties. In the Shakhty case and the Prompartiza trial the old engineering intelligentsia were blamed for unavoidable failures in the program of forced industrialization.
>
> The next purge hit the peasants. In what amounted to genocide between five and ten million people died during the forced collectivization of farming in the early thirties.

This painful confession could not be pleasant news to the citizens of the Soviet Union. Yet it must have been appreciated because as the newspaper warned, "If you forget the past it can happen again." It takes a fair amount of self-esteem to be self-critical in an honest way, yet it appears to be the only way individuals and nations can profit from mistakes and catastrophes.

Self-awareness, imagination, tolerance, altruism, and critical thinking are also useful processes in the long march toward peaceful relationships. In Chapter 4 we turn from the primarily psychological to the social factors involved in issues of peace and its disruption and examine the forms and consequences of competition and cooperation.

Chapter 4

Competition, Cooperation, and Peace

We have acknowledged earlier that people are not simple captives of biological impulses that push them into aggressive action. This will be evident as we observe different human societies. As we make these observations, it becomes clear that the variation in levels and forms of human aggression are immense. In this chapter we will examine the effects of cooperation and competition on issues of aggression and violence as opposed to social cohesiveness and peace.

Two Social Forms. Margaret Mead was one of the first anthropologists to write about these issues in a systematic way. In her classic *Cooperation and Competition Among Primitive Peoples* (1961), Mead finds certain groups with high degrees of competitiveness, such as the Kwakiutl Indians of the Pacific Northwest. On the other more cooperative side of the ledger we find societies such as the Iroquois, Zuni, and Dakota Indians. It is generally true (with some large exceptions) that people with very primitive technology are forced to be more cooperative to survive (Roberts and Brintnall 1982).

The word "cooperation" came into the English language in the

seventeenth century with the simple meaning of "working together."
The *Oxford Dictionary of English Etymology* (1966, 197) explains
that the term "competition" was not frequently used before the
nineteenth century. It comes from the Latin *competere,* which means
"to strive for something together with another."

Although these social forms have existed side by side in human
society for millennia, it may be no accident that competition is a more
recently constructed word than cooperation. In the nineteenth
century ideas such as competition, the survival of the fittest, and the
like began to be seen as the anchor of industrial society. By way of
contrast, the ancient hunting and gathering peoples of the world
stressed cooperation in food gathering and hunting. Individual
competition was regarded as detrimental to group survival.

Still, the twentieth century seems to be the century of competition
on all levels. In the industrialized world the polite word for competition
is success seeking, the impolite word is greed or selfishness.
Competition pervades economic life, sports, scientific achievement,
sexual pairings, and everything other than individual value. On the
larger scale, nations compete for prestige, economic gain, and military
superiority.

In our discussion of competition, we will always refer as well to
cooperation. They are in a sense paired concepts such as war/peace.
It is impossible to discuss one side of the relationship without
making reference to the other. They are, of course, opposite ways of
settling various human problems.

When we discuss these two social forms we must remember that
we are simplifying a very complex world in our effort to understand
it. In most aspects of our lives, friendship, politics, or whatever
competitive and cooperative relationships are intertwined. Thus
when we discuss these processes we must untangle them from other
social relations.

Reactions to Scarcity. In one sense both cooperation and
competition represent different ways of dealing with a lack of the
good things in life. We call this lack *scarcity.* Scarcity can represent
a lack of physical necessities such as food or it can relate to intangible

things such as prestige, love, or honor.

A classic study relating scarcity to competition was done by the social psychologist Muzafer Sherif (1961), who set up a summer camp called Robbers Cave in the mid-1950s. The twelve-year-old campers were divided up into two groups—the Rattlers and the Eagles. The boys were normal preteenagers and did not know each other before the camp. As the camp began the Rattlers and Eagles competed against each other in football, tug-of-war, and baseball. Prizes were given to the team winners of the day. Moreover, artificial scarcity was injected into the situation when desserts or privileges were denied the losing teams. Sherif had hypothesized that this competitive situation coupled with scarcity would generate aggression by the boys toward each other. Indeed it did. There were food fights, burning of each other's banners, verbal insults, and physical attacks. Sherif's experiment began to get out of hand. He attempted to influence the two groups to break down their mutual antagonism for each other by uniting them in competitions against other camps. This worked only temporarily. Eventually, Sherif was able to end what had become a vicious rivalry by setting up what he called "superordinate goals" for the boys to meet. These involved the cooperation of all the boys in various tasks such as fixing the water system or pulling a truck up a steep hill. Eventually, Sherif did report success in ending their aggressive conflict by structuring and requiring cooperative tasks.

The scenario we have just described was played out in a much more serious and tragic way in the late 1960s in East Africa. Colin Turnbull (1972, 31), an Africanist and anthropologist, has written about the fate of the Ik people in Northwest Kenya. The Ik were driven into the mountains by their government. They had been hunters and gatherers, and like other hunting and gathering tribes in the area they exemplified "those characteristics we find so admirable in man: kindness, generosity, consideration, affection, honesty, hospitality, compassion [and] charity. . . . For the hunter in this tiny, close knit society, these are necessities for survival; without them society would collapse."

For the Ik, collapse is precisely what happened. The mountains into which they were driven were barren of food and water and their few cattle died. They occasionally stole cattle from the Turkana people but were unable to raise any of their own. Their family units had almost completely broken down. Children were pushed out to fend for themselves at the age of three or four. Old people too sick and feeble to protect themselves were attacked and robbed by young boys. Young girls gained food by prostitution with other tribes but became so "aged" by eighteen that they were no longer seen as attractive. The ancient religion of the Ik declined as well.

Colin Turnbull attempted to aid the sick and hungry but often the food he provided was snatched from his hand. Turnbull returned to America from this nightmarish situation viewing our own society in a different light. "Our society," he concluded, "has become increasingly individualistic. We even place a high value on individualism and admire someone who gets 'ahead in the world' tending to ignore the fact that this is usually at the expense of others" (Turnbull 182). Turnbull believes the reduction of human relations to the individual's survival is a sort of mad exaggeration of tendencies in our own society. These are the tendencies toward competition in the extreme. As the Ik continue to destroy themselves, it would appear that they would agree with the prominent sports figure who said: "Winning isn't everything, it's the only thing." This is simply another way of describing the world as the political philosopher Thomas Hobbes did as the *bellum omnium contra omnes* (the war of all against all).

There are ways of understanding this competitive social form and its relationship to war and peace. Morton Deutsch (1985, 85) has studied competition in experimental situations for nearly thirty years. He sums up the findings of many studies with the observation: "In a competitive relationship, one is predisposed to cathect the other negatively, to have a suspicious, hostile, exploitative attitude toward the other, to be psychologically closed to the other, to be aggressive and defensive toward the other . . . to see the other as opposed to oneself and basically different." This aggression Deutsch speaks of is generated by some condition of scarcity and a competitive way of dealing with the problem. In a competitive situation the level of empathy for the competitor is clearly reduced; it must be, to win. Contempt for the other is a sort of by-product of intense rivalry.

In competitive social forms this contempt is often mixed with envy for the winners and a distrust of all other players in the competitive game. In relationships that are not at base competitive such as friendships, the satisfaction and reassurance received from the friend build empathy. While it is true that many friendships may have a competitive element, friendship clearly becomes a different sort of relationship altogether if competition comes to dominate.

Alfie Kohn (1986, 140) reports "A 1968 study of nursery school boys found that those who were less generous in giving away candies also seemed more competitive while playing a racing game with dolls. Conversely . . . high generosity seems to be a part of a pattern which involves less interpersonal competition."

Of course it follows that generosity would emerge from a system that does not promote scarcity. Generosity is a human capacity that flows from a lack of fear. The fear engendered in competitive systems is based on the idea that you may injure yourself by helping others. Actually, in competitive systems where rewards are limited by "doing in" one's opponents, generosity might be seen as a mental aberration.

There is, of course, the possibility of *contractual competition,* or competition in which the participants have agreed to follow formal rules to vie for agreed upon goals or recognition. Many sports and games have these characteristics. Under such conditions individuals or teams may be pressed to maximize their efforts or their skills. The victor and the other participants may also develop mutual respect and a degree of empathy. But this variety of competition takes place in a larger context of cooperation, which is a contract to compete in a limited way. Even here, competition often leaps the boundaries of a "gentleman's game," and the game becomes a more serious conflict.

For some people, working or playing in isolation would be the lesser evil than solving problems through competition. If isolation were an option for nations in competition for scarce resources through war, it would be a fine thing. This policy was an option the United States followed with some notable exceptions during the nineteenth century. Clearly, an isolationist policy became less possible and less likely in the twentieth century.

This brings us yet again to the other aspect of successful problem solving, that of cooperation. There are two ways to sum up the research and thinking about cooperation. The first involves a scientific approach. David and Roger Johnson (1984, 75) have done a rather complete analysis of 98 studies published between 1944 and 1982 which look at cooperation between individuals as well as groups. They explain that "cooperative experiences promote more positive relationships among individuals from different ethnic backgrounds, between handicapped and non-handicapped individuals, and more homogeneous individuals than do alternatives such as: cooperation with intergroup competition, interpersonal competition, and individualistic experiences."

There is a more poetic way of expressing these findings. An old rabbi asks the Lord to show him heaven and hell. They enter a room where a group of people are seated around a large pot of stew. Everyone is frantic with hunger. Each of them has a spoon that reaches the pot but is too long to reach their mouths. The wailing and knashing of teeth was loud and the suffering was horrible. The rabbi asked to leave.

"I will show you heaven now," the Lord replies to the rabbi. Again they enter another room. This time they see a pot of stew, another group of people, and again the same long spoons. Here everyone looks healthy, happy, and well nourished. The rabbi is puzzled. "Why are they happy here when the people were miserable in the other room and everything was the same? I don't understand." The Lord smiles. "Oh," he says, "don't you see? Here they have learned to feed each other" (Crum 1987).

Where We Are Today.

It may be argued that all studies on competition and cooperation are interesting but irrelevant to the world of today. After all, the world we live in is competitive in economics, diplomacy, and of course in the technology of the arms race. That is the way the world is. It will not change simply because we might like it to. Moreover, it is legitimate to ask if we could ever remove competition from our social life even if we liked.

Even if competition brings out the worst in us. It may appear to be asking too much to expunge it from our lives. Bertrand Russell (1964) had an interesting commentary on this problem. He argued that there are two distinctly different sorts of competition in which we can engage. They correspond to impulses basic to human nature. The first he terms the *possessive impulse,* which aims at acquiring private goods that cannot be shared. The second, or the *creative* or *constructive impulses,* by definition, are shared. The creative impulses or competitions would result in scientific discoveries, artistic creativity, or interpersonal skills. In this latter case, an individual enriches the world by sharing his or her creations. It is the possessive competition that is the source of most human conflict.

If one class of people has great wealth they decide not to share with underlings, social conflict is generally on the horizon in some form or other. In contrast, if a person is knowledgeable in a science, that knowledge is not kept from others. "You may kill an artist or thinker," Russell tells us, "but you can not acquire art or his thought. You may put a man to death because he loves his fellow man but you will not by doing so acquire the love which has made his happiness" (1964, 12). Russell concluded that we should put great limitations and strictures on possessive competition and few if any on competition in the creative world. This he felt would lower the general intensity of social conflict in the world.

Of course the competition between nations for military supremacy may end life on our planet. That is the most diabolical form of competition to have ever captured mankind's mode of thinking.

Carl Sagan (1986) and others have argued that competition by the superpowers in the nuclear arms race could be reined in by establishing mutually cooperative ventures such as the exploration of Mars by the United States and the USSR. It would be mutually advantageous for Soviets and Americans to prevent the spread of nuclear weapons and materials to Third World nations. Cooperation would clearly be in the interests of both giant nations. Opening more trade in cooperative ventures would doubtless aid both powers. If we follow Bertrand Russell's suggestions, cooperative exchanges in art, culture, and nonmilitary science seems easy enough to put in place.

What about the more difficult situations, however, where real economic and military competition are present in concrete situations? Here we can turn to some remarkable studies by Robert Axelrod (1984), who has done research on competitive games in his laboratories at the University of Michigan. Axelrod's work is based on a game called "the prisoner's dilemma," which involves two competitors attempting a task while having the power to block or cooperate with the others. What is the best strategy to use in this situation? After thousands of games with large numbers of contestants, Axelrod found the strategy most likely to win games in the long haul. He calls it the "tit-for-tat" strategy. This technique which players found to be effective after innumerable games is based on cooperation with a cooperative opponent; it dictates retaliation against betrayal of trust but opposes holding grudges. This strategy requires the player to remember the actions of the other players and take them into account but does not seek to punish the other side. It is a strategy that can be trusted.

Dietrich Fischer (quoted in Sommer 1985, 108) has applied Axelrod's principles to an international policy between the antagonists of the modern world. Those principles are:

1. Never initiate conflict.
2. Don't passively accept negative behavior but respond quickly.
3. Don't retaliate excessively. Having made your point, return immediately to a cooperative stance.
4. Let your strategy be simple and transparent so that your adversary can learn to rely on your responses and act accordingly.

What happens is that a kind of trust evolves between both players (or both nations) where a cooperative ethic appears to be in the interests of each. We note here that this result is the exact opposite of the politics of confrontation and escalation. These failed techniques use mutual terror and unpredictability to win the day. The idea here is that the less secure your opponent is, the greater will be your gain. Are the United States and the USSR more secure because they each have weapons that can be undetected by the other's radar? Are they more secure because they have other missiles that can be in enemy territory in no more than six minutes? The studies we cite argue against such an assumption, as does common sense. Thus it appears that people may come to recognize that their security may be directly related to their enemies' security. That is simply another way of talking about cooperation.

Chapter 5 will look at one way in which cooperation is hampered, namely in the deformation of language and thought. We will learn that in the interest of ideology, former friends can become enemies, enemies can become "objects," and objects can take on "human" qualities.

Chapter 5

Deformed Thought
and Deformed Language

But if thought corrupts language, language can also corrupt thought.

—GEORGE ORWELL

George Orwell's great antitotalitarian novel, *Nineteen Eighty Four,* shows how the control of language is used to control human beings. Orwell understood that most of our knowledge about the world comes from language and that most of our misunderstandings come from the same source.

In Orwell's futuristic and nightmarish society, history is always being rewritten to conform to the changing needs of the elites running the government. He who controls the past, controls the present; the past is controlled by those who can selectively interpret and change the records of history. We are reminded again of closed societies such as the Soviet Union in which Trotsky and later Stalin were "written out" of history and unofficially became "nonpersons" at one time or another.

Orwell knew that the impulse to control the past by ignoring it or distorting it was not limited to any one society. In an essay entitled "Politics and the English Language" (1946), Orwell tells us:

> In our time, political speech and writing are largely the defense of the indefensible. Things like the continuance of British rule in India, the Russian purges and deportations, the dropping of the atom bombs on Japan, can indeed be defended, but only by arguments

which are too brutal for most people to face. . . . Thus political language has to consist largely of euphemism, question-begging and sheer cloudy vagueness. Defenseless villages are bombarded from the air, the inhabitants driven out into the countryside, the cattle machine gunned, the huts set on fire with incendiary bullets: this is called *pacification.*

Orwell was prophetic both in a general sense and a specific one. The term pacification was used to justify the most brutal violence by supporters of the American war in Vietnam in the 1960s and 1970s, supporters of the Soviet war against rebels in Afghanistan in the 1980s, and supporters of the government of El Salvador as it fought an utterly ruthless war against its own peasant guerrillas in the 1980s. How is it possible that such a peaceful sounding word as pacification can be used in such a warlike way? The answer is that it is the intent of policymakers, and the euphemism is a way of cooling off the unpleasant emotions associated with the mass violence of total war. In this chapter we will view two forms of language manipulation as they relate to issues of war and peace.

Manipulation of Words: Heating the Emotions. Many of the

studies done on why men fight in war show that the reasons are, in the main, very concrete and immediate. That is to say, most troops fight for their own personal survival and for the survival of their buddies in battle (Stouffer and Lazarsfield 1949). Nevertheless, most if not all governments engage in the kind of propaganda designed to enflame both combatants and the civilian populations alike.

They Are Not Like Us. In preparation for war the two propaganda tasks of rival governments have traditionally been to glorify one's own side while casting doubt on the humanity of the enemy. Two weeks after the Japanese attack on Pearl Harbor, *Time Magazine* (December 22, 1941) described the differences between the new enemies of the United States, the Japanese, and the new allies, the

Chinese people. *Time* was extremely certain about the differences between the two peoples. Although it may be a source of embarrassment to the magazine today, this was *Time's* analysis in 1941: "Japanese are seldom fat, they dry up as they age. Japanese walk stiffly erect, hard-heeled. Chinese more relaxed, have an easy gait. The Chinese expression is likely to be more kindly, placid, open; the Japanese more positive, dogmatic, arrogant. Japanese are hesitant, nervous in conversation, laugh loudly at the wrong time."

It is quite easy to forget that all humans share most of the important characteristics that can be called good or evil. In time of war or preparation for war, a terrible simplification takes place in which all good qualities are appropriated to "our" side and all evil is transferred to the "other." There are two problems with this idea. First, it is simply not true. Even in World War II, which provided the clearest moral choices of any modern war, atrocities were committed by both sides and the needless deaths of noncombatant civilians resulted.

The second flaw in the "all or nothing" reasoning is that it portrays the enemy as having none of our characteristics, just as we have none of theirs. When we look at Nazism—the most destructive and hideous of social movements—we may feel better if we believe that its ranks were composed solely of crazed monsters. However, it is likely that most Germans joined the party for fairly ordinary reasons: economic deprivation, nationalistic fervor, social status, racial prejudice, etc. Note well that these are all fairly common reasons for activities among those fighting the Nazis. This does not mean that it was wrong to fight the Nazis; quite the reverse, it means that we should fight the potentials for Hitlerism in our own societies and in our own minds.

Thus when President Reagan referred to the Soviet Union as "the focus of evil in the modern world" (March 8, 1983), he was implying that evil was not a problem of the Western world. Carried to its logical extreme, this can lead to the premise that hunger, homelessness, and violence are not problems if they are not brought about by Soviet policies.

When preparing a country for war, these deceptive simplifications are commonplace. In Iran in 1986 the United States was still being called the "Great Satan of the Modern World." The United States shared this dubious title with Iraq, which was at war with Iran. Clearly, external enemies, especially Satanic ones, become useful to the powerful in societies such as Iran's, where shortage of food and basic goods make day-to-day life hellish for ordinary people. Pointing the finger at an external enemy solidifies support for the leadership of most countries and that is why pointing at people "not like us" is done so often.

Ad Populum *Appeals.* Whipping popular passions into warlike sentiments is a fairly easy task if the times are right. In the *ad populum* technique the propagandist takes commonly held values and uses them to promote war or mass violence. In World War I, German troops wore belt buckles that said "Gott Mitt Uns," meaning that God is with us or is supporting our cause. Religion is often used as a spur to war especially with the ancient idea of the "Jihad" or Holy War in Islam, or the Crusades in Christianity.

Other deeply held values can be tapped as well to promote hatred or violent behavior. In the American South, violence toward black men was often called forth by real or imagined sexual contact between black men and white women. Often the mass violence of lynchings was encouraged and justified in the name of racial purity. In one sense, this was odd because miscegenation has been characteristic of racial relations between blacks and whites since their initial contacts.

Appeals to religious values or sexual possessiveness are powerful motivations for war or violence and can be manipulated by people with many other motivations. One of the oddest varieties of the *ad populum* manipulation occurred in the 1960s. In 1966 the *Realist* magazine satirized the religion-war connection, producing a button boldly and satirically stating "Kill a Commie for Christ." Whether or not it was in good taste, the slogan was the source of much levity. However, the next year, 1967, a pro-Vietnam War march carried a placard with the above slogan just behind effigies of the Virgin. The slogan had turned from parody to reality and another *ad populum* slogan had been born.

The ad populum appeal often carries with it the *illusion of universality,* which means that it is framed in such a way as to convince the population that everyone supports violent action. In lynchings, for example, participants in mass violence stated they felt no personal responsibility for their activities because "everybody was doing it" (quoted in Ginsberg 1965). We will see this diminished sense of responsibility in various mass activities including war itself.

Manipulation of Words: Cooling Out the Emotions

Bureaucratic Euphemisms. If George Orwell had lived past 1946, he would have lived to see further distortion of the language he loved for causes he disliked intensely. Orwell knew that some variety of bureaucracy was needed in modern society. He did not want to retreat to some untouched forest away from the modern world. What bothered him about bureaucracy was its possible use in destroying humanity. He knew full well about the bureaucratic order of Nazi death camps and how their perverse reasoning had facilitated the "efficient" deaths of perhaps seven million human beings. The death camps were not, of course, called death camps; rather, they were termed relocation facilities or labor camps. That was a way of cooling out the reality that the camps were, in point of fact, death factories. The German people of the time were not anxious to ask questions about the activities in the camp, thus mass murder continued unabated.

With the unparalleled growth of weapons unimagined by earlier generations and with the recurrence of wars of rebellion in the Third World, new terms have been devised by military and governmental bureaucracies to give meaning to the new actions, weapons, and possibilities of the modern world. New words, as Orwell understood, do not always give us more complete knowledge of the world nor are they always intended to do so.

The new words that follow are not considered obscene by most English speaking people (certainly not in the same sense as those Anglo-Saxon terms we say in fits of anger). These terms (Table 5.1) are found in current documents from the Pentagon and the Defense "think tanks" which inform social policy in the United States.

Table 5.1. Euphemism and Ordinary Language

Bureaucratic Euphemism	Translation into Ordinary Language
1. Circadian deregulation	Death
2. Alternative hostility	Nuclear war
3. Broken arrow	Nuclear accident
4. Bargaining chip	Nuclear weapons
5. Bird	A nuclear warhead
6. Pacification	Removing an enemy from an area by destroying resources and materials
7. Termination with extreme prejudice	Murder
8. Dynamic processing environment	A zone in which all people are thought to be enemies and hence killed
9. Air support	Bombing
10. Peacekeeper	MX missile

The purpose of these bureaucratic phases is more to hide the reality of mass human destruction than to aid our knowledge. When nuclear war is conceived as a game with winners and losers, it follows that the terms associated with it will be emotionally cool rather than heated with emotion. Robert Jay Lifton called this process "psychic numbing" (1979). C. Wright Mills called it "crackpot realism" (1959). Whatever it is called, it involves a technique in which horror and tragedy are glossed over with the language of technical problem solving.

Old time problems of ethics, morality, and the like are not given much significance in these words. Moreover, words and phrases such as "a lie" or even "a damned lie" are replaced in political discourse with terms such as "disinformation," "inoperative statements," "spin control," or "lowering the accuracy standards."

When discussion of war and peace are absorbed into the military bureaucracy, deformed language destroys the human context of discourse. The struggles for war and peace are in part the struggle to control language. Are "freedom fighters" really "terrorists?" Are "terrorists" really "patriots?" It depends, of course, on whom one asks. If words are only tools for persuasion and not ways of deepening our knowledge about the world, we are indeed approaching George Orwell's greatest fears. Most of us do not speak the bureaucratic lingo we have shown above. Most of us have realities that are not totality grounded in bureaucratic realities. However, the individuals who plan "war games" with computer simulations of nuclear wars that involve the planning for "megadeaths" (millions of deaths) do seem to fall into this pattern. Ethics and concern for human welfare are seen as incidental to large "game plans." As Schell (1982) tells us: "Once the 'strategic necessity' of planning the deaths of millions of people is accepted, we begin to live in a world where morality and action inhabit two separate, closed realms." We would add to Schell's idea that when planning for the deaths of millions becomes a strategic necessity, words also become separated from meaning.

Earlier, we defined peace as nonharmful relations between people. A recent report from the Pentagon continued a slightly different approach to the concept; it defined peace as "permanent prehostilities."

Objectification. Another way of treating emotional topics of war and peace without emotion is through the process of viewing humans as "things." The French word for this process is *"chosefication"* which literally means "to thingamafy." To escape this awkward construct we will use the word *objectification.*

When one person complements another as having a "million dollar smile," the human quality (the smile) is connected to a nonliving or dead thing—money. When a medical doctor examines an individual and says that "the throat" shows infection, he is separating the throat from "your body." He has depersonalized the throat in a way that medical people tend to do. In one sense, we want to be treated as an object in a physician's care because (excluding psychiatric care) our bodies are living machines. Given the choice between a caring incompetent doctor and one lacking a sympathetic bedside manner, most of us would prefer the latter.

Nonetheless objectification is a part of the psychological process we use when rationalizing violence toward the potential enemy. No one knows for certain why in most human societies there is a strong prescription against killing or murder. It could be an innate part of our humanness, or it could be learned. Whatever the case, almost all killers suggest they were acting in self-defense. Our most extreme case, Adolf Hitler, justified his attack on Poland in 1939 as a defensive act. The Poles, he claimed, had attacked a German radio station. That this charge was not true is beside the point. The German people were not to view themselves as aggressive predators of humans even if their government was leading them in that direction.

When one prepares to do battle with another group or even an individual, it helps to view the enemy as something less than human. That, essentially, is the essence of objectification. It closely parallels the "They are not like us" syndrome. "They" lack the essential human qualities, brains, ethics, courage, the ability to feel pain. As Ronald Reagan said in *The Los Angeles Times* (March 6, 1980), "We have a different regard for life than those monsters [the Soviets] do." In reality, both the Soviets and Americans and all other groups on earth have the capacity to hold life in great regard and also to act as "monsters." Calling the other side nonhuman names is not rare in wartime, but it is quite rare when nations are at peace.

If America is "the Great Satan" as the Shiite faction ruling Iran believe, then it becomes easier to kidnap, torture, or even kill Americans. Americans have become "antihuman" things.

When humans become abstract caricatures of humanity or are called names such as "Chick" (woman), "Gooks" (Vietnamese), "Sand-Nigger" (Arab), or "Buck" (a young Native American or black man), the name-callers have taken a step toward violence. The humanity in these categories is diminished and symbolically "no one" is left. "I see nobody on the road" said Alice. "I wish *I* had such eyes," the King remarked in a fretful tone. "To be able to see Nobody! And at that distance too!" Lewis Carroll's *Through the Looking Glass* (1956) gives us an important insight into objectification. It is a form of emotional or real distance we put between our selves and our enemies when we label them as "nobodies" or things.

Naturally enough, this is worsened during wartime and the process of objectifying the enemy is quite calculated. The following is a marching cadence given to one of the authors by a Vietnam veteran; it was taught to the troops in boot camp before they left to fight in 1970:

NAPALM STICKS TO KIDS

We shoot the sick, the young and the lame
We do our best to kill and maim
Because the kills all count the same
Napalm sticks to kids.

Flying low across the trees
Pilots doing what they please
Dropping frags on refugees
Napalm sticks to kids.

See the farmers over there
Watch me get them with a pair
Blood and guts everywhere
Napalm sticks to kids.

Flying low and feeling mean
See that family by the stream
Drop some Napalm and hear them scream
Napalm sticks to kids.

A squad of Cong in the grass
But all the fighting's long since past
Shooting peasants planting rice
Napalm sticks to kids.

Napalm, son, it's mighty fun
Dropped in a bomb or shot from a gun
It gets the gooks on the run
Napalm sticks to kids.

It must be noted that this attempt to harden or psychically numb the American GI's in boot camp was only partially successful. It was an attempt, however, to dehumanize the enemy. In this dehumanizing process, we symbolically turn ourselves (as "killing machines") into objects as we objectify the enemy. In the psychology of objectification in war, everyone receives scars.

As we have explained, in war or in revolution dehumanizing symbols or labels justify violence. Through the distorted simplification of conflict in Vietnam, some American troops began to see "Gooks"— not human beings sharing a different culture. "Wasting a Gook" was not equivalent to "killing a man" in an emotional sense. In the Soviet Union in the late 1920s "enemies of the State" or political dissidents were labeled "renegades," "deviationists," or "opportunists." Those labels represented death sentences, although in Stalinist terms individuals were not killed, they were "liquidated."

Bernard, Ottenberg, and Redl (1970) have summed up the dehumanizing tendencies in modern warfare, charging that warfare produces:

1. *Increased emotional distance from other human beings.* This has been discussed at some length already.
2. *Diminished sense of personal responsibility for the consequences of one's actions.* This refers to the "I was only carrying out orders" syndrome. In a bureaucracy such as the military it is difficult to place the blame on any one individual for an act of violence.
3. *Increasing involvement with procedural problems to the detriment of human needs.* Here the potential human victim is seen as a statistic of little importance in the move/ countermove strategy of war games. Personal ethics are irrelevant to the tasks at hand.
4. *Inability to oppose dominant group attitudes or pressures.* This occurs in any bureaucracy, but in the military it is difficult to oppose dehumanizing trends because one's loyalties are questioned. "Troublemakers" are excluded from positions of power and are punished for their troublesome activities.
5. *Feelings of personal helplessness and estrangement.* The individual feels small, alone, and impotent to change things in a military bureaucracy and develops a fatalism (which we discuss in Part II) stemming from the idea that most if not

all people are corrupt, evil, or unjust. Often this estrangement
lasts long after the war has ended.

Strange Case of the Defense Intellectuals. In a remarkable article
in the journal *Signs* (1987), Carol Cohn describes a year she
spent studying planning with a defense institute at a prestigious
university. She was quite amazed to hear and later participate in
discussions of "clean bombs" (fusion bombs), "collateral damage" in
nuclear war (human deaths), as well as "countervalue attacks" or the
incineration of enemy cities. We have already described this sort of
language. It is the classic idiom of objectification and dehumanization.

Yet there was more to come. Much of the language Cohn heard
in the defense institute used sexual metaphors to describe the
artifacts and tactics of nuclear war. There was the discussion of
"vertical erector launchers," "soft lay downs," "deep penetration,"
"thrust to weight ratios," "getting more bang for the buck," "the
Russians being harder than we are," and so on. This language
reveals a connection between the incredible power of nuclear weapons
and the male ideal of sexual potency. This should give one pause to
consider what the relationship is between the masculine mind-set of
the war planners and wars of the future. Is nuclear war planning a
kind of surrogate for sexual activity or is the question deeper than
that? Some Freudian psychologists have postulated a relationship
between love and death. This analysis seems like a monstrous joke.
When Herman Kahn (1960) described the ultimate nuclear war as a
"spasm war" or a "wargasm," we begin to wonder if the joke is on all
of us.

At one point in her studies Cohn visited the nuclear submarine
base at New London, Connecticut. Cohn was invited by the officer
granting the tour to "pat the missile." She thought this very odd
indeed, because to "pat" something is usually a sign of intimacy or
affectionate domination. One typically pats babies, small dogs, or a
loved one. When one pats a missile, it becomes symbolically not the
potential means of wiping out the lives of millions of human beings
but a sort of friend or perhaps a sort of security blanket.

Cohn found that the longer she interacted with the defense
intellectuals in this sort of discourse, the easier it became to accept

their assumptions. This of course frightened her a great deal. Language creates it own reality.

Reification. In one sense reification is the mirror opposite of objectification. If we understand objectification as the taking away of human characteristics from humans, *reification* means the giving of human characteristics to things or ideas. Like objectification, reification is deeply rooted in our language and thought.

When we say that "money talks," we are giving a dead object life and human characteristics. When we say that "society cries out for revenge against terrorists," we are giving an idea, "society," human characteristics. Perhaps many people cry out for revenge against terrorists, perhaps most. Nevertheless, society is an idea we carry in our head. No one has ever seen "society." We do see *people* make demands. Society is a useful concept or idea with which to supply the world. Having said this, we must also say that ideas cannot act independently of humans (even if we find "an idea whose time has come").

Human beings alone are capable of creating valuable things for human use. Nevertheless, we often attribute the way we live to "fate," "luck," or "the stars." When people answer advertisements in tabloid newspapers for lucky charms and magic potions, they are attributing a human attribute (power) to a thing. They are also acknowledging their own helplessness to change their lives in ways that could make things better. This is the hidden secret of reified thought: as it attributes human power to things or ideas, it robs humans of the power they have to change their own lives. The following are examples of reified thinking and how they affect issues of war and peace.

1. The Naturalistic Fallacy. This logical error outlined by the philosopher G. E. Moore (1904) argues that because something occurs in nature it should therefore be an ethic in human society. If some form of mass violence exists in the world of animals, this logic would maintain there is nothing we can do to rid its influence on human affairs. Here "nature" (whatever that may mean) shows that violence and "war"

have always existed in nature, therefore it is useless to try to remedy the situation. Even if "the war of all against all" is the rule in the natural or prehuman world, there is no reason why that "should" prevail in the world today. Human beings have powers of reason and self-reflection that animals do not. We are not captives of nature the way ants are. Still, if we accept the naturalistic fallacy as being true, we can develop a comfortable pessimism that takes away responsibility for working toward peace.

2. The Error of Historicism. When individuals tell you that "history proves" this or that, they are speaking the language of reification. Only humans can prove things, and often as not they are wrong about what they attempt to prove. If history is seen as preordained or predetermined, then humans have no control over it. When Marx predicted the inevitability of communism and "the leap from the realm of necessity to freedom," he fell into the error of historicism. In reality the world could become communistic, capitalistic, something in-between, or we could exterminate ourselves.

In the 1980s another kind of historicism by some Christian sects predicted that nuclear war was inevitable; it was the Armageddon threatened by God in the Bible. Others interpreted the Bible to deny nuclear war as a possibility because the end of time is described differently in the Bible. These two forms of historicism or historical determinism have one thing in common, even if they reach different conclusions—nothing human beings do makes a difference. History is preordained and the time has been preset to activate the world's destruction. This gloomy view of the world has one "advantage" to it—the advantage of all reified thinking—one need not get involved in making life better. Since factors, history, fate, nature, or luck are in control, personal responsibility is unneeded.

Sometimes reified thinking is appropriate. It is appropriate whenever one must be passive. In war itself phrases like "If a bullet has your number on it, you'll go," or the Korean War favorite "That's the way the ball bounces," make sense. When a person has a terminal disease for which no more medical help is possible, it is sometimes useful or necessary to be passive or even fatalistic.

However, in the human struggle against mass violence, injustice, or extermination, reified thinking is a cop-out, a running away from the reality that we are free to change ourselves and to some degree the world. Hegel described the "unhappy consciousness" of medieval peasants by saying that seeking success in the afterlife, they guaranteed themselves failure in this life. To the European peasant, heaven was real and the day-to-day life in their time was not. Hence they saw few ways to make their lives on earth less oppressive.

Reified thought, like objectified thought, numbs our feelings about our possibilities and those of others around us. The disadvantage for people active in seeking peace is that they may fail. The reified thinker can always tell them their dreams are impossible anyway.

Moving Away from Deformed Thought. We have argued that

deforming our language is a serious threat to peace. The way we speak does shape the way we feel about each other. We must watch our language for more than reasons of politeness. If we fail to demystify the language of nuclear annihilation, we make it sound more acceptable. Would it not be better to describe nuclear war as "holocaust" or "extermination"? The words we use are important because they shape the way policy is made. The ways hatred is inflamed must constantly be exposed. Name-calling is often a preliminary to domestic fights in family life. It is also the preparation for mass violence or war. In that sense it is a rehearsal for violence.

Language should be used to "rehumanize" our opponents. Our ideological enemies must be seen as the sons and daughters, the fathers and mothers of families. When we use these words we connect our enemies to ourselves in a way that makes hatred more difficult. Furthermore, it is difficult to objectify an enemy when you have seen them face-to-face. The potential enemy lives, suffers, loves, hates perhaps in the same proportion as other human beings. With electronic warfare, the destruction of the enemy takes place without a glance at their humanness. The same technology that produces long-distance death through bombs, missiles, and death rays can also increase the communication possibilities between potential enemies. Abbie Hoffman once suggested that in wartime soldiers be forced to eat whomever they kill. This gallows humor has a point. Most damage inflicted in modern war is faceless and is therefore easier to commit. One way or another, images of the faces of those killed must get through to the other side. Real cultural exchange before war breaks out can solve this problem to a certain extent. Breaking down objectification means stressing the humanity of those very different from ourselves. This may enable us to limit the violence we do to each other.

Finally, it is important to rise above reified thinking to take responsibility for your own life and in a different way to take responsibility for the survival of the planet. It is not certain that we will succeed if we do try. It is certain that if we allow events or fate to determine history, we will not succeed.

The bad news that we have created the nuclear weapons to destroy ourselves should be tempered with some good news. It was not fate or nature or God who put us in this situation. We or our progenitors did so. This means that if we decide to use our will and reason to solve the problem in a timely way, we can indeed control our fate. In that process we will of necessity have to reformulate our language and thought. Such a reformulation requires understanding basic principles and patterns of communication as they occur between individuals and between nations. In Chapter 6 we will examine communication patterns and mistaken communication that leads to problems in personal as well as international relations.

Patterns of Communication and Mistaken Communication

One view of the current world situation is that we hang by a thread over the edge of the precipice of thermonuclear war. In this view the thread that secures us is the correct communication of intent by the nuclear powers. A single mistaken communication about atmospheric events by a computer or a misattribution of intent in military activities could sever that thread and plunge the species into extinction. In such a scenario, a mistaken communication is not the cause of conflict but a precipitating event. A whole structure of causes—nationalism, ideology, economic interest, territoriality, innate aggression—are seen as bringing the final outcome. Failure to communicate is but the last sad note in the human song.

Another view is that failure to communicate is endemic to the current world situation. It is the miswoven thread in the fabric of human life that runs across interpersonal as well as international relations. Indeed, some patterns and problems of human communication are similar between individuals and between nations. Where they are the same, similar understandings can enlighten us to improve communication and similar "therapeutic" remedies might be applied.

Communication and Metacommunication. *Communication* is the transfer of meaning. Its content is the *message*. In a sense, all behavior that is perceived is communication in that meaning may be transferred to the perceiver. If all behavior is communication, then the possibility of not communicating becomes remote. In fact, when behavior can be observed, try as one might, it is impossible to not communicate (Watzlawick et al. 1967). Because communication occurs between two or more parties and entails systems of response and feedback, it usually generates observable patterns.

When we speak about communication or examine particular patterns or problems of communication, we are *metacommunicating* (Watzlawick et al. 1967). This chapter is a metacommunication. Those concerned with resolving conflict must be metacommunicators and engage adversaries in metacommunication.

Metacommunication is not interpretation of what is observed so much as it is objective observation. It does not suggest why a message is emitted or why a particular pattern has developed but rather points to it. This qualification is important because whether interpersonal or international, nonverbal communication usually has particular meanings for the communicator instead of a universally understood meaning. Psychotherapists often try to help clients understand in a more conscious way what they communicate, to help identify and resolve conflicted feelings. Diplomats and negotiators often have similar goals. Such explicit communication forces both individuals and nations to test the reality of their assumptions and to understand the other party's perspectives.

What develops when we are forced to communicate more explicitly is facility in *meta-awareness* (Keefe 1983). Communicators have varying awareness of their own responses, the responses of the other party, and the patterns that develop between them. Meta-awareness watches patterns and responses. It is invaluable to clear, direct communication patterns and to the detection of problematic patterns.

Communication Patterns. The patterns of communication we examine here occur between individuals and between nations. In each case their sources are similar and their problems are similar.

We are concerned not only with intentional communication but also with all observable behavior emitted by a *system* (a set of interrelated parts within a boundary) and the responses it evokes in the other system(s).

Complementary Patterns. Complementary patterns of communication develop when the behavior of a system evokes a dissimilar behavior in a second system. Often this pattern can be seen as developing from a one up–one down interaction. Between two people an example might be, "You're awfully silly for one your age!" "Yes, Sir, I'm afraid I am, pardon me." Patterns of coercion and withdrawal are frequently observed in marriage partners and follow a complementary communication. In essence, the two responses while dissimilar are also mutually necessary for the pattern to persist.

There is nothing inherently bad or wrong with a complementary pattern unless one party is always one up and the other always one down. Such a *rigid complementary pattern* blocks the potential for new communication. It eliminates behavioral options for one or both parties. In a marital pair, the withdrawing spouse may seek gratification outside the marriage. Among nations such a pattern might be endemic to a colonial or imperial relationship.

Symmetrical Patterns. A symmetrical pattern can be envisaged as two mirrors facing each other; the behavior of one system evokes a similar behavior in a second system. Between two people an insult is met with an insult or a complement with a complement. If the content of the messages or behaviors are mutually beneficial, a symmetrical pattern is a system of mutual reward. A symmetrical communication pattern can *escalate.*

In lovemaking the escalation of a symmetrical pattern is functional and pleasurable. In a conflictive situation insults can turn to blows or territorial incursions can become military actions. An escalating symmetrical pattern can be found in the nuclear weapons race between the two major nuclear powers.

In his compendium, *Arsenal of Democracy III*, Gervasi (1984) has catalogued what can be seen as a symmetrical, escalating pattern between the United States and the Soviet Union. In 1942 the United States began the world's first artificial nuclear chain reaction. In 1946 the Soviet Union initiated its first nuclear chain reaction. In 1946 the United States conducted its first atomic bomb test. In 1949 the Soviets countered with a test of their own. Soon the United States deployed tactical nuclear weapons in Europe to counter Soviet military buildups in Eastern Europe. Not to be outdone, the Soviets placed tactical nuclear weapons of their own a few years later. The United States launched the first nuclear submarine in 1955 and was matched by the Soviets by one of their own in 1959.

The Soviet Union, feeling inferior status in numbers and capability of manned bombers, launched the first test of an Intercontinental Ballistic Missile in 1957. The United States followed immediately with a test of their own in 1958. Technical advance was met with advance and weapon with weapon. In 1960 the first strategic reconnaissance satellite took target identification into space. This American first was countered by a Soviet satellite in 1962. The United States initiated a series of nuclear weapons firsts in subsequent years only to be met with a similar behavior by the Soviets in almost every case. These included independently guided missiles, solid missile propellant, testing of an antisatellite weapon, and test and deployment of multiple reentry vehicles (warheads for missiles) in increasing levels of sophistication.

The neutron bomb and an operational cruise missile are more recent innovations of the United States awaiting similar Soviet responses. The federally funded research for "defensive" weapons in space, including laser weapons capable of incinerating cities in a matter of minutes (Star Wars), threatens to carry the symmetrical escalation into space (Scheer 1986).

These escalations have heretofore acknowledged that each of the major nuclear powers did not find it in its own self-interest to attack the other for fear of unacceptable retaliation. This mutually assured destruction provided a kind of stability to the communication pattern, not unlike two people who have agreed to posture and threaten by showing strength and resolve but never threatening to destroy the basic rule not to hit first.

This basic pattern changed. The Soviet Union deployed large

city–destroying missiles within range of European cities. The United States deployed highly accurate nuclear missiles in Europe capable of striking Soviet missile bases and cities in a matter of a few short minutes; long-range cruise missiles that could hit missile silos and cities in an undetected coordinated attack; and large, accurate, silo-busting missiles on submarines. The new behavioral message was, "We are preparing to hit first." Far more ominous than the previous pattern, a new form of symmetrical escalation was underway.

REVERSING ESCALATION. One way a psychotherapist tries to aid a marital pair with a symmetrical communication style that sometimes escalates out of control is to teach one or both partners responses dissimilar to the behavior and responses of their mate. Hence when a shouting match begins to heat up, the option of turning away and leaving the house for a brisk walk and a cool down is suggested. If one of the parties to the symmetrical escalation is able to come up with a novel and dissimilar response, the chance for improved communication and relating is introduced.

In preparation for arms talks with the United States in late 1985, the Soviet Union proposed a unilateral freeze on nuclear testing. Soviet Premier Gorbachov stated that there would be no further Soviet tests until the following year. If the United States joined in the moratorium, there would be no further testing. Very late in 1985 after several postponements, the United States tested another weapon with wide publicity after inviting Soviet scientists to come and watch. After the unilateral moratorium deadline, the Soviet Union extended its moratorium another three months. Reagan administration Press Secretary Larry Speaks said, "We're suspicious of Soviet moratoriums on testing. . . . We feel that for the moment the Soviets have an advantage and don't need to test. The United States feels that for own national security it's important that we do test" (*Des Moines Register* 1986, 9A).

While this initial attempt at a dissimilar and reverse escalation response was unsuccessful, at this writing there is some cause for optimism in the attempt to break the symmetrical pattern. As the public in both the Soviet Union and the United States continue to endure the economic hardships and the terror of the arms race, they have begun to play the role of therapist. They have begun to demand novel and reverse escalation responses on the part of their respective policymakers. For this to persist, a meta-awareness of other problematic communication patterns must begin to develop on a mass basis. These patterns include discrepant punctuation and the illusion of alternatives.

Discrepant Punctuation. In their classic text, *Pragmatics of Human Communication,* Watzlawick, Beaven, and Jackson (1967) describe the problematic interaction of a couple. Each partner justifies his or her current behavior on the basis of the behavior of the other. The wife's control of events is cited by her mate as the reason for his passivity. The husband's passivity is the cited cause of the wife's controlling behavior. Despite mutual dissatisfaction, each punctuates the other's behavior as the necessity for the perpetuation of their own part in the relationship. Hence the partners maintain very different views about the source of the conflict.

Watzlawick et al. observe the same patterns in international relations. At any level of communication, individual or international, the ongoing circularity of the communication system makes the attribution of cause an error. Each partner uses the other's behavior as the cause of their own *discrepant punctuation.* Each nation arms itself in response to the other's obvious preparation for war. Their own behavior may be undesirable, but it is an eminently necessary reaction to the other's behavior.

Between the superpowers the origins of mistrust are hardly obscure. In addition to conflicting political ideologies, military actions have fueled mistrust. In 1920 the United States sent one of five expeditionary forces to Russia in an attempt to overthrow the new government. In postwar Eastern Europe Soviet armed forces maintained a dominating influence. These sources of mistrust, however, pale by comparison to the ongoing justifications for each party's part in the arms race.

The job of military planners is to prepare for the worst case scenarios that might develop in relations with the other side. The job of political leadership is to prevent the worst scenarios from developing. However, to garner the support of their populations, the political leaders of each government point to the military plans and preparations of the other as evidence of the "real" intent of their adversary—and as evidence for the need to continue vast military expenditures and arms buildup.

Discrepant punctuation between the superpowers manifests as propaganda and manipulation of the populace to garner continued support of the problematic behavior of massive expenditures for arms. The Soviet leadership can document thirty military interventions by the United States in this century as evidence of evil American intent (Gervasi 1984).

American leaders can document the Soviet invasion of Afghanistan and shooting down a civilian airliner, KAL 007, as compelling huge military expenditures. Social programs are dismantled and government debt grows at geometric rates. If international events cannot suffice to generate justification of continued preparation for war, then bomber gaps, missile gaps, and windows of vulnerability can be concocted to create the necessary insecurity to justify further escalation.

Just as in the problematic relationship between the marital pair, the origins and the discovery of initial cause is not relevant to the perpetuation of the circular communication system. What is important is the way in which discrepant punctuation allows the pattern to be perpetuated. Like a therapist, the people of Eastern Europe have begun to demand new leadership. Peace activists in both the Soviet Union and the United States have begun to demand that the leadership find reasons to try new and reverse escalation behaviors—real alternatives. To respond to such therapeutic demands, however, the choices must be real rather than illusory alternatives.

Illusion of Alternatives. Paradoxical communication creates the illusion of alternatives. One form is the *double bind.* One communicator is given a choice between two equally poor alternatives. So long as both communicators define their circumstances by the limited, illusory alternatives there is no escape.

At the interpersonal level, a double-binding illusion of alternatives is theorized to exist for the schizophrenic in his other important formative relationships. When told by his parent for example, "Go out and play with your friends! It's no wonder they don't like you!" the child's paradoxical options are limited to playing with friends who don't like him or remaining inside and insuring they will continue not to like him. The only escape from the bind would be to laugh at the paradox, deride it, and thus transcend it. Of course this would be quite a task for a young child to accomplish with an all-powerful authority like a parent.

But adults also confront such injunctions to choose between the equally noxious. Hence, in the symmetrical runaway communication pattern that is the strategic arms race, we are asked to choose first-strike MX missile deployment, first-strike D-5 submarine missiles, and other dangerous escalations or face being invaded, bullied, or manipulated by the Soviet menace. To perpetuate the illusion of alternatives, Americans were told repeatedly that they must choose "Star Wars" to defend against the "Evil Empire" that shoots down innocent people on civilian airlines. In this later case, for example, they received only belated and one-time reports of the fact that KAL 007 was tracked while off course for two and a half hours by at least four American military radar stations, each of which had the capacity to warn the pilots they were dangerously off course (Gervasi 1984).

Conclusion. Patterns in communication between individuals or nations can be problematic to relationships or international relations. Our ability to recognize these patterns and even to begin to alter them in the interest of communication can serve the cause of peace. As we turn to Part II, such patterns can be seen to play a role in the religious, economic, and cultural issues we will address.

Part II

Social Forces

In Part II, we take up questions, issues, and perspectives based on social, economic, and historical realities. We look briefly in Chapter 7 at perspectives on war and peace from the world's major religions. Next we address the question, "Why war?" and examine its kinds and causes. War and preparations for war, with the excesses and misuses of the military, affect the social and economic fabric of society. The nature and extent of this impact on human rights and welfare is the concern of Chapters 9 and 10. The study of peace must now entail confronting the spectre of nuclear war, and in Chapter 11 we take a hard look at this uncomfortable problem with a hint at paths for its solution.

Chapter 7

A Glance at
Religious Perspectives

Several years ago a group of social scientists attended a social gathering held in my home. Among those present was a political scientist who had been born to a Hindu family in southern India. He struck up a conversation with a sociologist who had grown up in a Jewish family in Austria. The Jewish professor had barely escaped with his life from the Nazi terror; many of his family had not been so fortunate.

In the course of their conversation the Indian professor observed he found it interesting the three world religions that were most warlike and militant were all born in desert countries. Further, he offered the opinion that Judaism, Christianity, and Islam had all tried to convert people by the sword to their way of thinking. "Was this not a result of the harsh struggle for life in the desert?" he asked. Buddhism and Hinduism, he explained, originated in a more temperate climate and were more given to peaceful activities.

The Jewish professor took issue with his new acquaintance and suggested that desert peoples and their religions were neither more nor less violent than other peoples and religions. The Indian professor decided to press the issue further by asking if the ancient Hebrew idea of the chosen people of God was not a potentially exclusionary and warlike idea. The Jewish professor vigorously rejected this characterization, saying that the ancient Jewish idea of an exclusive "chosen people" was a corruption of ancient Hebrew beliefs. In response he argued that the caste system of ancient (and modern) Hinduism was an even more deadly and degrading way to organize human life. He went on to argue that the role of the "untouchable" in Indian society showed the inhumanity of the Hindu system. At this point the Indian professor shook his head violently. "No, no," he said, "this was not an original part of Hinduism. As Gandhi and many others have pointed out, this was corruption of Hinduism."

With that comment the conversation turned to less exciting topics. Is there a lesson to be learned here? Indeed there are several. First, we should not be too bold in making generalizations about complex religious traditions. It would, of course, be impossible to prove that the desert religions produced more mass violence and war than the ancient Norsemen or Chinese or Aztecs.

Beyond that there is another aspect to consider from the conversation just described. It amounts to this. From an outsider's point of view, one cannot tell the differences between core beliefs of a religion and the corruptions that may have followed those beliefs. All we have is the history of the religion—for better or worse.

World religions such as Judeo Christianity and Islam carry many conflictual tendencies within their faith and practice. Nowhere is this more true than with issues of war and peace.

War Making and Peace Taking in World Religions. All world religions have recognized the dangers of war. Clearly war and the love of war can lead to blood lust and chaos. Yet at times war seems to become necessary, and at times it even appears to be commanded by God. For example, in the Book of Numbers, Chapter 31, in the Old Testament, Moses is commanded by the Lord to "Avenge the children of Israel of the Mideonites" (31:1). "And they warred against the Mideonites as the Lord commanded Moses and they slew all the males" (31:7). And Moses said unto them, "Have ye saved all the alive?" (31:15). "Now therefore kill every male among the little ones and kill every woman that hath known man by lying with him. But all the women children that have not known a man by lying with him, keep alive for yourselves" (31:17). It goes without saying that this extraordinary outrage violates the spirit of the second commandment, "Thou shalt not kill."

One of the central ideas in Jewish history and scripture concerns the concept of the Messiah or the "anointed one." The messianic age was to come in the future when justice would return to the Jews who had been scattered from their earlier kingdom. One philosopher of religion observes:

> While one cannot speak of a straight line in the evolution of the prophetic thought from the earliest to the later prophets, it is nevertheless possible to say from the first Isaiah onward, the basic vision of the messianic time is more clearly and fully expressed than before. Perhaps its most important aspect is peace. When man has overcome the split that separates him from his fellow man and from nature—then he will indeed be at peace with those from whom he was separated (Fromm 1966, 100).

The Jewish messiah is sometimes represented as a man, other times as the Lord, and sometimes as a collectivity of people (Klausner 1956, 73). In a future messianic age, peace is to come as humans overcome their fragmented knowledge of their world and come to live in harmony with each other. The Hebrew word for peace, "shalom," also means completeness. The completeness we long for is symbolized by the Garden of Eden in which man and woman lived in peace with each other and with the world of nature.

The messianic age as seen by the ancient Jews was one of the first utopias created by mankind. The idea is given poetic shape by the prophet Isaiah (11:6–9):

> The wolf shall dwell with the lamb and the leopard shall lie down with the kid, and the calf and the lion and the fatling together, and a little child shall lead them. . . . The suckling child shall play over the hole of the asp, and the weaned child shall put his hand on the adder's den. They shall not hurt or destroy in all my holy mountains; for the earth shall be full of knowledge of the Lord as the waters cover the sea.

Thus humankind, "full of knowledge," lives at peace with nature, which has ceased its war of all with all. Justice has come to the world.

The prophet Micah offers the prediction that peace among men and women will carry with it the destruction of all weapons of war. For in the messianic age

> they shall beat their swords into plow shares and their spears into pruning hooks; nation shall not lift up sword against nation, neither shall they learn war anymore; but they shall sit every man under his vine and under his fig tree, and none shall make them afraid; for the mouth of the lord of hosts has spoken (Micah 4:3–4).

Of course, this peaceful world is to occur in the future. For Israelis fighting Arabs on the Gaza Strip in 1988, this prophetic injunction would seem to have little relevance. Yet among some of the early proponents of Zionism, such as Rabbi's Hillel, the prophetic concept of peace was an achievable dream, even if it took many generations to gain the wisdom to bring it about.

In historical Christianity the ideal of war and peace is a melange of idealism, practicality, and compromise between the two. Theologians of many stripes have argued for centuries as to the teachings of Jesus on the issue of war and peace. To be sure, there are a number of contradictory passages in the New Testament. For example, in Matthew (10:34) Jesus says, "I have not come to bring peace but a sword." A few chapters later he follows that military metaphor with this warning: "All who take the sword will perish by the sword" (Matthew 26:52).

Ultimately, however, it is the peacemakers rather than the war makers Jesus calls "blessed." St. Paul, following Jesus' teachings, gives this rather rigorous ethical fiat:

> Bless those who persecute you, bless and do not curse them. . . . Repay no one evil for evil, but take thought for what is noble in the sight of all. . . . If your enemy is hungry, feed him; if he is thirsty, give him drink; for by doing so you will heap burning coals upon his head. Do not be overcome by evil, but overcome evil with good. (Romans 12:14–21).

These high ethical values seem, at first blush, to be more appropriate to the messianic age than our own. It is these pronouncements, however, that have given Christian pacifists their guidelines.

Leo Tolstoy published his argument for Christian pacifism in Russia in 1911 entitled *The Law of Love and the Law of Violence.* He put forth the concept that early, and thus purer, Christians practiced a pure sort of nonviolence. "The Christian communities of the first four centuries declared categorically, from the mouths of their pastors, the prohibition of all murder, individual or collective—that is to say, war" (1948, 61).

Nevertheless, St. Augustine argued that for Christians pure pacifism was unworkable (Bainton 1962, 37). Since the fall of Adam and Eve from the Garden of Eden, human beings are tainted with original sin. This, actually, is much like the twentieth century argument that humans are naturally aggressive. Sometimes Augustine argued that peace must be broken to protect the weak or to achieve justice. This led to Augustine's concept of the "just war," which the church was to look to as a standard for conduct for the ages.

Criteria for a Just War as Set Down by St. Augustine

1. The war must be declared by a legitimate authority.
2. The war must be carried out with right intentions [revenge or blood lust is wrong].
3. The war must be undertaken only as a last resort.
4. The war must be waged on the basis of proportionality. The evil produced by the war must not outweigh its good.
5. The war must have a reasonable chance of success.
6. The war must be waged with all the moderation possible.

The just war ideas of the church were an attempt to merge morality and ethics with the reality of warfare. It goes without saying that this is a difficult task to perform. Once the dogs of war are unleashed along with the human passions of warfare, moderation, "right intention," and proportion are unlikely to be maintained for very long.

By the beginning of the nineteenth century conservative Catholic thinkers such as Joseph de Maistre (1754–1821) began to view war as the inevitable punishment of God upon wicked people (Roberts and Kloss 1979, 196). All the while, denominations smaller than that of Roman Catholicism were advocating nonviolence as the true Christian ethic. The German pietists who formed the Anabaptist movement in the sixteenth century gave birth to many Christian sects whose communicants would not go to war under any circumstances. This group included the Mennonites, the Amish, and many others, along with Quakers and later Christian groups such as the Jehovah's Witnesses who followed this path.

By the 1980s many of the mainline Christian denominations were advocating a kind of "nuclear pacifism," arguing that the use of nuclear weapons had no justification for any reason. The Methodist bishops' *In Defense of Creation* (United Methodists Council of Bishops, 1986) and the Catholic pastoral letter *The Challenge of Peace: God's Promise and Our Response* (American Council of Catholic Bishops, 1983) take this position.

Islamic Law. Not surprisingly, by the 1980s many Americans were to associate the Islamic culture and faith as a violent and warlike tradition. Largely ignorant of Islamic beliefs and practices, Westerners fell back on stereotypes and prejudices to understand the turmoil in the Middle East.

When the Prophet Muhammad was born in what is now Saudi Arabia in 570 A.D., his people had clustered into a few hot dusty cities along long caravan routes across the desert. Muhammad's earliest preachings carried a forceful message about the worship of the one true God and the need for ritual and strict ethics in day-to-day life. Muhammad did not hesitate to unsheathe his sword against unbelievers. Yet he also exhibited great tolerance toward the other "People of the Book"—Jews and Christians.

In the Koran he prophesied: "Behold, Muslims, Jews, Christians and Sabeaens—whoever believes in Allah and the last day and acts righteously, his reward is with the Lord, and no fear is upon him neither shall he morn" (Quoted in Wismar 1927, 17). In fact, as Islam became a world power in the eighth, ninth, and tenth centuries, it exhibited great tolerance and respect for learning. Jesus was seen as a sanctified figure, although not the son of Allah.

With Muhammad, however, came the idea of the holy war, the jihad against the enemies of Allah. The missionary vision of the new faith blended with the organized violence of war to carry out Allah's will. For several schools of Islamic law, the jihad was to be undertaken only if unbelievers had begun the war and only if there was a reasonable hope of winning it (Jansen 1979, 28). The last serious call to jihad was made in 1914 when Turkey came into the European war on the side of Germany, which ended in failure (Peters 1973).

The reasons for Islam's current association with violence are complex but there are two explanations. First is the simple ignorance of Westerners. It is no more just to evaluate all of Islam on the basis of the Iran-Iraq War than to evaluate all of Christianity on the basis of the Protestant-Catholic conflict in Northern Ireland. Yet there is a more compelling reason for the association between Islam and violence in the 1980s. Western economic systems and cultural values have penetrated Islamic society. Great disparities between the rich who often assume Western ways and the poor are often worsened. A return to a purified, revitalized Islam is often accompanied with violence designed to keep Western capitalism out of Iran, Egypt, or other Islamic states. Often the return to the old ways is done with the extremism of the newly converted.

It is interesting to compare the militarism of Iran or the Arab states to other tendencies in Islamic thought. During the nineteenth century a reform movement in Shiite Islam was led by the prophet Bahã U llah. This religious movement, which later broke from Islam to form its own religious identity, was called Bahaism. One of its central tenants is world peace, and its members practice total nonviolence and pacifism. This, too, is another aspect of the ideological inheritance from Muhammad.

Peace Within: Eastern Perspectives. The contemplative smile of Buddha, the slowly opening lotus flower of the Hindu texts, and the Taoist sage who chooses a pastoral life over an appointment as a prime minister, each reflect an ancient perspective on peace that departs from Western perspectives. The common thread among Eastern perspectives is peace as an internal condition, which is realized in the perfecting of the individual. Peace is an experience and a perspective that is ultimately independent of what the Westerner might call historical or social conditions. Such perspectives can be criticized as requiring a denial of reality, a monastic life, or, worse, a self-delusion. But if war, social chaos, oppression, and suffering are the conditions of life, we must find a beginning and an inspiration for the realization of peace from somewhere.

Ancient Eastern perspectives have combined elements of religion, philosophy, and psychology. Each element is involved in the individual's quest for peace, which often begins with conflict and suffering and develops into an attempt to understand or resolve the absence of peace throughout the world.

Peace of Renunciation and Devotion. The Hindu Bhagavad

Gita, written about 200 A.D. from a much older oral tradition, places its chief protagonist, Arjuna, in an untenable position (Prabhupada 1972). Arjuna is a prince who must lead his army into battle with another army that includes kinsmen. With the two armies arrayed on the plain about to do battle, Arjuna turns to a dialogue with his charioteer, Krishna, who is also an incarnation of Vishnu or God.

Arjuna's concerns are not unlike those of anyone who questions the necessity of war and suffering. Arjuna's options include: (1) not acting in his own interest and refusing to defend himself; (2) carrying out his duty, dispassionately participating as a small part of a larger process not subject to his personal values and desires; or (3) acting in accord with complete devotion to God and thereby achieving a peace of the spirit in the midst of the duality and suffering in the world.

There are many interpretations of this great work. But Arjuna's quest led away from and even shunned worldly attachments in favor of devotion and an ultimate peace of the spirit despite the world. For the *yogi,* or student, the consciousness and spirit are bound to the senses. As higher levels of consciousness such as compassion and wisdom and ultimate identity with a godhead are pursued, the senses must be renounced along with their accompanying desires. The conditions of the world are at best teachers for the individual. In such a quest, peace is of the inner self and of the spirit but not of the world.

Peace of Nonaction. One of Arjuna's options was to not act. This

hints at the position of some Taoist and Buddhist perspectives on realizing peace. The nonaction of the Taoist is a product of inner peace. Nonaction is not passivity but rather acting without ego involvement. It is action for its intrinsic sake. External reward divides the self between skillful actor and one who strives for a prize or to win. Attachment to social status or political rank is seen as one of the traps that separates you from your natural, peaceful self. A peaceful self springs from an inner tranquility that has its roots in a sense of the Tao or the natural whole of life. The Taoist sage Chuang-tzu, when told he was to be appointed to the position of prime minister by the prince's chancellors, declared that instead of becoming a venerated object, he would instead live "as a plain turtle dragging its tail in the mud" (Merton 1965, 94). Such a perspective, usually captured in the context of a simple and pastoral existence, is seen to generate harmony both within and without.

Peace of Nonattachment. Siddhārtha Gautama led a protected life, never seeing suffering and pain until early adulthood when he spied an old, sick beggar by the gate to his sheltered compound. This sight led him to a period of renunciation in order to resolve the question of why there was suffering in the world, which the sight of the beggar had brought home so starkly to his naive consciousness. Siddhārtha came no closer to his answer in the life of renunciation. Finally, he sat down to meditate beneath a tree, vowing never to move until he realized the cause of suffering in the world.

One interpretation of his realization beneath the *boddhi* tree provides a dual perspective on peace. Siddhārtha, now the Buddha, expounded what are called the Four Noble Truths learned through his awakening: (1) the condition of life is suffering, (2) the cause of suffering is attachment, (3) there is a way to end suffering, (4) the way to end suffering is the Eightfold Path. In other words, everything is impermanent; when we become invested in particular conditions their inevitable change will cause us unhappiness. The solution Buddha propounds holds the key to the perspectives on peace.

The Eightfold Path indicates that concentration on the tasks at hand in eight aspects of life including Buddha's insight about suffering, aspirations, communication, conduct, vocation, effort, attention, and meditation can lead to an end to suffering (see for example Burtt 1955). Peace is found in the moment of existence much like the experience of the Western existential philosophers. There is no identity with a godhead or doctrine. This *middle way* of living neither renounces nor indulges. Rather, it suggests that freedom from ego attachments and peace is synonymous with concentration on the ever-changing events and activities of life. But such selflessness also implies that there is an equivalent lack of attachment to values, and by extension, political positions or positions about peace.

This brings us to the second perspective on peace, which necessarily follows from the first. Selflessness implies an ego-free method of looking at the world. Such a perspective is cultivated in meditation (discussed later) wherein the mind and the ego are brought to rest. The realization, which is the heart of this philosophy and of Buddha's original awakening, is a simple realization of the undifferentiated awareness of consciousness that rests at the core of the personality and is always present despite the travails of the world. Those who share this perspective know by extension that such an awareness is shared by others.

Therefore other people, some would say all other living things, are fundamentally the same in the awareness we share. Buddhist compassion is born of this discovery. It is the basis of peaceful action toward others and of the notion that to know yourself is to know others. It changes and reorders values. If we destroy, oppress, or delude others, we destroy, oppress, or delude ourselves.

Such an insight may at first seem trivial. The outline and roles of the individual's life remain the same. But the overinvestments and strident attachments become interests and concerns, no less sources for action, but much less sources of suffering and crippling rumination. It is truly noteworthy that for some 2500 years in human history no war has been fought in the name of Buddhism. Yet Buddhist monks have chosen to sacrifice themselves again and again in the cause of peace.

Split in the Soul of World Religions. Most of the religious traditions we have glanced at in this chapter reveal an ambiguity toward questions of war and peace. The reasons for this are many. One important reason is that leaders of the world religions we discussed have realized warfare leads to the lust for blood and inhumane and ungodly acts. Therefore, concern about war is great in all the world's Scriptures. Yet the high ethics and moral scruples put forth in these principles are often lost when fear, greed, or the desire for revenge give rise to extreme acts in war.

It can be said that all religious institutions move back and forth between the two poles of realism and compromise on one side, and the need for purity and reformation on the other. This, naturally, is manifest in their attitudes toward war and peace.

There is yet another variable which has come into the consciousness of many of the leaders of world religions in the last half-century. With the advent of the nuclear age and weapons of unimaginable destruction, there is the possibility of mankind doing away with itself—leaving no one to worship God in any form. With this in mind, thinkers from all of the world's religious traditions attempt to work out ways of bringing mankind together, if not in love, at least in survival.

The key to survival in our nuclear age may be learning as much as possible about those elements of our world that threaten survival. War threatens the survival of individuals, families, communities, countries, and even species. What causes war? Beyond the biological and psychological factors, what social and historical elements are related to war? In Chapter 8 we will define war, learn about its different forms, and examine theories about its causes.

Chapter 8

Why War?

As we learned in our discussion of aggression and violence, human instincts and human nature have been suspected as causes of war. Other single factors that have been suspected include greed, territoriality, male socialization, and so on. Yet to attribute the cause of war to any single factor is a vast oversimplification. War, in addition to its biological and psychological aspects, is a social phenomenon with many complex causes. Furthermore, there are several kinds of war afflicting different levels of social systems, each with its set of causal factors. Finally, the causes of war may change through time, so that factors contributing to war in one era may be different from those contributing to war in a later time. In this chapter we will briefly review the varieties and causes of war. Based on our review, we speculate on the possibilities of future wars because we believe at least a beginning acquaintance with the causes and possibilities of war is useful to those concerned with realizing peace.

Kinds of Wars. The word *war* is derived from the Old High German word *werra* meaning strife. In French it became *la guerre* and in

Spanish, *la guerra*. *Webster's New Twentieth Century Dictionary of the English Language* (unabridged, 2d ed.) defines war as, "Open armed conflict between nations or states, or between parties in the same state, carried on by force of arms for various purposes; a conflict of arms between hostile parties or nations." This definition is distinctly modern in that it is tied to the notion of the nation state. It is inclusive of *civil war* such as the American Civil War, *revolutionary war,* and *bilateral* and *multinational* or *world war,* such as World War I. When the casualties of war extend to civilian populations or when significant portions of the population are engaged, affected by, or identified with the war (Morgenthau 1948, 1978), it is called *total war.* More recent varieties include *nuclear war,* so named by reason of the predominant weapon to be employed, and *policing war* or *guerrilla war,* so named by reason of the nature of the combatants and strategies. Furthermore, there are *client state wars* in which small countries fight with the support of more dominant world powers, and finally, the *cold war,* which is more a state of protracted animosity and threat of war between the superpowers and their allies.

Prior to nation states, there were wars of city states such as the war between Athens and Sparta. There were religious wars such as the Moslem *holy wars* in the seventh century and the Christian Crusades from the eleventh to the fourteenth centuries. There have been wars among tribes and clans well into the era of the nation states. When we consider the varieties of war and the different character of the warring entities, we can surmise that while there are probably some common causes, there are also probably many different factors causing the different forms.

Causes of War. In the absence of scientific data, we seek simple and global explanations for recurring social phenomena. It is no surprise, therefore, that simple and global explanations for war have been with us for some time. Let us begin with a look at these and move on to the more complex social explanations fitted to particular kinds of war.

The Beast. Machiavelli's famous advice to Lorenzo "the Magnificent" de' Medici included this counsel:

You must know, then, that there are two methods of fighting, the one by law, the other by force: the first method is often insufficient, one must have recourse to the second. It is therefore necessary for a prince to know well how to use both the beast and the man (Machiavelli 1513/1980, 92).

The beast is present in the unspoken assumptions of others besides Machiavelli when they turn to the subject of war. Hobbes's "war of every man against every man" was checked by the absolute sovereignty of the state, which prevented this natural evil.

Whether described in Greek classical myth as the animal portion of the centaur, in Freudian psychoanalysis as the Id instincts (Freud 1924/1975), or by sociobiologists as biological predispositions, the beast in humankind is a perennial causal assumption as the basis of war.

The "beast" is held in check in these views variously by law, rationality, public opinion, conscience and socialization, and social learning. When these factors fail, war is among the evils loosed upon the world. In these classical views, failures are the cause of or synonymous with the failure of the state or society. But as we have observed in our discussion of aggression and violence (Chapter 3) there are those who see the state or society as the reservoir of social causes of war and the individual as a social and loving creature corrupted by social forces of the state or society into mass violence and war (for a review of the Frankfort School or Freudian Left position see Brown 1973).

In this view the social forces, generated by economic or material processes, are at work on a basically loving or neutral creature. It follows that if we were to examine war at its most basic social level, that of tribal warfare among small primitive societies, we might see the interplay of material and social forces and human nature at work. We might learn something about the basic nature of war.

Material Causes. Economic and other physical processes interact with the nature of the societies subject to them. In a materialist view, these material processes help to shape social institutions and phenomena such as religion or war. If we look at less complex societies, we can learn something about the nature of the processes and shaping postulated in the materialist view.

WAR AMONG "PRIMITIVE PEOPLES." In reality, there is no such thing as a primitive culture. The subtle nature of all human interaction is complex. It is true, however, that some cultures have not developed complex technologies, and it is these hunting and gathering people we call primitive people.

The most primitive peoples seem in general not to be warlike. For example, anthropologists believe that warfare was absent from the lives of the Shoshoni, the Yahgan, and the Mission Indians of North America. War was unheard of among the Adaman Islanders and the Tasaday people of the Philippines (Lesser 1968; MacLeish 1972).

Other hunter gatherers were known to make war, but it is not clear if this was an original part of their culture or an invention due to their contact with Europeans (Divale 1974). What is clear is that hunting and gathering people put strict limits on the damage that could be inflicted by warfare. Most common is a great amount of excitement, spear throwing, and the hurling of insults. After one or two casualties, the enemies would retreat to discuss the significance of the battle. Often their "wars" were based on personal grievances, and hostility was directed at one or two individuals in any case. The small numbers of people in these hunting and gathering bands must have been a moderating influence regarding war. Moreover, very little surplus wealth was available to fight over.

With the creation of villages and the invention of agriculture, warfare became much more brutal. Among agriculturalists war became more organized and far more deadly. It may start over charges of witchcraft, an idea equivalent to the modern holy wars among the more sophisticated nations of today. Napoleon Chagnon (1974) estimates that one-third of all the deaths by young men among the Yanomanmo Indians of Brazil are caused by war. This sort of warfare does keep the population down in areas unable to maintain dense populations. To the modern mind there are, of course, less brutal means of population control.

For better and often for worse, the low-technology peoples of the world often find themselves in direct contact with the outside world. At this point, conflicts that have simmered for years boil over with tragic consequences. In Mozambique, for example, rivalry and occasional violence between the several tribal groups have been transmuted into the full-scale destruction of a nation in a guerilla war. One ethnic group predominates in the Frelimo party, which runs the government and allies with the Soviet Union. The guerilla faction, the MNR, is supported by South Africa and the United States.

Needless to say, both sides in the conflict are armed with the latest weapons. Lina Magaia describes the slaughter in the countryside:

> And I saw my children ground, disemboweled, rent with bayonets or with their heads blown open by a burst from a machine gun. And I heard it being said that their was a civil war in Mozambique. Civil War? . . . There's no civil war in Mozambique. In Mozambique there is genocide perpetrated by armed men against defenseless populations. Against peasants (1988, 3).

When major modern military powers supply the peasant people of the world with sophisticated weapons and declare them to be a surrogate enemy, the probability of their extermination in is nearly absolute.

MODERN WAR. By 1917 sociologist Thorstein Veblen blamed the competitive demands of national business interests as a cause of war. Marxian analysts placed the causes of imperialist wars in the dynamics of the capitalist economic system. While the identities of major corporations remained with particular nations, one could make the case, for instance, that the wars of exploitation and colonization of Third World nations by the dominant industrial powers served the interests of business. As raw materials were extracted to be shipped home and processed into manufactured goods, new markets for these goods were being created in colonized countries. To the extent that nations blatantly competing for such markets and sources of raw materials resorted to war, we could say that such wars certainly had an economic basis.

A related process becoming evident prior to World War II and persisting today is that in which arms merchants sold to all sides of a potential war. A race for the latest technology may have contributed to the growing mistrust among adversaries. A version of this process persists today as we find the major powers, including the Soviet Union, United States, France, Britain, and Germany to be the largest arms merchants to the Third World, selling to the largest arms importers including Iran, Libya, and Iraq (Earle 1980). Adversaries who would have had to resort to machetes thirty years ago now have the latest combat aircraft and small missile technology available for a price.

In addition to the suspicion and fear that continual arming generates, it contributes to the impoverishment of domestic populations and thus to political instability in the "consumer nations." In Chapter 10 we will examine the dynamics of economic exploitation and injustice as a destabilizing factor contributing to war.

In his critique of capitalist industrial society, *Capital,* Karl Marx observed the inherent nature of capitalist economies to continually expand (Marx 1867/1974). This process of expansion—rather than the personalities or greed of capitalists as is sometimes surmised—necessitates the discovery or creation of new markets for goods produced in the capitalist system. If new markets cannot be found or generated, a crisis of overproduction of goods can cause economic and political disruption and widespread suffering from unemployment and related problems. Consequently, the quest for new markets is seen in this view as one of the chief causes of wars. Here the opening of new markets or the protection of markets are the overt or covert factors of contention.

Militarism and Authoritarianism. At first thought, militarism and authoritarianism might seem to be singular causes for war. Yet both are complex social phenomena with characteristics that can engender war.

Authoritarianism is taken here as the mode of thinking and behaving in which the individual perceives the world in fairly rigid hierarchies of rank and power (after Adorno 1950). Other people are seen as either superior or inferior on some dimension such as military rank, intelligence, or racial background. There is minimal tolerance for ambiguity. Those not allied are enemies. One's comportment is characterized by deference to authority and aggressive condescension toward subordinates. There is an attraction to rigid, hierarchical social organizations, like the military. A propensity to attribute blame for problems on scapegoats or outsiders marks the authoritarian personality and the authoritarian society. Uncritical acceptance of the authority of the leader can precipitate national movements at a leader's behest. And generally war on an enemy can help consolidate support behind the leader.

Historian John Stoessinger, examining the genesis of war, turned to a brief speculation about Adolf Hitler: "I am convinced that the secret of Hitler's charismatic grip on Germany had its roots in the authoritarian structure of the German family" (1974, 60). Stoessinger noted the ambivalent feelings—a mixture of love and hate—that the German youth held toward authority manifest in rebellion and obedience. Following an analysis by Erikson, Hitler did not fill the image of a father figure. "Had he done so, he would have elicited great ambivalence in the German youth. Rather, he became the symbol of a glorified elder brother, a rebel whose will could never be crushed, an unbroken adolescent who could lead others into self-sufficiency— in short, a leader" (Stoessinger 1974, 62).

Authoritarian characteristics whether the product of authoritarian, paternalistic family patterns, the pervasive fear of economic crisis, or of rigid bureaucracy may predispose people to accept and foster military solutions to problems. The military is attractive to an authoritarian mentality in that it provides a clear hierarchy of authority, lends itself to straightforward if simple answers to complex problems, and is predisposed by function to focus on an enemy. If an authoritarian leader derives power from the military in society and fosters military solutions to internal and external national problems, an authoritarian populace may be predisposed to support that leader.

Moreover, such leadership will naturally consult with and give great weight to military advisors regarding national and international relations. Like any group, the military will usually provide council in keeping with its own self-interest and its own perceptions about solutions to problems. We can recall here the famous example of the attempt by the German Kaiser Wilhelm II to influence Helmuth von Moltke, his chief of the German general staff, to consider turning the trains headed south and west loaded with the German army toward the east and Russia. Moltke's response was in keeping with his years of preparation for war, "Your Majesty, it cannot be done" (Stoessinger 1974, 23). Looking more deeply at the eleventh-hour crisis, military historian Alvin Sunseri observed that militarism, military rivalry, and the consequent arms race and manpower competition between the European powers contributed to the causes of World War I (Sunseri 1985).

While some see the military and militarism as necessary to the prevention of war, others see them as neutral tools, and still others see them as causal factors in war. As military budgets grow larger and as arms sales and procurement become more and more a part of the world economic processes, the means of war persists as a leading cause of war.

Leaders and Their Misperceptions. When we advance the idea that leaders cause wars, we must determine if those leaders are seen as independent actors subject to the whims of their personalities and perceptions, or if they instead embody the character, will, and perceptions of their people. Such a determination is difficult at best and will cause a perennial debate. Laying the causes of war at the feet of individuals may fill a human need to see history as a consequence of self-determined actors rather than chaotic or impersonal if patterned forces. Whatever your position is on such questions, there are some generalizations historians have made concerning leaders and their perceptions as causes of war.

Stoessinger studied the cases of World War I, Hitler's attack on Russia, the Korean War, the Vietnam War, the India-Pakistani conflicts, and the Thirty Years War and extracted generalizations about the causes of war. Stoessinger identified the personalities of leaders as being crucial in the outbreak of war:

> I am less impressed by the role of abstract forces such as nationalism, militarism, or alliance systems that traditionally have been regarded as causes of war. Nor does a single one of the six cases indicate that economic factors played a vital part in precipitating war. The personalities of leaders, on the other hand, have often been decisive (1974, 222).

The lack of rationality in Kaiser Wilhelm II, Adolph Hitler, the ego involvement of Douglas MacArthur in Korea and two American presidents with Vietnam, and the volatility of Gamal Nasser in the Six Day War are examples of personality variables as causes of respective wars.

Perceptions of individuals are closely connected to their personality. Stoessinger's case material reveals that the most important single precipitating factor in the outbreak of war is misperception. The leader's image of himself, his view of his adversary's character, intentions, capabilities, and power can be distorted in ways that lead to decisions to go to war (1974).

We might generalize that leaders must continually test the reality and communicate to reduce the adverse influence of personality and misperception. One of the great barriers to both reality testing and communication can be overarching belief systems that exclude the reality and communication of others.

Belief Systems. Whether belief systems such as religion or political ideologies are causes of war or convenient socially acceptable reasons given to cover real material and economic motives is a matter of debate. Was the American Civil War fought over slavery or was it fought because of conflict between two competing economic systems? Was the Thirty Years War between Protestant and Catholic countries a matter of religion alone? Was World War I a war to make the world "safe for democracy?" Such questions might never be finally answered. Nonetheless, today ideology is cited again and again by national leaders as reason for war.

Maurice Cranston, in an article on "Ideology" for the *Encyclopaedia Britannica* (1975), has traced the history of the appeal to ideology as a justification for war. When wars were fought by the dominant classes by professional soldiers there was little need to justify war to the civilian populations. When the casualties of more recent total war mounted and civilian populations became increasingly involved, appeals to ideological reasons for war became more common. While early religious wars had a communal nature and appeals to beliefs or abstractions were made, modern wars to

stop communism or fascism or capitalistic imperialism have such
appeals as a dominant theme (1975).

Power and National Self-Interest. Among the abstractions to which
leaders might appeal is the interest of the nation. While
nationalism might be seen as a causal factor to the extent that it
motivates the populace and combatants, it has been seen also as an
organizing political entity. Hans J. Morgenthau saw nations as
acting to protect their own self-interests in a world where power was
a chief variable in international relations. In this "realist view"
expressed in Morgenthau's classic book, *Politics Among Nations,*
war becomes more likely when a rapid rise to power by a new nation
is met with rigidity by dominant nations who see their vital
self-interest threatened (1948/1978).

REALIST SCHOOL. The appeal of power as a chief variable in
international relations in this analysis rests on an amorphous
"principle of political realism," which "believes that politics, like
society in general, is governed by objective laws that have their roots
in human nature" (Morgenthau 1948/1978, 4). Unfortunately, human
nature is never explicitly defined as would be hoped in a science of
politics, which rests so heavily upon it. However, economic processes
as causes of most wars, both those prior to capitalism and those after
capitalism, are dismissed. In their place is a pervasive appeal to the
vision of a world in which nations—much like fish in an aquarium—
vie for dominance variously challenging or defending the status quo.

War, in this analysis, can be the result of imperialism, which is
the endless pursuit of economic and political power. The inducements
for imperialism and hence for war, become winning a war, revenge
for losing a war, and weakness—to carry our aquarium analogy
further—as the weak or injured fish must become the next meal of
the healthy survivors. Power must fill a vacuum. The natural
extension of this realist analysis is that peace is to be maintained, if
at all, by a balance of power.

This balance of power becomes a convenient metaphor in a time
when two power alliances are seen to dominate the world, the
democratic states and the communist block. Hence, in this realist

school that has held sway for some thirty years in American foreign relations, "The balancing process can be carried on either by diminishing the weight of the heavier scale or by increasing the weight of the lighter one" (Morganthau, 1948/1978, 185). Such a view has appeal and power and has, for better or worse, served a generation of American leaders and diplomats. But with such an analysis, in which the causes of war lay in the murky depths of human nature and the implicit view of that nature is not unlike a struggle for dominance in which power is preeminent, what are the prospects for peace?

Morgenthau suggests the answer. "In a world whose moving force is the aspiration of sovereign nations for power, peace can be maintained only by two devices. One is the self-regulatory mechanism of the social forces, which manifests itself in the struggle for power on the international scene, that is, the balance of power. The other consists of normative limitations upon that struggle, in the form of international law, international morality and world public opinion." Morgenthau sees neither device as "keeping the struggle for power indefinitely within peaceful bounds. . . ." (1948/1978, 25). Such a vision has within it the seeds of continual war. Perhaps this would not be the intentional nuclear war, which would be against the self-interests of the participants in a rough power balance. More likely it would generate the smaller wars that are the natural extensions of foreign policies designed to insure hegemony of more powerful states. This would be especially true in parts of the world where control is unclear.

The trouble with the realist analysis lies in its basic assumption. If we can attribute human and therefore national motives to a mystifying hypothetical entity, human nature, we do not need then to search for deeper causes for war. We can dismiss economic motives. We can ignore the appeals of oppressed populations unless they resort to arms. If they challenge a government aligned with us against the other powers, they can be dispatched by force. We do not need to search for economic solutions to their plight. We do not need to reconsider trade policy or attempt to find solutions to their social and economic problems in the complexities of trade policy, economic aid, development, and cultural dynamics. The trouble with the realist analysis is that it is not realistic. It is based on myth. It was necessary to hold the myths of Id instincts, astrology, and the flat earth in abeyance while we searched for scientific explanations for behavior, replaced horoscopes with telescopes, and searched for new trade routes by sailing around the globe. As long as we believe the myth of human nature and act upon it, we will not look further for the causes of past and possible future wars.

Causes and Cures of Future Wars. From our brief survey of

the kinds and causes of war we will speculate about the causes and cures of possible future wars. Several of the varieties of war already mentioned may persist in decades to come. Populations and historical claims may push some countries to contest for territory, and economic interests may cause others to fight for sources of vital materials. Religious, racial, and political ideologies may motivate wars between smaller nations and between the client states of the superpowers. Yet the dominant powers have come to recognize that war is less and less in their self-interest. Nuclear war is a self-destructive endeavor. The short-term profits of arms sales may become increasingly recognized as a source of economic waste, injustice, and political instability in the Third World. Our hope— new visions of international relations that consider the complexities of traditional territorial claims, culture, economics, national identity, belief systems, authoritarianism, and militarism—will begin to gain influence.

Meanwhile, the advantages of peacetime commerce will become increasingly evident to regional leaders, such as Arias of Costa Rica in Central America, who promote peace despite meddling by dominant powers. The transnational corporations will continue to evolve an international perspective that may be a force against aggressive nationalism. Communication technology will inform common people as well as their leaders about disruptions and possible war within hours of their development, allowing a quick survey of world opinion and rapid diplomatic response. Secret government policies of armed suppression and disruption will be harder to sustain on all sides. Ecological, energy, and economic threats to international stability will be increasingly seen as world problems calling for cooperative world solutions. Organizations concerned with the prevention of war are becoming more sophisticated in identifying steps to be taken toward their goal. For example, the Center for Defense Information identified halting warhead and missile testing as the first step in ending the arms race where United States-Soviet arms agreements have not been effective (Center for Defense Information 1989).

Perhaps under such material and social force, war will be more readily seen as primitive and unnecessary behavior carried out by deviants in the international community. As John Stoessinger succinctly put this dawning of international compassion: "It is no longer quite acceptable to our sense of logic that throwing a human being into a fire is an atrocity, while throwing fire on many human beings may be designated as a military operation" (1974, 229). The causes of war will be increasingly a study of a social problem with solutions quickly sought by transnational economic interests and the dominant world powers. The attention and energy of the world community will turn more and more to the study of the causes of peace and its perpetuation.

One focal point for the study of peace and its perpetuation is the way a society distributes its energy and wealth. Serious questions have been raised about the relative investment in arms versus the direct welfare of the populace. In Chapter 9 we will examine this issue and what it means for people and for the future of our society.

Chapter 9

Welfare or Warfare: A Vital Choice

If we do not change our direction, we are likely to end up where we are headed.

—ANCIENT CHINESE PROVERB (quoted in Willens *1984*)

Vital choices require a sense of where we have been and where we are going. Both a sense of history and a sense of remote future consequences enable us to make those choices that auger for our survival. When we make decisions individually, we wish to avoid repeating mistakes and to optimize our long-term rewards. When we participate in collective decisions, the goals are the same. Yet with important societal decisions, such as the allocation of national wealth, both the past and long-term future consequences are sometimes neglected with catastrophic results. This neglect is compounded when the interests of the many are subordinated to the interests of the few. Such may be the case with recent decisions made about the allocation of national wealth to arms and to social welfare. Let us consider the historical context and current consequences of vital choices being made on this issue. Similar choices are being made in Third World countries and will be examined in a later chapter.

This chapter is based on an article by the same title in *Social Development Issues* II, no. 1 (Spring 1987):38–48.

Historical Perspective

Welfare and Warfare. In his classic book on social welfare, Romanyshyn sees welfare, "as including all those forms of social intervention that have a primary and direct concern with promoting both the well-being of the individual and of the society as a whole" (1971, 3). A more specific definition is, "government protected minimum standards of income, nutrition, health, housing, and education for every citizen, assured to him as a political right, not a charity" (Wilensky and Lebeaux 1965, xii). In the latter definition the government is given a central role in protection of the minimum standards for welfare. Hence the state can become the guarantor of individual and collective welfare; as such, it is sometimes called a *welfare state.*

For our purposes of this analysis, a *warfare state* is one in which the portions of the national budget, productive capacity, natural resources, and scientific endeavor given over to the military and weapons production are so large as to seriously distort and diminish social welfare, the economy, and prospects for long-term economic prosperity.

Historical Links. Ironically, the development of the welfare state and the warfare state seem to have had the same basic cause. While they overtly seem to be means to protect against different risks, they can also be seen as social inventions that preserve a particular economic structural arrangement within society. Thus the intervention of the state in the economy serves more than the poor. For example, Levitan (1986) points to tax exemptions and expenditures that enhance personal economic security, credit programs, price supports, and aid to financially troubled businesses as aspects of welfare provided by state intervention. It is also a hedge against organized political revolt that could be fueled by abject deprivation.

Paul Adams, in his analysis of social policy and war, recalls that the welfare historian Titmuss saw war as generating a need to guarantee a healthy and willing population. It follows that the more "total" war becomes, the more need for social welfare programs. Hence, World War II saw the development of several social welfare programs in Britain. Adams presents a framework for analysis that considers not only the nature of war but also the "balance of class forces at a particular historical juncture" (Adams 1977, 432). In this analysis, the need for a healthy work force, the organization, independence, and political clout of the working class, and the degree of threat to economic arrangements by the working classes are variables in the scope of social welfare policy choices. These linkages and variables must be borne in mind when we examine both historical and current welfare or warfare choices.

Different Paths. In both the United States and Germany of the 1930s the economic arrangements of industrial capitalism were under severe pressure. These included massive unemployment, alarming inflation in Germany, and in both countries organized political challenge from the left that might bring down private ownership and control of major industry. In the United States the New Deal with its public works projects, welfare, and social insurance programs has been seen as a plan to insure the continuation of capitalism (*Encyclopaedia Britannica*, 15th ed.). In Germany, Hitler built a warfare state through massive public works projects, regimentation, and later arms production (Pinson 1966; Neumann 1944). In Great Britain the invention and construction of the welfare state and meeting the contingencies of war were explicitly linked. Titmuss characterized the cradle to grave security of welfare programs and social insurance put in place during World War II as a "war strategy" in which British fighting the war would feel their system offered more than that of the enemy (Titmuss, 1969).

In the short run, both of the social inventions of welfare and warfare states were successful in their basic intent. The political challenge of collectivized, democratic ownership of industry was stifled. The position of the private corporate elites was consolidated, especially those involved in the manufacture of arms and war-related goods, as long as they were on the winning side, traded with all sides, or, as in the case of the Krupp family, used political power to eventually restore family wealth following defeat. Following the war, the Americans continued their welfare programs and their arms buildup without serious choices being made between the two. Since the war, American expenditures for social welfare as a portion of the national product have varied around 10 percent and up to 20 percent in 1976 (Gilbert 1986). Historian James Clayton examined the pattern of welfare and warfare expenditures in the United States and the United Kingdom from 1946 through 1975 and found ". . . no statistically significant correlation between defense spending and welfare spending over time in either country" (Clayton 1977, 408). These trends persisted in a period of general economic prosperity and stability for the majority of the domestic population.

Historical Break. Still in recent years in the United States the increasing allocation of the federal budget to military expenditures and the cuts in social programs with direct benefits to people in need breaks with history. Welfare versus warfare has become a forced choice.

Current prosperity masks a recent, growing investment in arms and the military that exacts a heavy price. The price is being paid by the poor, by Third World populations, and by future generations that will have to contend with the massive and growing debt and distortions of economies that expend their wealth in the manufacture of weapons. Weapons are goods that cannot be used to generate new wealth and, in the light of historical perspectives, threaten security.

Hitler's warfare state was carried on the backs of slave labor. It engendered the decline of labor unions. It fostered the demise of craftsmen and small businesses. It shunted the nation's wealth and intellectual resources into arms manufacture and the military (Pinson 1966; Neumann 1944). While the economy was briefly salvaged in this approach, if we assume that whatever goods are produced must eventually be consumed, the outcome of such an economic plan might be seen as inevitable. This approach has some disturbing parallels to policies in practice today.

Recent Choices. In the 1980s the United States generated an unprecedented peacetime military buildup. The buildup seems to have been fueled by the power of the military-industrial sector of the economy to maximize production costs to the government and to secure policy decisions that demanded ever-more expensive arms. The buildup was rationalized by a thin veneer of authoritarian conservative ideology that would pressure the Soviet economy by threatening its governmental stability. It simultaneously undermined liberal welfare institutions and policies in this country. For example, Levitan pointed out, "By combining rapid increases in defense spending and deep reductions in the federal tax base, President Reagan has intentionally created budget conditions in which social welfare expenditures appear unaffordable" (1986, 8). Yet the United States devotes a smaller proportion of its wealth to social programs than any other industrialized country (Levitan 1986). Such policies forced economic and personal choices with grave consequences.

Economic Consequences of Military Spending. Several consequences of an overinvestment in weapons were identified by Seymour Melman (1974/1985) in his book, *The Permanent War Economy.* Increased demands on raw materials make them more expensive for use in the manufacture of civilian goods. More expensive civilian goods do not compete as well on world markets. This adversely affects our balance of trade as well as our domestic market, which turns increasingly to cheaper foreign-made civilian goods. Third World governments borrow more money to pay for arms needed to defend against neighboring governments or their own populations that must bear the brunt of low wages and unstable markets as their natural resources are plundered by larger industrial countries.

The scientists, engineers, and managers who could be generating a millennium with new high technologies are instead increasingly absorbed by the arms industry. Finally, weapons manufacture is *capital intensive.* It requires far more federal dollars per job than are required in the civilian sectors of the economy. Melman (1974/1985) has demonstrated that the warfare sector of our economy is an expanding parasite that is dominant over the civilian sector. He observed that "In a permanent war economy whole industries and regions that specialize in military economy are placed in a parasitic economic relationship to the civilian economy, from which they take their sustenance and to which they contribute (economically) little or nothing" (Melman 1974/1985, 63). Reinforcing Melman's critique, the Congressional Budget Office estimates that ten billion dollars spent on the military creates 40,000 fewer jobs than if it were spent on anything else (Gervasi 1984, 9).

These consequences are aggravated by a growing national debt. Ironically, politicians elected to "downsize" the federal government placed more of our economy under the control or scrutiny of federal managers than ever before. For example, the national debt generated in recent times by military spending and inadequate income exceeded the debt of all previous federal administrations combined. Indeed Ruth Leger Sivard points out that between 1979 and 1988 defense outlays actually increased more than the increase in the budget deficit (Sivard 1987, 39).

Most of the discretionary funds of the federal government are allocations to social welfare programs and allocations to the military and arms contracts. For example, in the fiscal year 1985 the federal budget, excluding trust, funds allocated 54 percent to the military and debts for past wars. At the same time human and physical resources, including health, education, agriculture, transportation, and low-income programs, received 27 percent of federal spending with the rest going for all other expenditures (Sane 1985). The argument that money spent on weapons and the military would not necessarily go instead to social welfare sounds empty in face of this reality. The welfare or warfare choice has been underway for some time in what has become a zero-sum game where there must be winners and losers.

In the years 1982 through 1985 the United States authorized an unprecedented $889 billion in military spending. From 1981 to 1985, $120 billion of that money came from cuts in social welfare programs. The Reagan administration planned to spend $2.6 trillion on the military in the years 1982 through 1989 (Gervasi 1984). To begin to grasp the magnitude of this spending, it compares with estimates of 2.1 and 2.3 trillion dollars spent on the military for all of the years from 1946 to 1980 (Melman 1985; Gervasi 1984). From 1980 to 1990 the federal administration planned a 239 percent increase in military spending (Gervasi 1984). As history suggests, such policies have their likely destructive conclusions. However, the destructiveness is not limited to the aforementioned conclusions alone.

Consequences for People. The consequences of current military spending come close to home if we consider what the fiscal effect has been in recent history on the average American family of four. The per capita spending on the military by the federal government in 1980 was already $762.90 (Edelman 1985). This translates into an average expenditure of $2,061.60 per family. By the time of this writing, the expenditure for a family of four was $4,545.20. The projected per capita expenditure was to increase. At this writing political changes in Eastern Europe and the Soviet Union may slow expenditures as the apparently lessened military threat makes such increases harder to justify. As each poor and middle-class American family dug deeper into its financial resources, it lowered the standard of health and welfare for its children. Given the rates of taxation, poorer families were hit the hardest by the military spending spree. This massive military expenditure becomes an even graver specter if one considers what simultaneously happened to federal expenditures for the health and welfare of the children.

In 1980 the per capita expenditure for health, nutrition, education, and welfare programs for low-income families and children was $486.80. This translates into $1,947.20 per family of four (Edelman 1985). By 1986 the family expenditure for poor families dropped to $1,716.80. The projected expenditure per capita by 1990 was to fall to $395.80, an expenditure of $1,583.20 per family. As the Children's Defense Fund pointed out, "Every poor American child could be lifted out of poverty in 1986 for less than half of the proposed defense spending increase for that year alone" (Edelman 1985, 3).

THE POOR. While the costs to individuals and families for military spending accelerated, the numbers of children growing up in poverty accelerated as well. With the aid of a healthy economy, the Great Society programs of the 1960s and 1970s reduced the numbers of families living in poverty by nearly 27 percent. The time of accelerated military spending and cuts for welfare from 1979 to 1983 saw a 35.6

percent increase in the number of families living in poverty and 3.3 million more children fell into poverty (Edelman 1985, vii, 18). By 1985 there were 13.3 million children growing up in poverty in the United States (Edelman 1985, 33). That was one child in five.

The 35 million people living in poverty in the United States survive in part through the variety of federal services and programs instituted since the Great Depression. Reductions in these services and programs strike at the core of human needs that are not met in our society. The Children's Defense Fund documented some recent examples. The 1984 Physician's Task Force on Hunger in America found widespread hunger in the United States, particularly in the Deep South. Yet the federal food-stamp program and a special program designed to insure proper nutrition and growth in small children—Special Supplemental Food Program for Women, Infants, and Children (WIC)—were targets for cuts. Each reached only one-third of eligible persons.

The number of homeless people in the United States has been estimated to be between 300,000 and 3,000,000 (Roberts and Keefe 1986). In 1985 the number of children under 18 without adequate, permanent shelter was 66,000. There was a two- to eighteen-year wait for public housing in major cities in various parts of the country.

A little more than half the families living in poverty receive Aid To Families with Dependent Children benefits. Half the states will not pay benefits to impoverished families who have both parents living at home, even when both are unemployed. One choice that poor parents must make is to separate so that the mother and children can survive with AFDC benefits. Unfortunately, the burden of survival choices is not the only one that must be borne by the poor.

Paying for the Military Spending Choices. The choices being made between social welfare and weapons is manifest in many indirect ways in addition to direct cuts in social welfare programs for the poor. The poor have had to bear an increasing percentage of their income being taxed to help fund the military budget. Joseph Pechman of the Brookings Institution points out that taxes for the poorest tenth of the population rose from 16.8 percent of their income to 21.9 percent from 1966 to 1985. In the same years, taxes for the wealthiest tenth dropped from 30.1 percent or their income to 25.3 percent (Edelman 1985). During three recent years of military budget growth, 1980 to 1982, taxes paid by poor families increased by 58 percent (Edelman 1985). The Children's Defense Fund pointed out that in 1983, Boeing, DuPont, General Electric, and Texaco together earned 3.8 billion in profits yet paid no income taxes and received 321 million in tax rebates and benefits. Over 230,000 families at the poverty line helped generate those rebates and benefits at the cost of dropping into poverty (Edelman 1986, 51–52). By 1975 each of these corporations were in the top one hundred military contractors (Gervasi 1984).

THE MIDDLE CLASS. Of twelve major corporations paying no tax or receiving up to 283 million in rebates and benefits from 1981–1983, seven, earning 14.54 billion in profits, were major military contractors by 1975 (Edelman 1985; Gervasi 1984).

There is some evidence to conclude that most of the American middle class does not benefit from military spending. Since military spending is capital intensive and produces relatively few products, the manufacturing sector of the economy has been hurt rather than helped by such spending.

Workers in the manufacturing sector of the economy have traditionally made up the largest category of middle-income workers in the United States. They have hit hard times with the general slump in manufacturing in the United States. Military spending creates large profits and high salaries for professionals such as engineers. Still it does not employ great numbers of workers as did the auto industry and other manufacturing giants.

By the mid-1970s a great increase in military spending was generated by the U.S. government. Average weekly earnings of U.S. workers declined 14.3 percent (when adjusted for inflation) from 1973 to 1983 (*New York Times,* Sept. 5, 1986). There are, to be sure, other factors influencing these tendencies, yet military spending policies do appear to redistribute wealth from the middle class to the wealthy. For example, the gap between the two groups began to increase rather dramatically in 1977, and by 1984 the middle-income groups in the United States had gone from 20 to only 17 percent of the share of the national income.

Summary and Conclusion. In recent times it has become clear that through cuts in social welfare expenditures, higher taxation, and higher costs for basic goods the poor and the middle class carried the burden of the choice for massive increases in military expenditures. While spending on welfare and warfare have been relatively independent phenomena historically, clearly a choice for warfare has been underway in the United States in more recent times. The military related industries and the wealthy have prospered as never before. Yet, the casualties of the choice for warfare have begun to mount. The economic health or our society has been gravely affected. The federal debt that will have to be paid by future generations has reached stunning proportions. The health, welfare, and structure of families in and near poverty have been severely stressed. All the while the waste of our wealth on arms is making us less and less secure. Historically, this choice has led to terrible consequences for industrial economies and people's lives. The changes in the Soviet Union and Eastern Europe may provide a historic opportunity to reverse our recent societal choices and avoid adverse economic and social consequences.

The United States has not been unique in this distribution of wealth and energy. The Soviet Union has by their own admission been saddled with the same choices. Even more profound in its effects is the shift from social to military expenditures with even more and graver casualties that is underway in the Third World. We turn to this next.

Chapter 10

Lessons from the Third World

Letters from a Violent Place. In the late 1950s a vicious and terroristic guerilla war broke out in the French colony, Algeria. The conflict was between the French government and the native Arab population. The two million French settlers or *Pieds noirs* had developed a good deal of racial hatred toward the Arabs. The French were by and large middle class, while the Arabs remained in poverty and squalor. As the Arabs agitated for political independence, violence was soon to wrack the unhappy country. Arabs planted bombs in public places where the French were likely to congregate. The French retaliated with killer raids on villagers suspected of harboring guerrillas. Moreover, the French applied methods of torture to suspected Arab agitators that came very close to techniques the Nazis used in World War II.

Franz Fanon, a black psychiatrist from Martinique, was hired by the French government to work with the French police in Algiers. It appeared that French officers who were torturing Arab suspects were exhibiting psychiatric symptoms and were suffering from insomnia, anxiety, and suicidal obsessions. Some had awakened in the night in the act of choking or beating their own wives.

Fanon was repulsed by the violence, but he began to analyze it in his *The Wretched of the Earth* (1965). Fanon had come to believe that violence was a necessary component of a colonial system. It seemed to him that violence by the oppressed was the only way out of the system of colonial domination.

Another French-speaking intellectual, Albert Camus, had great interest in the struggle in Algeria, where he was born. During World War II he fought in the French resistance against the Nazis, but by the late 1940s, he had became a pacifist.

In 1946 he stated his position in this fashion:

> All I ask is that in the midst of a murderous world, we agree to reflect on murder and make a choice . . . over the expanse of five continents throughout the coming years an endless struggle is going to be pursued between violence and friendly persuasion. . . . Henceforth, the only honorable course will be to stake everything on a formidable gamble: that words are more powerful than munitions (quoted in Weinberg 1965, 122).

As the conflict intensified and Franz Fanon became more identified with the Arab rebels' cause, he received several letters from Camus. Camus expressed to Fanon his hope France would grant the liberation and justice that had been denied the Arab population. He argued that the dialectic of increased violence on both sides could not be justified by *any* future goals—no matter how noble. Nonviolent change, negotiation, and gradualism were seen as the only way to future justice. In any case, Camus argued that pacifism must become the ethic of humankind or humanity would not survive (O'Brien 1970).

Fanon's reply to Camus was quick and to the point—only a middle-class intellectual such as Camus has the option for pacifism. For the Third World poor, "the wretched of the earth" as Fanon called them, violence is part of everyday life. It is embedded in the hunger of children and in the humiliating insults of the rich. When people of the Third World struggle nonviolently for a better life, the mask of civilization falls off the oppressor and violent repression must ineluctably follow. No, Fanon argued, pacifism was not a choice for those in the Third World. On the contrary, it is a possibility only for those with means enough to stay above the struggle for existence. Violence is the only possibility for those denied a hearing in polite society. Violence is the only possible way to express your humanity when your skin is the "wrong" color and you are stripped of political power. In other words, justice is more important than compassion (Geismar 1969, 121).

Camus' response was that violent justice leads only to violence. It is not at all certain that justice can come out of it. Violence nearly always escalates, even after its original causes are forgotten.

These two thinkers have set out the issues we now address, namely, how violence happens and is shaped in the impoverished parts of the world. Finally, and with some trepidation, we will offer some solutions to the problems of violence and peace in the Third World.

The lessons that the Third World learns regarding violence are generated in economic and social processes. They are manifest in the consequences of these processes for people and are driven home by military responses to social and political instability.

We will outline these processes, consequences, and responses in search of a global view of violence that can serve as a basis for peace. This will inevitably lead us to look at the gaps between the rich and the poor countries and between the rich and the poor people within countries of the Third World. It will require a critical look at economic developments and relations between developed and underdeveloped countries. And finally it will require a focus on the increasing use of military violence and suppression to control the tensions created by the gaps or disparities in wealth between countries and between people and the dynamics of their relationships. From what we encounter in our overview of the conditions and processes, we will suggest modest goals that may be of use to those concerned with the distant objective of realizing peace in the world. The main benefit of this analysis is likely to be a sensitization to the conditions and processes that generate profound violence in the world.

How the Third World Came To Be. What we call the Third World as opposed to the worlds of developed capitalistic and socialistic countries has a somewhat common and often tragic history. In almost all cases Third World countries were colonized by Europeans in the eighteenth and nineteenth centuries. Systems of forced or cheap labor fueled large-scale plantation systems all the way from Indochina to Latin America to East Africa.

The economies of these societies were developed around the needs of the colonizing nations. Thus the economies of the Third World produced for export rather than internal consumption. This pattern continues today in spite of the prevalence of hunger as a real issue for many of the poor in Third World countries.

Colonialism meant that Third World people were ruled directly or indirectly by foreign people who were often unconcerned about the welfare of the people they ruled. However, European ideas such as freedom, democracy, and equality were quick to take root in these oppressed countries. As a result of this and other factors, anticolonial struggles dominated the nineteenth as well as the twentieth centuries. These struggles were often bloody, especially when racist notions fueled the fires of hatred.

Racism and physical distance from the Third World's poor allowed tragedies such as occurred in the Belgian Congo at the turn of this century. English missionaries began to tell about the frightful slaughter of the native population in areas ruled by King Leopold of Belgium. Vast rubber plantations were worked by the native people in which

> Each village was ordered by the authorities to collect and bring in a certain amount of rubber—as much as the men could collect and bring in by neglecting all works for their own maintenance. If they failed to bring in the required amount . . . native troops many of them cannibals were sent into the Villages to spread terror, if necessary by killing some of the men. . . . They were ordered to bring in one right hand for every cartridge used (Russell 1964, 401).

Less extreme tragedies of this variety were commonplace in remote parts of the colonized world during the nineteenth century. Eventually, local elites came to dominate the Third World as colonialism retreated. Nevertheless, they too became dependent on the money and power of the outside world as new forms of economic dependency took over in the Third World. Few legal colonies exist in the world today, yet the external domination of Third World countries by outside powers is commonplace. When we attempt to understand this reality today we can conclude that "absentee landlords don't care much about their tenants." Foreign investors in the Third World often know or care little for the welfare of the work force or the ecological problems in a distant nation.

Gaps. Richard Estes, a researcher into social and economic problems of the Third World, cautioned that unless global social change was undertaken, "The development gap between rich and poor nations will continue to widen with the result that, by the end of the present century, the world will have become vastly overpopulated, overly urbanized, and increasingly less safe with poverty, starvation, and the dangers of war and destruction increasing daily" (1985, 61). This bleak picture reflects the nature of current realities about the gap between rich and poor nations.

By 1977 the major capitalistic countries had two-thirds of the world's income and 20 percent of the world's population. The underdeveloped nations had less than 13 percent of the world's income and more than 50 percent of the world's people (Harrington 1977, 16). This condition is but one point in a long historical trend. The income gap between industrializing countries and agrarian countries was 2 to 1 in 1850, was 15 to 1 by 1960, and is projected to be 30 to 1 by the year 2000 (Brown 1972, 42). Another way to indicate the gap is to note that in 1985 the poorest fifth of the world's population living in the poorest countries had a 1.6 percent share of the world's total gross national product while the richest fifth living in the world's richest countries had a 74.2 percent share of the world's total gross national product (Sivard 1987, 21). Indeed, the richest 40 percent of the world's people share 90 percent of the wealth while the remaining 60 percent divide the remaining 10 percent (Sivard 1987, 21).

International Stratification. However, if we consider the gap between rich countries and poor countries alone, we will miss a significant aspect of the vast differences that exist between the rich and poor people of the world. Townsend asserts that we can understand the relations between rich and poor countries only if we envision a system of *international stratification* in which the wealth of some societies is linked to the poverty of other societies and to the poverty within the wealthy societies (Townsend 1971, 42). Such a system analyzed in detail by Michael Harrington led him to comment about the wealthy class in Brazil, "the upper class lives in the First World, the masses in the Third World" (Harrington 1977, 149).

The gaps between the rich and the poor countries and between the rich and the poor people of the world are extreme, but they are also part of a process. The process has euphemistically been called Third World development. A critical focus on this process gives those of us in the developed world new insights into both the scope and nature of violence and the necessity for peace.

Economic Development as Violence. The development of the industrial world took place as part of a long historical process in Western Europe as it emerged from feudal society (Harrington 1977). In this context as more efficient means of producing goods developed, unemployed workers and growing populations could find work as the investment of profits in new technologies created jobs. The ideal of an economic trend of perpetual self-generating expansion would indeed raise all levels of society. Periodically, economic recession and depression would wreak havoc among working people, but the system survived.

Underdevelopment. By contrast, "development" in the Third World proceeded not from processes within each country but from external influences by the already industrialized nations (Harrington 1977). The story of the extraction of natural resources from Third World nations to fuel production in the industrial world is well known.

But there is much more to the process, which is sometimes referred to as the development of *underdevelopment* (Hoogvelt 1977). Understanding the general outlines of this process is key to understanding the genesis of violence in the Third World.

One dynamic in this process is that observed by Harrington

(1977). Very simply stated, the Third World worker is paid a wage that may be many times less than that paid a First World worker for production of similar goods. The advantage for the company owner or multinational corporation is that the goods produced so cheaply will be sold at First World prices. Moreover, the profits are not necessarily reinvested in the Third World country in which they are made. If demand for the goods drops or if production becomes more efficient causing decreased demand for workers, the unemployed and excess population is impoverished. They do not reap the benefits of the wealth they have created. They do not find employment in new industries created by technological innovations.

Add to this dynamic a couple of other factors. First, people in traditional agrarian societies often secure their old age with many offspring—children are their social security. If there are high infant mortalities, they are likely to produce many children (Grant 1988). The populations continue to increase placing ever-increasing demands on resources necessary to basic human needs. Second, as already suggested, the elite classes who control wealth in Third World countries are oriented toward the First World. Investment opportunities are most attractive in the more stable First World. As Harrington explains, "the upper classes in the impoverished lands often subordinate themselves, politically and culturally, to the rulers of the affluent countries" (Harrington 1977, 138–39). The net result of these processes and others related to them is to create what are called *enclaves of modernity* in Third World countries (Harrington 1977, 145). An urban area is created with some intense production of goods for the First World by low-wage workers surrounded by poverty worsened by the fragmentation of their traditional agrarian society and modes of production.

The Rich Get Richer and the Poor . . . After indicating that a remarkable feature of underdevelopment in India and elsewhere in the Third World is the continued impoverishment of the lower-half of the population and an even further drop in income of the poor as in the Philippines, Kim observes, "likewise, studies and reports from many different sources invariably point to the fact that the benefits of economic development have accrued exclusively to the rich and the power elites of the developing nations" (Kim 1985, 4).

This is not the way economic development is supposed to proceed according to traditional views. Everyone should eventually prosper from the new wealth and opportunity generated by investment and the production of goods. But because of the processes of underdevelopment this old assumption, which generally held up in industrial countries, does not prevail in relations between the First and Third World.

The consequences of underdevelopment can be expressed in economic and social indicators that portray a form of violence unfamiliar to the life experiences of the majority of people in the developed nations. Earlier we defined violence as physical force employed so as to damage or to injure. We need not stretch this definition very far to encompass the force of conscious economic decisions and the special violence resulting in the Third World.

Debt. The continual outflow of capital from the Third World in profits has been balanced partially by direct aid from industrial countries to the developing countries. Yet this aid plus the wealth that developing countries generate is now far from sufficient to overcome the imbalance between the rich and the poor. This occurs because in their struggle toward development along the same path as the industrial nations, Third World nations have borrowed greatly from them. One source calculates the loan debt from developing countries to developed countries has grown from $750 billion to $1 trillion from 1982 to 1986 (Isbister 1987, 7).

The net effect of this debt and the associated interest payments is that in 1985, taking into account foreign aid, loans, interest, investments, and returns, the developing world transferred over $30 billion to the industrialized world. Only five years before the flow of capital had been $40 billion in the opposite direction (Grant 1988). This massive debt has been accumulated by the extension of the underdevelopment process along with a few added problems. Competitive international banks functioned with only partial awareness of each other's investments. Consequently, too much money was lent and borrowed between the First and Third World in the 1970s (Isbister 1987). Oil price increases adversely affected the financing and economies of the Third World in the 1970s as well (Isbister 1987). Thus many Third World countries are in the dangerous position of having to borrow to pay off the interest on their debts while the debts increase at 8 percent per year. Indeed, we now live in a world in which the developing countries are financing the growth of the industrialized countries (Isbister 1987).

Violent Consequences. And what is the response of Third World governments to this crisis of increasing debt? They are in the position of having to roll over their debt, default and lose credibility, or "tighten their belts" in an effort to extract more productivity from their people—who are experiencing lower wages and less governmental social spending to meet basic human needs. This process produces a kind of violence because physical and emotional damage is inflicted as a direct result of financial and political decisions.

In Latin America restrictive government policies put in place in an attempt to finance the debt forced incomes to decrease 10 percent in five years. The poorest people in those countries have lost 25 to 40 percent of their incomes (Isbister 1987, 5). United Nations sources indicate that seventy governments have adopted "economic adjustment" policies including cuts in social services and subsidies for staple foods (Grant 1988). In one estimate almost three out of ten people in developing countries have experienced a stagnation or reduction in their incomes since 1970 (Sivard 1987).

THE DEATH OF CHILDREN. Such income reductions and cuts result in violence to the children who are most vulnerable and to the most vulnerable among the poor. "One death in every three in the world is the death of a child under the age of five. And each week more than a quarter of a million young children still die, in the developing world, from infection and undernutrition" (Grant 1988, 1). The results of these economic changes is a "measurable deterioration" in at least thirty nations. In one sample of ten nations there was increased malnutrition in five, increased child deaths in three, and school attendance falling in eight (Grant 1988, 1). Diarrhea related to impure water is the leading cause of child mortality. Infectious diseases that can be prevented by vaccination claim 3 million lives each year. Acute respiratory infections claim the lives of 3 million children under the age of three. Undernutrition accounts for one-third of the deaths (Grant 1988). Since most of these deaths are preventable and the result of economic decisions, they can be seen as a form of violence. It is the violence of small children and infants dying in their mother's arms as the rest of their family looks on. It is the violence and destruction of the future for diverse cultures and ways of life. It is a form of violence that we notice merely in passing in the First World. It is preventable death but death ignored by those who decide what is most important.

UNEMPLOYMENT. Since 1960 unemployment has increased twice as fast in Third World countries as in developed nations. Outside of China, 90 million are unemployed and some 300 million are underemployed, working in part-time jobs such as handymen, running errands, or selling flowers (Sivard 1987). The consequences of unemployment in developed countries include increased stress as well as deterioration in physical and psychological health, and it is correlated with increases in spouse and child abuse, alcoholism, and homicides (for a summary of effects see Keefe 1984). To the extent that the consequences are similar in developing countries, unemployment has disastrous consequences in these large populations without even considering the deprivations of basic needs for people living close to the edge of starvation.

DETERIORATION OF THE FAMILY. One of the economic shifts taking place in the developing world observed by Estes in his research has been the steady erosion of the extended family as the basic social welfare institution in the majority of the world's developing countries (Estes 1987). In periods of less governmental involvement and support of basic welfare, deterioration of the family as a unit of mutual support through death, dislocation, migration, and war is a subtle but real form of violence that is difficult to repair. As such violence grows, people are oppressed, but they will not remain passive victims.

Instability and the Military Solution. Research substantiates the intuitive assumption that the wider the gap between the rich and the poor, the less stable the established order (Hashimi 1985). With economic development processes, Third World debt and pervasive violence to the poorest populations, social unrest, and political instability are likely to follow. One response to instability born of economic deprivation is economic assistance or welfare. Another, of course, is to attempt to control unrest or potential unrest through military threat and military violence.

Economic aid is a form of welfare for Third World countries. It is noteworthy that it is linked closely to military aid and military government. This linkage of aid and arms reveals something about the relationship between the industrial and the Third World— additional sources of violence. As Sivard points out, "most of the major recipient countries had higher than average incomes and a higher than average ratio of military expenditures to GNP. The largest share of aid went not to countries in the most extreme poverty, but to middle-income countries, many of them associated with major military alliances or in areas of high military tension" (Sivard 1985, 23). In a sense, the military sectors of the Third World receive the most aid.

Why is the demand for arms so great? Why are the already indebted nations so inclined to spend so much on arms that only add to their debt and produce little or no new wealth?

Coup d'état *and Military Control.* Part of the answer lies in the changing nature of Third World governments. Sivard (1987) defines military control of a government as key leadership by military officers, martial law, extrajudicial authority by security forces, lack of political control of the military, or occupation by foreign military forces. Sivard found that 26 percent of developing states were under military control in 1960; by 1987, 52 percent of 113 developing countries were under military control.

These governments have more militarized countries—two and a half times as many men under arms—and spend twice as much on arms as other developing countries (Sivard 1987). From 1960 until 1985 there were 138 successful military coups, that is, sudden overthrow of governments by a small group using military troops (David 1987). Africa, Latin America, and the Far East lead the regions of the world with military governments (Sivard 1985).

Sivard points out that there is a proliferation of very advanced weapons in underdeveloped, politically volatile nations. She observes:

> The weapons are in many cases more sophisticated than the general level of industrial technology in Third World importing countries. The education and training that they require, often assisted by the exporting countries, has helped to create a favored group in the Third World which uses elite status, as well as the weapons themselves, to assume political control, and in turn to expand military power and prestige. The system builds on itself (Sivard 1985, 14).

One of the ways that the system builds is through the military coup. One reason that coups d'état take place is the sense of the military that it is different from and better than the society from which it comes (David 1987). Also the military may believe that it acts in the national interest or that it is preserving the position of the armed forces *vis-à-vis* civilian leaders. In any event, the coup d'état is the most common form of extralegal government change in the Third World (David 1987). The clear transition in the Third World is to military government. The clear means is by coup. The human consequences are also clear.

Human Consequences. The violence generated in the dynamics of underdevelopment and increasing debt is compounded by the violence generated by the military. This additional violence is derived from the demands of military spending in terms of *human need* and by military oppression in terms of *human rights.*

DEPRIVATION. It is disheartening to note that the world's largest arms exporters, the Soviet Union and the United States, are the stingiest with economic aid as a portion of their GNPs (Sivard 1985). It is disheartening when we note that figured in man-years of income the military burden of military expenditures in the Third World is three times what it is in the First World (Sivard 1987). Indeed, the Third World's military expenditures in one year equal the income of people in the forty-four poorest nations (Sivard 1987).

Again, Ruth Sivard enumerates the comparative costs of arms and the costs of meeting human needs. To raise school enrollment to the level of First World countries, 230 million children would have to become enrolled—an enormous number. Yet an expansion of this magnitude would cost less than one-third of the $150 billion that developing countries are spending on the arms race in a single year (1987).

At the cost of $5.00 per child, 3.5 million children could be saved each year through vaccinations. Fourteen million children could be saved each year through low-cost measures. Half of the Third World's people do not have safe drinking water. Eight million more physicians would be needed to bring health care to the levels of developed countries. Half a billion people suffer from anemia, nearly 800 million do not eat enough food for an active work life. And yet government budgets for health average only one-fourth their military budgets (Sivard 1987, 1985).

SUPPRESSION. A most telling finding of Sivard is the documentation of human rights violations by military governments. Among fifty-nine military governments identified, fifty-seven violate human rights employing torture, brutality, disappearances, and political killings (Sivard 1987). By contrast, while violations of human rights existed under civilian Third World governments, Sivard reported there were ten times as many civilian governments as military with no violations on record (1987). Sivard concludes, "Militarized government survives on repression. Fear-inducing tactics are used to subdue the opposition, bottle up change, and ensure the control of resources that nourish power" (Sivard 1987, 26).

The military solution to instability generated by extreme poverty actually exacerbates the living condition of the people. It is much like putting a cover on a boiling kettle in the hope that it will prevent its boiling over. But there is more.

WAR. Briefly stated, the numbers of wars in the world have increased radically in this century and in the last decade. In 1960, 52 percent of the deaths in these wars were civilians, in 1970, 73 percent, and in the 1980s, 85 percent (Sivard 1987). But the most telling fact is that since World War II only one war has taken place outside the Third World. The other 119 were or are being fought in the Third World (Sivard 1985).

We must add to the civilian casualties the massive dislocation of people who become refugees, the many who starve because of separation from their means of producing food, and of course the survivors who suffer grief and terror. Table 10.1 provides examples of Third World violence in Central America that typify the violence we have discussed.

From Violence to Solutions. We have seen that the process of underdevelopment begets violence in the Third World, and this violence begets instability and militarism both to control unrest and

Table 10.1. Examples and Varieties of Violence in One Part of the Third World in the 1980s

---

1. Hunger

From 35 to 70 percent of Central Americans are malnourished. Three out of four children are malnourished.

In Central America the number of landless peasants tripled from 1960 to 1987.

Eighty-five percent of the best farm land in the area is used to grow crops for export.

The average rural wage of $2 to $4 a day is not enough to pay even half a family's minimal food, shelter, and clothing costs.

---

2. Violent Repression

The increasing use of death squads to control peasants in El Salvador, Guatemala, and Honduras.

Guerrilla warfare in El Salvador, Guatemala, and Nicaragua.

The use of torture and mutilation as social control by the governments of Guatemala, Honduras, and El Salvador.

---

3. Environmental Poisoning

The "dumping" of unsafe pesticides in Central American countries.

Few or no regulations on the uses of pesticides or other harmful chemicals in these countries.

Sources: Robert G. Williams, 1986, *Export Agriculture and the Crisis in Central America* (High Point: University of North Carolina Press); Tom Barry, 1987, *Roots of Rebellion: Land and Hunger in Central America* (Boston: South End Press); *Torture in the Eighties,* 1985 (London: Amnesty International Publication).

to secure the process and its perpetrators. The costs of the increasingly applied military solution include enormous arms expenditures, destruction of human rights, and the death, dislocation, and terror of war. We must find better solutions and new ways of relating between the First and Third Worlds.

Toward Prevention and Peaceful Ends to Violence. If we think of preventing and ending violence in the Third World, the tasks seem monumental. We must remember that it is violence born of human activity, and thus human action can end it. It is not a condition beyond human control.

One way of addressing such an endeavor is to think in terms of preventing a disease or problem that occurs in a population. *Primary prevention* creates conditions that would not allow the violence to occur. *Secondary prevention* would limit the spread of violence and its effects already underway. *Tertiary prevention* would rehabilitate the existing victims to the extent possible (after Bloom 1980).

Primary prevention of Third World violence would address the dynamics of underdevelopment. Can the basic approach to development be changed? Is a different model for development possible? Solutions at this level are more global and general. Kim argues that we must look for a model advanced by the new international economic order that is oriented toward a first priority of meeting human needs (Kim 1985). Myrdal (1970) argues that the social inequality generated in economic inequality is detrimental to development and that equality and social justice are conducive. What is needed is a model of social development that places human needs and human rights at the center and allows each country to develop along paths in keeping with its culture and history. As the quality of life improves and people begin to prosper, economic investment can have a *mutually* beneficial effect.

Goals are needed such as international guarantees of human rights and international programs of consciousness raising that use the ever-more pervasive electronic media. First World countries could develop policies born of democratic pressure that require such actions as redistribution of the land; plowing a percentage of profits back into countries in which they are earned as a prerequisite to domestic tax advantages; or use of their economic influence to force Third World countries to reduce the income gaps between the rich and the poor, to reduce the power of the military, and to broaden political participation (David 1987). The international community could collaborate in more comprehensive programs for immunization of all Third World children against the main infectious diseases, purification of the water supplies, and supplying adequate prenatal and postnatal nutrition.

Secondary prevention would address the problems of hungry, illiterate, underemployed, exploited populations. A uniform food policy by producing nations would help. Foreign aid could once again be tied to human rights protection and establishment of democratic institutions. First World countries could stop supporting military insurgencies and train Third World military officers in less violent disciplines such as government, civics, and economics.

Tertiary measures would consist of international demands for reparation payments to survivors and refugees by victors in Third World wars, oral rehydration therapy for children, and vocational education systems for peoples whose traditional economic production methods have been disrupted by "wrongful investment" and market exigencies.

Conclusion. In sum, the Third World peoples are victims of a multiplicity of afflictions. They inhabit the poorest, most violence-prone parts of the earth. We can surmise that if a World War III were to come forth, it may spring from some conflict in the Third World. Thus it is in the interests of the developed nations to see that peace breaks out in these troubled parts of the world.

The lesson the Third World has to teach us is that some sort of economic justice or equity is a necessary prelude to peaceful times in the Third World. It is obviously not true that the developed countries can make over their poorer neighbors in their own image. In the recent past, conflicts between the poor and other groups in Third World nations have often been used by the major powers to test theories and weapons of "low-intensity warfare." When this happens

Table 10.2. Ways to Reduce the Sources of Violence in the Third World

Sources of Violence and Poverty	Examples of Possible Solutions
1. Concentration of land in a few hands and landless peasants	1. Land reform and redistribution
2. Increasing external debt	2 Renegotiation or cancellation of debts by foreign sources (elimination of protectionism)
3 Dependence on only a few cash crops	3. Diversification of rural economies
4. Lack of organization among peasants for self-development	4. An end to the repression of grassroots and local organizations of the poor
5. Torture and death squads directed at the poor	5. Support for international observers via United Nations and Amnesty International, etc.
6. Bad drinking water, preventable diseases	6. International aid for development coupled with grassroots organizations
7. Guerrilla wars	7. Inclusion of all classes of people in government—egalitarian reform
8. The use of modern weapons by third-world governments in local wars	8. International agreements not to use the Third World as surrogate for first and second world conflicts.

the violence of poverty is compounded by the violence of modern warfare. Yet having said this, we must also point out that the technical expertise and tools of the rich and developed world are desperately needed in those countries containing the wretched of the earth.

For the peoples of the Third World, survival is a daily question to be answered through struggle. For the people of the rich industrial societies the question of survival is an abstraction, a denied fear, a spectre that is usually not confronted. In the next chapter we turn to face this spectre, to confront its threat, to learn its potential. In confronting these possibilities, we believe we take a necessary first step toward understanding and eventual control over the nuclear menace to our survival.

Chapter 11

The Spectre
of Annihilation

A spectre is haunting mankind. It is the spectre of annihilation in a thermonuclear war.

—ERIC HASS (1958)

The words thermonuclear annihilation, nuclear war, Armageddon, and the like call up different but usually intense reactions in people reading or hearing them. They mean death. They mean personal death but something more. The thought is enormously difficult to deal with. Ours is perhaps the first generation since the threat of the Black Death in the fourteenth century that has had to contemplate the end of humankind. But as we shall see, thermonuclear annihilation threatens even more; it threatens to end life itself.

So we who are aware of the threat have a choice. We can defensively charge that such thoughts are too farfetched by reason of their magnitude to be considered at all and accuse those who raise them as being shrill alarmists. We can fall into a chronic, dark mood beneath the spectre of the mushroom-shaped cloud. We can adopt a life-style of immediacy without plan or concern for a future that may not come. We can repress all thoughts of such possibilities and live our lives in a slightly panicky repression of what haunts us, perhaps making its success more likely. Or we can turn around and look Death, dark Thanatos, in the face and proceed with caution and confidence on the way toward using part of our lives to deal with this most pressing of problems.

In this chapter we will take the latter course and confront the problem. There is wisdom in discovering what each of us can do in our own small way to help solve this problem. The first step is to become informed.

Possibilities. There are a variety of ways that nuclear war could begin by accident. By 1984 the United States and the Soviet Union each possessed well over six thousand and ten thousand strategic nuclear warheads respectively (Gervasi 1984, 92). And as we will soon discover, there are several more countries with nuclear weapons and more countries are joining the nuclear club all the time. Are current superpower policies leading to more dangerous possibilities for nuclear war? Could one or more of these weapons be launched without the intent of the political leadership of its country of origin? What are the possibilities?

Drift Toward Armageddon. Consider a scene in which two knights stand in a field eyeball-to-eyeball. Their swords are in their scabbards. Can a battle be forestalled? Consider a second scene in which the two stand in the same position but each has drawn his sword and is slowly raising it to a position to swiftly strike the other. What are the chances for peaceful resolution now? It may seen simplistic to characterize the development of nuclear arms relations between the superpowers as analogous to these scenes, but they do bear a resemblance.

MAD. The first nuclear bombs were used against cities. This was a continuation of a trend in warfare in which civilian populations became targets as a part of a strategy of "total war" (Dyer 1986b). The Eisenhower administration developed the doctrine of *Massive Retaliation* in which an aggressor could expect to be destroyed. As the Soviet Union developed its nuclear capacity, it became clear that massive retaliation was possible for both of the nuclear powers. An attack of one side against the other was sure to be met by a massive destructive counterattack from the other. This condition was called Mutually Assured Destruction (MAD) by Secretary of Defense Robert

S. McNamara (Chant and Hogg 1983). Like knights in a field, the two superpowers stood eye-to-eye with swords ready but not yet drawn, daring each other to strike and see if he could survive the retaliatory blow.

This policy seemed to stabilize superpower relations in the sense that a third world war has not occurred. Yet the condition of MAD was not really the product of wise and intelligent policy so much as it was the result of technological developments. As we have learned, the nuclear missile made the cities of each country vulnerable. Without an adequate defense the MAD policy was inevitable. Just as inevitable was the deterioration of this condition as weapons technology progressed.

FIRST STRIKE. Inevitably missiles became more accurate and warheads more powerful. Soon even the land-based strategic weapons of both sides were vulnerable to the other side's weapons. This created a new condition and hence a new strategy and accompanying policy. If one country strikes first and "decapitates" the other by destroying their command and control and strategic weapons before they are launched, then "victory is possible" as two strategists put it (Gray and Payne 1980). If we add the ingredients of the Reagan administration's deployment of Pershing II missiles only a few minutes from Moscow, superior and more accurate submarine launched missiles, MX "silo busting" missiles in silos that cannot withstand a Soviet first strike, and of undetectable cruise missiles, then there is a possibility for a nuclear *"first strike"* that would catch the enemy unprepared. Should a few enemy missiles be launched and get through, the country could recover. Of course the Soviet Union began to match the U.S. capability in each new area thus sending first strike signals of its own. Had the knights now begun to draw their swords?

These developments were coupled with rhetoric about the "immorality" of MAD in which cities were threatened first rather than military targets. Soon buzz words like "counterforce" (targeted against military targets) and "collateral damage" (human victims) were part of the manipulation of consciousness by governmental spokesmen. Assuming that the highest authorities of each government were aware that such strategies disregard the effects of radiation, nuclear winter, the destruction of the ozone layer, and the severe disruption of the exosphere, why did they pursue such strategies and policies and use such rhetoric?

The reality is that the military of both sides—as well as the other nuclear powers—prepares for the worst case. The political leadership of both sides points to the opposing military plans as indicators of the intentions of the leadership of the other side. Meanwhile technology continues to develop and lead the strategies and "policies" of all sides. Wisdom, political leadership, and common sense seem to be absent and policy seems adrift.

Occasionally we hear on either side that the grand scheme is to bankrupt or to economically bury the other side and force a political change in its leadership. This is a rationalization for a terrible game being played for profit and propelled by mindless bureaucratic processes. This seeming lack of human wisdom and control magnifies the possibilities of unintentional nuclear war.

Madman Scenario. One of the earliest and most abiding fears of the nuclear age is the fear that a madman in a position of responsibility for the care or launching of nuclear weapons might start a nuclear war by firing his weapons. After all, we have more destructive power on a single nuclear missile submarine than was unleashed in all of World War II. Suppose the captain was to become insane? Or the pilot of a nuclear bomber? Or a megalomaniacal chief of state? This is the fear of those who tend to trust the "system" and see its failure as the genesis of evil. What exactly is the "system," and how does it prevent the actions of a single or few madmen? A good review of the system in rough outline is provided by Chant and Hogg in their book, *Nuclear War in the 1980s* (1983).

The system or systems of the major nuclear powers are a series of checks and codes that are designed to prevent accident by usurpation of authority. First, persons who operate nuclear weapons are carefully screened to determine emotional stability and suitability. Second, in most cases, the nuclear warheads and their launch systems are separated until such time as their joining is authorized. Third, no nuclear weapon can be used without its code that can only be given by higher authority. Without the permissive code, individuals who have the means to launch a weapon cannot do so. Fourth, the launch of a weapon requires the cooperation of two people who are physically separated. The system is elaborate and redundant. It may be the most reliable link in the vital chain that secures the world. The military usually keeps its lines of authority clear and inviolate. But what about those in authority? Who are they?

Assuming that the system works to keep the operatives in line, can we rely absolutely upon the stability and suitability of the decision makers? Only the president of the United States has authority as commander-in-chief to authorize the use of nuclear weapons. But, according to the *Defense Monitor* (1986) of the Center for Defense Information, unlike the nuclear warheads of the Army and Air Force, the some 9,500 nuclear missile warheads, bombs, and antiaircraft and antisubmarine weapons aboard U.S. ships and submarines did not carry as of that writing Permissive Action Links that must be unlocked before the weapons can be armed. The captains of any nuclear-armed ship or submarine could launch nuclear weapons without permission from the president (*Defense Monitor* 1986). Even more unsettling is the possibility of these captains being deceived by error or intent.

Mistaken Strike. The Center for Defense Information reports that between 1977 and 1984 there were six serious false warnings requiring threat assessment conferences, one lasting six minutes (*Defense Monitor* 1986). Could a flight of Canadian Geese, a meteor shower, or other natural events at a time of international crisis set off a nuclear war? Until now human decision makers have assessed the circumstances and discovered the false alarms in time.

But the time for decision making grows shorter and shorter. The major nuclear powers are deploying weapons such as the Pershing II with only a few minutes flight time and Cruise Missiles that are low flying and very difficult to detect. Under these conditions it is increasingly alarming to find that more and more of the process of responding to possible attacks is given over to computers.

LAUNCH ON WARNING. One natural extension of this process is the so-called "launch on warning" option. This policy option would turn the decision to launch nuclear weapons completely over to a computer. Presumably, the preprogrammed decision would be based on computer analysis of data indicating an enemy attack. The "advantage" of such an option would be to shorten the decision time so as to insure the launching of missiles before the enemy warheads arrived to destroy them. United States military planners have stated that such a policy is a viable option. The United States' powerful and accurate MX missiles were to be placed in vulnerable silos, which appeared to make sense only with a "launch on warning" policy (*Defense Monitor* 1986).

Analysis, communication, and decision by political leadership involves less and less time. It may even be turned over to artificial intelligence. Deception and failed technology becomes a greater possibility.

ESCALATION OF SMALL CONFLICTS. A global first strike, where something benign is mistaken for an all-out nuclear attack, is but one way a mistaken retaliation might occur. Another possibility would be a misinterpretation and escalation of a conventional attack during a tense period of military maneuvers, posturing, or limited conflict.

A forward observer could easily mistake a conventional weapon explosion, with its fireball and cloud, for a small yield nuclear device. The observer would dutifully radio his observation to his command post. The commander would then forward the possible nuclear strike to his theater command and so on up the chain of command. An American president or Soviet premier would be faced with a decision of waiting to check out the reports or to take action quickly enough to allow most of his weapons to be launched before they are hit by the possible enemy first strike. Under these conditions a mistaken launch is possible.

A former secretary of defense, Morton Halperin, enunciated the doctrine of the North Atlantic Treaty Organization (NATO), which makes the Soviet premier's decision more troublesome. "The NATO doctrine is that we will fight with conventional weapons until we are losing. Then we will fight with tactical nuclear weapons until we are losing. And then we will blow up the world" (Halperin 984, 7).

We can add the unsettling possibility that a provocateur could fire a nuclear device in a region of tension such as the Middle East that would be interpreted by one or more nuclear powers as the start of an attack requiring rapid retaliation. As columnist M. R. Montgomery (1986) observed about the potential for building a triggering device for a primitive bomb, "Any Third World country with one MIT graduate and an American Express Card could put together the trigger of a very skinny Fat Man (an early atomic bomb)." One or more such nuclear devices set off in the major cities of a nuclear power could likewise begin a massive nuclear exchange.

Nuclear Proliferation. The United States exploded its first nuclear device in 1945; the Soviet Union followed with one of its own in 1949 (Gervasi 1984). They were later joined by France, Great Britain, and China. Seeing the danger of proliferation, a Nuclear Nonproliferation Treaty was signed in 1970 to stop the spread of nuclear weapons to more countries (Chant and Hogg 1983). The treaty was not sufficient to stop the spread of nuclear technologies such as nuclear power plant fuel reprocessing, which can be a step toward the development of fissionable materials necessary for nuclear weapons. Such technology would enable countries to develop their own nuclear weapons, so less formal agreements among some of the more technologically advanced countries to tighten up on the spread of nuclear weapons related technology have been attempted (Chant and Hogg 1983).

The International Atomic Energy Agency (IAEA) of the United Nations furthers efforts to prevent proliferation by the diversion of peaceful nuclear energy research for military purposes (Tirman, 1985). Despite the Nuclear Nonproliferation Treaty, the IAEA, and other attempts to stop the spread of nuclear weapons and the capacity to make them, India has developed and exploded a nuclear device. Several other countries are approaching nuclear weapons capability including: Argentina, Brazil, Egypt, Iraq, Israel, Libya, Pakistan, South Africa, South Korea, and Taiwan (Chant and Hogg 1983). As of this writing, six of these countries are not signatories of the Nuclear Nonproliferation Treaty.

Among the several dangers that contribute to the possibility of nuclear war, the proliferation of nuclear weapons and the capacity to make them is the most ominous because it increases the possibility of the other scenarios taking place as more and more players enter the nuclear arms game.

Human and Ecological Consequences of Nuclear War.

The human and ecological consequences of nuclear war are of course inextricably linked. The links between the human species and our environment are complex and extensive. Both are threatened by the possibility of even a limited nuclear exchange. Some human factors are artificially separable from ecological factors for discussion. The first of these, human consequences, is often overlooked.

Human Consequences.

CURRENT CONSEQUENCES. In a sense a third world war has already begun and has exacted many human casualties. It has begun in the sense that the superpowers' preparation for nuclear war has exacted a massive toll on the wealth of nations and upon their people. For example, 17 million lives of very young children could have been saved for $100 per child (UNICEF 1981); the total cost compares with the cost of six weeks of world arms spending or a single $1.793 billion Trident submarine (Gervasi 1984, 107).

Another kind of consequence that is just becoming clear is the psychological effects of the threat of nuclear war. Those of us who were born about the same time and after the explosion of the atomic bomb have grown up in a very different world from those of the past. We can within reason contemplate the end of not only humankind but of life itself. This reality may have an impact upon our worldview, our optimism, our unconscious life, and our behavior. Exactly what the impacts are and their magnitude are not yet manifest in extensive empirical research. Still, we do know some of the implications, and they are quite naturally troubling.

We know that fairly young children in the United States and the Soviet Union are aware of the threat of nuclear war (Mack 1982/ 1984). We know that this awareness sometimes affects their dream life (Mack 1984). We know that it sometimes affects their view of the future and their personal future (Schwebel 1982; Escalona 1982; Yudkin 1984). Family therapists report that like sexual abuse or adultery, the threat of nuclear war has become a family secret not to be discussed within families who seek counseling (Bloch 1984; Zeitlin 1984). The possible effects of such awareness and secret keeping are a wholesale mistrust in the elder generation's capacity to deal with very important life-threatening issues.

So there is the possibility of a kind of "learned helplessness" in which a threatening and noxious circumstance is seen as not amenable to any efforts to deal with it (Maier and Seligman 1976). If a whole generation grows up believing in their own impotence as a result of identifying with and modeling their parents and other adults, the possibility of its dealing with the threat is even more diminished. Children must see adults coping with the issue of nuclear war. In essence, they must learn that what is created by human beings can be changed and controlled by humans in a rational, democratic way.

IMMEDIATE EFFECTS OF A NUCLEAR BLAST. The immediate consequences for humans of a nuclear blast vary with their distance from ground zero, the point of detonation. Sometimes these immediate consequences are standardized by discussing the effects of the detonation of a one-megaton nuclear bomb over a major city.

A one-megaton bomb is about sixty-six times the power of the atomic bomb dropped on Hiroshima. The Union of Concerned Scientists and others have described the effects of such a detonation (UCS 1981; Chant and Hogg 1983). Its fireball would be 1,000 feet in diameter. Fifty square miles of the city would be totally destroyed by blast and fire. Unprotected people within 600 square miles would be killed. This would amount to 500,000 fatalities and 750,000 immediate casualties. In an area the size of Rhode Island all persons looking at the fireball would be permanently blinded. An area the size of Connecticut, 4,000 square miles, would be blanketed with radiation. In a full-scale nuclear war, as many as 50,000 nuclear weapons would be detonated. In excess of 100 million people in the United States and in the Soviet Union would be killed immediately. Because medical facilities would be destroyed, survivors would be without medical assistance. They would be subject to widespread epidemics and starvation. Industry, agriculture, and communications would be destroyed.

The flash, heat, and blast including high winds would take their toll of immediate victims. Less immediate victims would suffer the effects of varying doses of radiation. Ionizing radiation changes the electrical charges of elements in the body (Chant and Hogg 1983). This adversely affects the chemical processes and cell reproduction. Those receiving an initial large dose of radiation from the fireball or a large dose from fallout will experience nausea, vomiting, and diarrhea within a few hours of the exposure. This would be followed by fever, delirium, and death within a week (Chant and Hogg 1983, 140). Those receiving lower doses will experience hair loss, bleeding of the skin and mouth, an ulcerated gut, loss of appetite, rapid weight loss and fever, anemia, bleeding, and vulnerability to infection due to the suppression of white blood cells, which places the surviving individual at further risk. Leukemia is a long-term risk. Victims within half a mile of the blast at Hiroshima suffered sixty times the rate of leukemia than would be expected in a normal population (Chant and Hogg 1983).

We can guess that the psychological effects of nuclear war on individuals would be equally devastating as the physical ones. The loss of home, loved ones, and normal life; witnessing the effects on people and the environment; having to cope with the demands of an unprecedented, even unbelievable, situation; and lacking resources for medical and physical needs and social support would be overwhelming. Such would be the devastation that many have said the survivors would envy the dead.

The human consequences alone would suggest that assertions about survivability, limited nuclear war, and the economy regressing to the 1920s seem naive or crazy. But when the human consequences are linked to the probable environmental consequences, the absurdity of such assertions becomes clear.

Environmental Consequences. We might think of the biosphere of the Earth as a single organism with its interdependent parts and systems that enable the whole to survive. Some process that severely affects parts of this organism affects the health of the whole.

FALLOUT. We knew early on that the fallout effects of nuclear war would be widespread and profound. After a nuclear war, fallout would cover most of the United States and the Soviet Union. Air, water, and land would be contaminated. The radioactivity of some of the elements—uranium and plutonium—in the fallout would persist for thousands of years (Chant and Hogg 1983). But as has become increasingly clear from scientific study and projection, fallout is but one catastrophic ecological consequence.

OZONE DEPLETION. Jonathan Schell, in *Fate of the Earth* (1982), documents the dynamics of the ozone layer of the atmosphere and life on the planet. The layer of ozone gas in the upper atmosphere has the property—or function—of preventing ultraviolet radiation from the sun from striking the earth with its full intensity. Because the ultraviolet radiation would have adverse effects on higher life-forms as well as varieties of marine life, the ozone layer plays a vital role in the biosphere system. When higher life-forms are plentiful, nitrous oxide generated in their metabolic processes will diminish the ozone layer. When higher life-forms are depleted, the single cell organisms produce more ozone to replenish the layer and block out more ultraviolet allowing the flourishing of more higher forms, and so on.

This delicate and complex process would be seriously disrupted should a nuclear war occur because the air bursts of even a small number of nuclear weapons would deplete the ozone layer. This rapid depletion would admit sufficient ultraviolet radiation to blind all sighted animals. Ultraviolet radiation would devastate the complex systems of food chains in the oceans and on land. Other complex processes would be set in motion that could adversely affect the ozone layer and the climate (Schell 1982).

NUCLEAR WINTER. One climatic effect that was noted by Schell and has subsequently been investigated extensively is the effect of the lofting of dust and smoke from the incineration of cities by nuclear bombs. The "nuclear winter" phenomenon could be triggered by the detonation of only 1 percent of the current nuclear arsenals. The lofted dust would come down only very slowly and would be of sufficient density to block sunlight for months. This would lower temperatures sufficiently to change summer conditions of northern latitudes into those of normal winters (Ehrlich et al. 1984; Sagan et al. 1983). The effects could be such that all higher life-forms would die of starvation and cold in the northern hemispheres and human life would cease everywhere.

The combined effects of radiation, ozone layer depletion, and atmospheric dust would seriously threaten the life of the organism Earth. Indeed, contemplation of the effects of nuclear war on humans and on the ecosystem is disheartening. But in light of such information one fact becomes clear: surviving a nuclear war can be accomplished in only one way—by preventing it.

Prevention. In the domain of prevention, the most knowledgeable authorities are public health workers who are responsible for the study and carrying out of prevention measures for disease. When they turn their perspective to contemplation of nuclear war, their vision is simple and direct. Dr. Howard Hiatt of the Harvard School of Public Health shares his version of the contemporary reality of nuclear war, observing: "War must be dealt with as an untreatable epidemic for which there is only one approach—that of prevention. In this new and frigid atmosphere, that is still the only reality" (Hiatt 1981).

Just as we have focused our attention on the reality of nuclear war—its possibilities and its consequences—we must also look clearly at prevention. We must know what prevention is, and what it is not. It is important, therefore, that we first recognize plans and assertions that masquerade as prevention but are something else.

Crackpot Realism. C. Wright Mills (1959) identified "crackpot realism" as the assertions of those who wished to sound authoritatively realistic but had personal agendas that simply confused the actual reality. There are some contemporary suppositions about nuclear war that are generally known and contribute to the distortion of the reality of nuclear war. Usually such plans or positions support an ideological or political position.

Often they play on the psychological defenses we all harbor about nuclear war.

SURVIVABILITY. Until the 1970s when the realities of "overkill" and ecological catastrophe became increasingly clear, the civilian populace was nurtured on the notion of survival after an "atomic attack." The phrase, "When you see the flash, duck and cover," was the first step toward survival after the bomb. In the *Woman's Home Companion* of May 1951 a variety of survival measures for the "woman at home" were proffered that characterize the can-do attitude about coping with the bomb. Some practical measures were suggested such as raking up leaves and throwing away paper that might ignite from the heat of a bomb, storing water, and building stout tables for cover. "Blast and heat are the greatest menace in an atomic attack, not radiation" (Anthony 1951, 22). As we shall see, this is advice that seems to have stuck with some of the experts of today. Children are to be given name tags to wear whenever they leave the house. "Civilian defense authorities recommend beginning air-raid drills in your home now. Some child-care experts believe children should be spared this for as long as possible. But if war comes, there is no question. Begin the drills at once. Explain to children that it's like a fire drill in school. No one really expects a fire in school—and you don't expect a bomb to fall on your house" (Anthony 1951, 24). The last rule for survival, "Keep calm—panic can kill more people than the bomb" (Anthony 1951, 26). We can see the silly placidity promoted by the government propaganda of this period. Yet in a sense people had some right to feel safer in that period than in today's world. Few nuclear weapons existed. The warning time was much greater than now.

The line of propaganda fostering the notion of the survivability after nuclear war reemerged during the late 1970s and the 1980s to justify the deployment of first-strike weapons. The myth that there would be a world worth surviving for and survivors with a moderately regressed standard of living had to be perpetuated. Such a myth had to disregard the reality of radioactive fallout, nuclear winter, depletion of the ozone layer, and a host of ecological consequences. One expert asserted that a small trench covered with a couple of doors and shoveled over with dirt would allow people employing such measures

to survive a nuclear war. The phrase, "If you have enough shovels
. . ." became the hallmark of this folly (Scheer 1983).

LIMITED NUCLEAR WAR. A closely related notion is that of a
limited nuclear war, trumpeted under such titles as, "Victory is
Possible" (Gray and Payne 1980). The basic idea here is that the
United States and the Soviet Union could have a limited nuclear
exchange after which a peace would be negotiated favorable to the
United States. Another version would be the use of small, short-range
weapons in Europe that would not lead to the use of strategic
weapons against the Soviet and United States territories.

The overt threat in this notion is that the United States is
prepared to fight and win a limited nuclear war. Mutually Assured
Destruction was demeaned as a policy—even as amoral (Gray and
Payne 1980). The covert threat was to force the Soviet Union to
devote a greater amount of its wealth to military preparation and
weapons. The net effect of this covert threat would be to create an
economic crisis that would precipitate internal insurrection and
force a new form of government. The folly of this approach was
pointed out in a brief analysis by Gwynne Dyer (1986) that showed
the Soviet economy could keep up with the United States even
without significant loss of consumer goods production and
consumption. Dyer observed, "The Soviets would eat grass, if
necessary, to stay even with the Americans in the strategic
competition, but there is little evidence that grazing is necessary"
(Dyer 1986a, 7A). As recent events suggest, economic efficiencies
and political openness are better incentives for internal change.

Behind these overt and covert political and military messages of
survivability and limited nuclear war are the motivations of expanding
of the military bureaucracy and military dominance of the federal
budget. Moreover, the idea of winning a war even if it is a nuclear
conflict has great appeal to those who hold to nineteenth century
ideas about military domination. Such motives become more clear as
the crackpot realism becomes more and more suspect.

STAR WARS. The *Strategic Defense Initiative* has several
questionable assumptions and doubtful feasibility. It probably could
not be deployed, given the resources available. It might not work if

deployed. The Soviets would find effective and cheaper countermeasures. And the nation's wealth would continue to be squandered. But if the policy is pursued, the profits will still be made, and the military hegemony of space will be more likely. Other civilizations have had their military defense follies. The Chinese had their Great Wall, which as a defense did not prevent the periodic conquest by tribal conquerors. The German tanks and trucks quickly ran around the Maginot Line. Crackpot realism is not new. We must be critical in our consideration of all preventive plans. Having said this, prevention is possible; we must determine how to achieve it. Let us look at some attempts and some directions.

Nuclear Treaties. The cynical view of the nuclear treaties signed so far is that each simply sanctifies the existing status quo and allows newly proscribed avenues for the development of weapons and the perpetuation of the nuclear arms race in different and more deadly directions. Another view is that the existing treaties are small first steps toward a faraway goal of eventual elimination of nuclear weapons. Perhaps neither view is totally realistic. Let us look briefly at existing treaties and at possible directions for urgently needed future agreements.

In response to the serious consequences of radioactive pollution of the atmosphere and the political pressure of peace and environmental activists, the *Partial Test Ban Treaty* was signed in 1963. Other treaties that placed some limits on underground testing followed in 1981 (Chant and Hogg 1983). The *Nuclear Nonproliferation Treaty*, previously discussed, became effective in 1970.

When it became apparent that missiles that could intercept strategic ballistic missiles coming to their targets at speeds in excess of 20,000 mph were not likely to be effective in stopping an overwhelming barrage, an *Anti Ballistic Missile* system treaty was signed. Economic pressure and the probability that the explosions of the ABM missiles themselves would be quite destructive played a role in bringing about the ABM treaty. The treaty was signed and went into effect in 1972 (Chant and Hogg 1983).

The *Strategic Arms Limitation Treaty,* SALT I, which placed some limitations on offensive weapons, was signed in 1972 (Chant and Hogg 1983). SALT II, placing other limitations, was signed in 1979 but has yet to be ratified by the U.S. Congress. The terms of this treaty were nonetheless honored by both sides until 1986, when the Reagan Administration threatened to put into service the 131st B-52 bomber equipped with cruise launched guided missiles that exceeded limitations of the treaty (*Des Moines Register* 1986).

The *Intermediate-range Nuclear Forces Treaty,* signed December 8, 1987, and ratified by the U.S. Congress in 1988, had little military significance but made several political innovations. The treaty eliminated only about 4 percent of the world's 50,000 nuclear warheads (Defense and Disarmament News 1988). It reduced the number of the 10,000 nuclear weapons in Europe only marginally (see *Defense Monitor* 1988). However, the treaty's innovations included: the elimination of a whole class of weapons—intermediate-range land based missiles—elimination of some very new weapons, elimination of dangerous Pershing II missiles with flight times to Moscow of less than fifteen minutes and hence reduction in the necessity of a launch-on-warning policy, and introduction of both challenge and on-site inspection of factories producing nuclear weapons (Forsberg 1988). These innovations suggest future directions of shared security and shared information about nuclear arms. The value of the INF Treaty seems to lie in the new directions it sets. Perhaps these can be a basis for further arms reductions.

One can see that these treaties are the result of economic and political pressures. Some have had significant positive human benefit (the 1963 Test Ban Treaty), nevertheless technology allows the development of weapons by other means. Treaties seem unable to stop the development of novel kinds of arms. Areas in which there is potential for the development of intriguing new systems seem to be avoided by both sides. On the positive side, despite propaganda to the contrary, the Center for Defense Information reports that the Soviet Union, and until recently the United States, have carefully honored the terms of their agreements (*Defense Monitor* 1987).

In the future a *Comprehensive Test Ban* treaty to stop the development of new weapons would be an effective break in the arms race (*Defense Monitor* 1986). Despite a year's unilateral moratorium on the testing of nuclear weapons by the Soviet Union in 1982, the

United States continued to test weapons and such a treaty awaited a more positive political atmosphere in the United States.

Some Preventive Measures and Directions for Change.

There are definite directions in which the superpowers can proceed. The directions just hinted at below are ideas neither better nor worse than any others but they can provide a springboard to begin thinking about ways to back away from the precipice of thermonuclear annihilation.

Technological Change

1. Nuclear weapons technology and materials can be more closely policed by both sides to forestall further spread of the capacity to make nuclear bombs.
2. Political and economic sanctions can be applied against countries building weapons.
3. Arms control should begin with the removal of the most destabilizing weapons first. These would include those with short flight times, first-strike threats, etc.
4. With the development of nuclear missile submarines with missiles of great range and accuracy (*Defense Monitor* 1987), the potential for the abolition of all land-based strategic nuclear missiles has become possible. With no land-based nuclear missiles, the incentive to strike the cities and silos of the other side is significantly reduced. Sure retaliation from the sea would result. A giant step toward reversing the arms race would be taken.
5. Like leaving their six shooters at the door of the saloon, the banning of nuclear weapons—all weapons—in space by the superpowers should be continued.
6. Communication links between the likely chief actors in a nuclear crisis can be greatly improved. It should be as easy for the president of the United States to reach the Soviet premier as it is for him or her to reach the nuclear launch codes. (There has been some progress in this area to date.)

> Considerable preparation for dealing with troublesome situations or crises (such as terrorist use of nuclear devices) should be shared by the superpowers.
> 7. Nuclear war prevention symposiums composed of individuals from the nuclear nations with or without the sanction of their respective governments can brainstorm scenarios and recommend preventive measures.
> 8. Hiroshima and Nagasaki must become the completely known and universally memorialized common history of humankind.

A Path to Peace. These measures we suggest require a vision of a future without nuclear weapons and an epoch of peace. Such a vision was provided in an important work, "The Freeze and Beyond: Confining the Military to Defense as a Route to Disarmament," by Randall Forsberg (1984). Forsberg sees the path of peace as up to thirty years of sequential steps following neither the typical arms-control formulas or the pacifist unilateral-disarmament routes. She argues that nuclear weapons allow the superpowers to continue their interventions in the Third World without direct conventional warfare confrontation with each other, which could end in mutual destruction. So a confinement of the military over a span of time to defense only is prescribed.

Briefly reviewed, the steps to a peaceful future begin with a freeze on the testing and production of nuclear weapons that allows the technological arms race to continue. Large scale military intervention is ended. The nuclear and conventional forces in Europe, China, and Japan are cut 50 percent. Economic development in the Third World is continued seriously. Foreign military bases are abolished, and forces are restricted to conventional forces for defensive purposes. Nuclear weapons are abolished. National armed forces are eliminated and replaced with an international peacekeeping force (Forsberg 1984).

Average citizens concerned about the possibility and consequences of nuclear war may feel impotent in their desire to influence treaties and agreements among nations. Yet it is important to remember that perhaps the most significant and effective treaty banning testing of nuclear weapons in the atmosphere was the result of pressure by thousands of well-informed and active peace workers in the United States. There are directions that our governments can be pushed or led to by average citizens who have possibilities in mind and the courage to educate themselves and work for them.

Overcoming the Psychological Barrier. The issue of thermonuclear annihilation can be grappled with. Human effort has gotten us into this mess. Human effort can solve it. Crackpot realists will tell us we are not expert enough to have an opinion, much less act on our opinions. This, of course, is an antidemocratic sentiment. Solving this most pressing of problems cannot be left to the same experts who have gotten us into it. The largest barrier we face is one of attitude.

When Eric Mader canvassed American neighborhoods for the Nuclear Weapons Freeze Campaign in Madison, Wisconsin, in 1986, he collected some of the responses of persons who would not sign the petition to freeze nuclear weapons development and deployment. While these responses were "not the rule," they illustrate the subtle ways of psychological resistance to the issue. Some of them are the following:

"I don't think I want to be interested."

"What would the President think if he knew what you were doing?"

"I served in the Vietnam War. Serving in a nuclear war is your problem."

"We're still making payments on the pool."

"We need nuclear weapons because no one will enlist in the Army anymore."

"I'm all for nuclear war! How else will we know of the second coming of Jesus."

"Don't worry, God will destroy the Russians."

"You're scaring our kids!"

"Don't sign. They're KGB!"

"There's no one here right now, and I don't want to talk to you."

"Sorry, I'm neutral." (Mader 1986, 50)

On the more serious side of the problem of psychological barriers to dealing with the issue, Robert J. Lifton described what he called *psychic numbing* in survivors of the bombing of Hiroshima. He noted many survivors experienced a closing off of stimuli from the environment that were too strong and unacceptable for response. He observed that this closing off extended itself to become *psychic numbing*, or a chronic state of despair, denial, and rejection of the experience. The condition is still seen in many survivors who are unwilling to be reminded of the experience or to be involved in any way with political or other activities related to nuclear weapons (Lifton as reported by Thurlow 1982).

We are all survivors of Hiroshima and Nagasaki. We all experience images too strong and too unacceptable to respond to. To some extent we all are subject to psychic numbing with regard to thermonuclear war. What we must do is move beyond the images of death to images of alternatives—images to which we can respond and for which we can each work in our own way. In Part III we will lay out guidelines for peace work. We will introduce skills that can be developed and applied to peace work at various levels of social enterprise. But we must bear in mind that prevention, like war, begins with many small decisions made by many individuals. The key to facing and dealing with the threat of thermonuclear annihilation lies in each individual considering the links and consequences of his or her own actions on the job, at the polls, in conversations, on the streets, or with pen in hand.

Part III

Skills for the Practice of Peace

Part III involves a three-part compendium of skills that persons studying and working for peace can acquire. The intent is to identify valuable skills and to provide sufficient introduction to their origins and use to generate familiarity, interest, and further study and practice.

We begin in Chapter 12 with an essential exploration of skills needed to cultivate a "peace within" in both the child and the developing adult. In Chapter 13 we then identify skills for peaceful relationships including conflict-resolution skills. Recognizing the value that understanding and working with small groups of people holds for peace workers, we end the section with a practical guide to skills for working with small groups.

Chapter 12

The Peaceful Attitude: Self-Understanding and Socialization

For many, peace begins as an attitude of heart and mind. Realizing peace is in part realizing oneself as a peaceful entity. Earlier we examined the genesis of violence and aggression as parts of our biological and psychological makeups. Ultimately, each of us must come to terms with our own experience and attitudes about our basic natures in light of these issues and discoveries. To some extent this suggests the turning of our attention inwardly upon the personal and private. Such work need not separate us from the realities of the social world and the sources of violence and war which lie there. Perhaps work on the self is but a part of the work which must be done to realize peace in the world.

Work on oneself is also a prelude to imparting values and attitudes to those we are charged with bringing to participation in the social world—newcomers to society, children. Those whom we initiate into social consciousness and participation will perpetuate the work already done and initiate new hope for the future of peace.

The skills surveyed in this chapter affect individual attitudes, perceptions, and actions. First, we will examine those with particular relevance to developing attitudes of peacefulness. These skills arise from several philosophical traditions. The first of these skills is meditation.

Meditation. Meditation is a skill found in many philosophical
    traditions including Christian, Jewish, Taoist, Buddhist, Hindu,
and tribal religions. Of the varieties of meditation, the one portrayed
here is derived from the Zen tradition (Kapleau 1967). There is no
belief system or doctrine attached to the behaviors that comprise
meditation. However, an understanding of how the notion of a
peaceful attitude is associated with meditation is in order.

James Forest (1976) asserted toward the end of the Vietnam
War:

> What peace activists might learn from their Vietnamese
> counterparts is that, until there is a more meditative dimension in
> the peace movement, our perceptions of reality (and thus our ability
> to help occasion understanding and transformation) will be terribly
> crippled. Whatever our religious or nonreligious background and
> vocabulary may be, we will be overlooking something as essential
> to our lives and work as breath itself.

This essential something is best experienced rather than
described. But it includes an ability to calm the cognitive processes
and to focus attention. This is accomplished by pairing a relaxed
state of the body with an attentive focus of the mind. The result is the
development of—or discovery of, depending on one's orientation—
consciousness independent of visual and verbal symbols that
constitute thought. This capacity allows us to step behind the
actions, thoughts, images, social identities, and disruptive feelings
and to discover there a restful attentiveness. This attitude of mind
allows us to see the world with less bias and with more objectivity
and equanimity.

The attitude of mind that is cultivated in meditation, being
independent of thought, is unstructured by values or predisposing
bias. Consequently the experience of meditative awareness may
initiate a values examination in the form of questions like, "Where
do I go from here? As I step back from a value-free awareness, where
do I direct my energy and effort? What is most important?" Usually,
such questions are answered by the expectations and demands of
everyday life. Sometimes, however, direction and purpose is
discovered in the experience of undifferentiated consciousness that
meditation allows. Specifically, we recognize that consciousness is

something we share with other people and other conscious species (or as some practitioners of meditation would say, "other sentient beings"). Such a realization of this consciousness that we share with others can form the basis of compassion. To save, nurture, help, and protect others is ultimately the saving, nurturing, helping, and protecting of the same consciousness we hold within ourselves. There are other bases for compassion, but this is one. There are other values that contribute to an attitude of peacefulness and peacemaking, but compassion is one.

Let us be clear that we do not hold forth claims—as some have—that through meditation the material world will be transformed without the necessity of human effort. The promise of a new age of peace and harmony will come, if at all, through action. Meditation, like the other skills in this book, is seen merely as a tool to aid us in that long and critical journey.

Benefits of Meditation. Research and experiential evidence indicates that meditation can provide the practitioner with a set of mental skills. These include: a capacity to relax while remaining attentive; a capacity to discriminate the mental contents, such as memories, fears, fantasies, sensations; a capacity to perceive and respond to bodily processes such as the changes in breathing when stressed; an ability to mentally step out of the immediate social drama and to view events more objectively in relation to your own history; and an ability to have more profound empathy with others (for a review of the research and experiential evidence see Keefe 1986; Shapiro and Walsh 1984).

The technique briefly detailed here is a form of Zen meditation derived from Kapleau (1967). The general instructions are readily found in a variety of books.

Instructions for Meditation. Set aside a time and place where you will not be interrupted. Meditate for one-half hour each day. You should feel refreshed and relaxed as a result of meditation. If you feel anxious or depressed or otherwise uncomfortable, stop and work on some other skill.

The meditation posture is as follows:

1. A sitting position with the back straight, head balanced.
2. Sitting cross-legged with hips elevated on a high pillow is ideal if it is a comfortable position for you.
3. If uncomfortable, sit in a straight chair.
4. Hands should be folded in the lap.
5. The eyes may be open or closed. If open, they may be allowed to float and not focus on any particular thing.
6. The back should be straight for comfort since slumping causes cramping. However, you may find a big easy chair is best for you.
7. Loose clothing around the waist is suggested.

The major task of meditation is easily explained. Simply follow the natural, unforced, uncontrolled breath for the duration of each session. The focus of attention is best about one inch below the naval, following the rise and fall of the abdomen in rhythm with the breath.

Frequent intrusions of thoughts, memories, feelings, sounds, and physical sensations will naturally occur. The real task of meditation is to recognize when attention has strayed from the breath and to refocus. One should not push thoughts and sensations from awareness! Instead, recognize them and return to the focus of attention on the rise and fall of the abdomen in rhythm with the breath. This becomes a rewarding state of restful awareness. You should not cling to thoughts that will carry you from your focus. You should recognize them and let them go. The mind of the meditator is like an open hand. It clings to nothing; it forces nothing away.

Some additional hints may be helpful. Let the eyes float and the tongue relax. If you start to dream, you are falling asleep. You are not getting enough sleep. Go to bed.

Stressful thoughts and memories will loose their charge, relax. Don't push your breath. Let it flow naturally. Trust your body to breathe itself. If you push your breath, this may tell you how you are living your life.

You will remember creative ideas. You don't have to stop meditating to write them down.

If you get lost in a train of thought, you may suddenly realize this and have to refocus; it happens to all of us. If you ruminate about depressing things and feel worse for it, stop meditating. Try running.

The authors suggest four phrases to help remember the attitude of mind that is developed in meditation. Remember: become like an open hand, accept what comes, cling to nothing, give what is needed.

Meditation, like any behavior, can be transferred to other contexts and used at different times. Consequently, attending to the breath can allow one to sense physical stress or anxiety. It can also enable one to relax without obvious effort in different situations. The experience of the other possible benefits varies with the individual. But meditation can contribute to a relaxed peaceful attitude of mind.

The attitude of nonattachment is enhanced in those who meditate. This can contribute to more objective decision-making and sometimes to less suffering under the changing currents of life. The insight of nonattachment can give rise to a questioning of your values when they are seen as components of our egos. As we have suggested, a search for values is sometimes launched through the meditation process. In addition, involvement with peace-related issues and activities may require us to reexamine or defend our values. It may then be useful to briefly examine the process of values clarification as a skill.

Values Clarification. B. F. Skinner (1971) envisioned values as guides to behavior. They may be more than guides to behavior as well. But certainly many behaviors are the consequences of values we hold.

Dewitt Parker in his work, *The Philosophy of Value* (1968), observed that values are intimately tied to desire. A value is not a material thing or a specific goal or objective. It is the assuagement of desire. Thus a value is the satisfying activity that realizes a goal or objective. In these terms "realizing peace" is a value. Just where realizing peace may fit into your value hierarchy of importance, how important it is to you, and how it might fit into the patterns of your life can be determined through the process of values clarification.

Raths, Harmin, and Simon (1966) have developed a set of criteria for determining whether something is actually a value in your life. Their criteria has served as the basis of values-clarification procedures (Smith 1977; Simon et al. 1972). Whether a person is actually holding a value is determined by the following: (1) Is the value chosen freely, from among alternatives, and after consideration of the consequence of each alternative? (2) Is the value prized, being cherished by the holder who affirms the value publicly? (3) Does the holder act on the value repeatedly in the pattern of his or her life?

There are a plethora of strategies or exercises designed to detect people's values and the extent of their influence in their lives. A full examination of your values might make use of strategies for values clarification available in books designed for that purpose. A simple method is to list the things you enjoy doing in life and to rank order the list in order of importance. You can then ask of each item whether it meets the criteria for being a full value in your life. Those activities that fall short of all of the criteria may be a *value indicator* (Smith 1977, 15). A value indicator may develop into a full value as we grow and change. Realizing peace may be a fully held value or an indicator of a direction in which we may wish to grow. Beginning involvement with peace issues such as writing to the editor of newspapers or registering concerns about peace issues to representatives can suggest growth or change in the direction of peace as a value.

Critical Consciousness. Critical thinking that distinguishes between opinion and fact is a skill valuable in the scholar and lay person alike. Determining what is real—what we desire but is not real or not yet realized—is important for successful coping in everyday life. The idea of critical consciousness is an extension of critical thinking.

Testing the personal realities of everyday life can be extended to understanding the social and political issues and changes that affect our personal life by their effect on community life. Critical consciousness includes such understanding that leads to our participating in social and economic changes affecting community life. Realizing peace requires that we understand, participate in, and even help to guide the social and economic changes affecting peace. Thus this understanding and participation is *critical consciousness.*

People who are uncritically accepting and adapted to their social environment are submerged in changes that may beset it. Their consciousness is circumscribed. Paulo Freire observes that such a consciousness characterizes traditional South American communities before the advent of the social and economic changes of industrial capitalism (Freire 1973).

As social and economic changes get underway, people begin to experience a *transitive consciousness*. At first, their transitive consciousness may be characterized by oversimplification of problems, nostalgia, or underestimation of the common man. Their behavior is characterized by gregariousness, lack of interest in investigation, a propensity for fanciful explanations and to follow charismatic leaders, fragility of argument, strongly emotional style, the practice of polemics rather than dialogue, and magical explanations. These terms might be extended to any social system undergoing structural economic changes.

For example, such adjectives might characterize early stages of the antinuclear movement. However, as Freire observes, there can come a time when people who are literate and have some opportunity for democratic functioning in their own self-interest can become critically conscious. Critical consciousness is characterized by

> depth in the interpenetration of problems; by the substitution of causal principles for magical explanations; by the testing of one's findings and by openness to revision; by the attempt to avoid distortions when perceiving problems and to avoid preconceived notions when analyzing them; by refusing to transfer responsibility; by rejecting passive positions; by soundness of argumentation; by the practice of dialogue rather than polemics; by receptivity to the new for reasons beyond mere novelty and by the good sense not to reject the old just because it is old—by accepting what is valid in both the old and new (Freire 1973, 18).

Freire helped to teach the peasant populations of Brazil and Chile to read. His adult literacy campaigns enabled the people to better understand and participate in the economic and social changes going on in their countries and communities. Freire's efforts fostered the ability of people to master the currents of change in their lives rather than simply being the passive objects and sometimes victims of change. In other words, it taught individuals to connect their own personal problems and needs to larger social issues.

Consequently, another way of describing critical consciousness is learning to understand the interests that are at stake in changes that are underway. We can learn to participate in and direct those changes in our own and our community's interests. Another example of such participation might be identifying the amount of tax money a community contributes to military spending and questioning how a portion of that money might be spent on community needs. For example, public debate could help contribute to a reallocation of tax monies at the federal level aimed at supporting local community projects.

The changes underway in the late twentieth century concerning war and peace are technological, economic, political, and social. We have reviewed these changes elsewhere. They are changes that can be influenced, even directed democratically if sufficient numbers of people are critically conscious. This means that peace activists must be not simply literate but literate in a new sense. We must be familiar with the technological language of experts with vested interests in the perpetuation of the nuclear arms race. We must be conversant and informed about political spheres of influence and about how arms expenditures affect the amount of wealth left over for social needs in all parts of the world. The all too familiar cant that "the public" is not sufficiently informed to have an opinion on a subject affecting the lives of many people is a refuge for those who would manipulate change in their own interest.

Ultimately critical consciousness is a universal skill that leads to the refinement of other skills necessary to be informed, to not be intimidated, and to participate. This is part of the essence of the democratic process. The perpetuation of this process is the objective of the last individually focused skill for realizing peace we will address.

Parenting for Peace. One of the important functions of parenting is the *socialization* of children. *Socialization* is "the process of building group values into the individual. . . ." (Broom and Selznick

1963, 93). Just as it becomes important to clarify our values in the pursuit of peace, it becomes equally important to perpetuate these values in those who will carry a culture of peace into the future. We are subject to socialization throughout life as we enter or identify with new roles or new groups. But the early socialization of children is profound and very significant in the behavior of those children when they become adults.

Responsibility for Value Transmission. Skinner (1971) points out that to avoid or refrain from imparting values through rewarding those behaviors we find to be in keeping with our values simply leaves the shaping of behavior and values to random forces. Parents compete with the schools, television, motion pictures, other children, the implied behaviors suggested by toys, and other forces in the socialization of their children. Sometimes the values advanced by these other vehicles of socialization reinforce the peace-related values parents wish to inculcate. Sometimes they compete with those values.

The so-called "war toys" such as toy soldiers, guns, tanks, planes, missiles, and computer war games suggest violent roles and equate war with pleasure and glory. Mass media portray scenes of violence that sometimes exceed the imaginations of children. Political positions perpetuating popular support for small wars or the arms race are directly and indirectly espoused in the media.

Perhaps even more influential than the implied and expressed values contrary to peace coming from sources other than parents are the values parents themselves convey by example. Researchers and clinicians have studied the degree of awareness among children and the impact upon children of nuclear war and the arms race. Using a variety of terms, such as *psychic numbing, avoidance, fantasy,* and others, they have expressed concern that children may be learning a seriously dysfunctional value from the examples adults and their parents are setting regarding the threat of nuclear war and the arms race (Lifton 1979; Escalona 1982; Mack 1982; Schwebel 1982; Yudkin 1982; Zeitlin 1984). This value can be called *passivity* in the face of a serious and threatening social condition.

If parents are seen to be passive and to avoid even discussing such issues with their children despite their children's already present awareness and fears, then as the children model their parent's behavior, they learn passivity in the face of such issues. This is a dangerous value to impart in a democratic society, especially regarding a social issue that threatens our very existence. We would not want to raise a generation entrapped by a naive consciousness predisposed to leave the important issues including peace issues to the control of experts, while remaining passive, uncritical, uninformed, and easily misled.

The best antidote to this troublesome scenario is to perpetuate values of democratic functioning—participation, critical thinking, cooperation and constructive competition, peaceful ways of relating, conflict resolution skills, a habit of being informed about community and national and world issues, and alternatives to violence in the home.

Some Parenting Strategies. Kathleen and James McGinnis (1983, 23) believe "peace consists in creatively dealing with conflict." The creativity is resolution of conflict in a way that all the participants win and wish to cooperate more fully. In their book, *Parenting for Peace and Justice,* the McGinnises advocate nonviolent conflict resolution in the family on a day-to-day basis by recommending, for example, that parents stay out of the conflicts between children unless one is getting hurt or the parents' needs are being affected by the conflict. This allows children to work out their own conflicts. If parents do intervene, they suggest it be done in a way that allows the children to resolve the conflict themselves.

Nonviolent conflict resolution is carried out in a family atmosphere that emphasizes affirmation of other people, cooperation, and good communication skills including clear expression of desires and feelings and empathetic listening. Democratic family meetings facilitate these values and behaviors as well as providing alternative modes of disciplining (McGinnis and McGinnis 1983).

Avoiding violence in the media or explaining it, talking it over, avoiding war toys, and communicating with another family from a different culture are some of the ways the McGinnises transmit values in keeping with peace and justice to their children (1983).

Basic Beliefs. Sometimes what we think about the basic nature of human beings is reflected in our approach to children. Sometimes the violence in playtime at the nursery is seen as the natural unconditioned nature of children coming to the fore in their primitive relationships with one another. However, as we suggested earlier in our discussion of violence and aggression, this view may not be accurate. Indeed, our informal observation of children both as parents and as social scientists suggests to us that the basic nature of children is gregarious and loving. Hence, the source of interpersonal violence lies more in the examples that are provided children than in their basic natures. We are convinced that good examples of nonviolence and peaceful comportment and resolution of conflict give rise to the same in children, especially when they are seen to be more effective and better rewarded.

Therefore, parenting for peace places our own values and our ability to live in keeping with them on the line. While the methods and strategies are important, what we espouse and what we do will serve as a model for children. Being clear about our values and living them will underlay our parenting and teaching.

Conclusion. Meditation, values clarification, critical consciousness, and parenting for peace are skills introduced here that can cultivate a peaceful attitude. This is in part a discovery of yourself as a peaceful person, a development of the heart and mind. In this process of discovery and development of the self we not only generate the foundation for our present work in realizing peace in the world but also the capacity to transmit this ideal to children and the future.

The medium of such transmission of a peaceful attitude is made up of communications, relationships, and the resolution of conflict. We next turn to skills that enhance these aspects of life.

Chapter 13

Peaceful Relationships, Communication, and Conflict Resolution

Skills that help and repair relationships contribute to peace work in several ways. We cope with the world through our relationships with others. Skills that foster growth and change in personal relationships can therefore enhance our coping with problems we face. Most of us develop networks of relationships that serve as sources of identity and support. Skills that promote our relationships help to build strong networks of support. Whether it be political influence or grass roots organizing, we use both collaborative and conflictual relationships to achieve our goals. Skills, which enable individuals to better communicate and to recognize and resolve conflict, enhance the potential for working compromise and effort toward mutual goals.

We can identify and develop these various kinds of skills for use in relationships and for fostering communication and conflict resolution between groups and even between nations. Such skills can foster our individual effectiveness toward goals of realizing peace in our personal lives and in our work with others in which we collectively address peace issues.

The skills we identify will be exemplars of the many skills that can be acquired for peacemaking activities. Several of those skills can be applied at different levels of the social spectrum, from personal relationships to conflict resolution among nations. Some of them will be immediately applicable to everyday life. Others, especially some of the conflict resolution skills, must serve the reader as motivators to explore the kinds of careers in which these more advanced skills are developed and practiced as a part of a person's occupation or profession.

Relationship Skills. There are many aspects of our conduct that affect relationships. The skills we will focus on here are those that have been identified in research as useful in enhancing social networks and in conflict resolution.

Empathy. The first skill we will examine is *empathy.* It is a skill that enhances relationships, helps develop our social consciousness, and as we will see, can be extended to action within a community (Keefe 1976, 1978). *Empathy* is understanding and feeling with another. It is not sympathy, which sometimes has the connotation of being slightly superior to a more unfortunate person or people for whom one has a measure of concern.

Empathy is skill with two main aspects—understanding and feeling (Keefe 1976). First, to some extent the social roles, situation, and verbal and nonverbal communications of another person must be understood. Second, except for instances of physical or mental defect, each person shares the same physiological capacity for creating and experiencing emotion. While what we feel may be different, the capacity for feeling is something most people share. Therefore the capacity for feeling *with* others is present in each of us.

PHASES OF EMPATHY SKILL. *Understanding* and *feeling with* another person requires several behaviors and internal processes that when taken together comprise a useful relationship skill (Keefe 1983, 1976). Identifying each of these behaviors and processes will help us to learn and develop this skill more easily. We will identify these behaviors and processes in what we will call phases of empathy skill.

Each of us gives clues and cues as to what we are thinking and feeling. The content of what we say, our tone of voice, and inflection comprise our verbal messages about our feelings and thoughts. Facial expressions, gestures, body posture, interpersonal spacing, eye contact, and other behaviors decode information about our thoughts and feelings as well.

The *first phase* of empathy skill is *perception* of verbal and nonverbal messages and cues from the other person. When we try to enhance our empathy with others, a good place to start is with our perception. This is because empathy requires a particular state of mind that allows us to see the other person as he or she is, rather than through a filter of complex thinking and analysis. The other person is seen as another self that changes, feels, experiences, imagines, and self-perceives (Barrett-Lennard 1981). He or she is not an object. In other words, empathy is the opposite of relating to people as objects to be manipulated.

Here the other person is perceived passively without interference by our desires, biases, and complex cognitive processes (Jourard 1966). Such perception allows others to speak for themselves and to affect us as equals. It forestalls hasty categorization or ulterior responding. Our perception is open and focused on the other person. Meditation (see Chapter 12) has been suggested as a means of enhancing this quality of perceiving.

The *second phase* of empathy skill is allowing yourself to experience your own feeling responses to the other person based on your perceptions. To maximize empathy, we must allow our initial feelings toward another to remain as free as possible from intruding thoughts. Such thoughts would typically include stereotyping, value judgments, premature analysis with some theory, or defensiveness due to threat. Instead, we must initially allow the external stimuli from the other person to elicit or generate his or her feeling responses directly. We must momentarily allow our inner experiences to be controlled by the other's self-presentation. Meanwhile we hold complex thoughts in temporary abeyance. This, of course, is difficult to do when facing an adversary.

In the *third phase* we must distinguish between the feelings we share with the other person and those feelings we do not share but hold alone. If we get feelings we do not share mixed up with those we do, we end up projecting or placing our own feelings onto the other person. For example, someone may be very fearful of being beaten or abused by a third party and expresses this fear to us. In addition to the feeling of fear we sense in the other, we may also become angry at their victimization. They may not yet feel anger. If we respond to them as if they shared our anger, we loose a degree of empathy.

Just how you separate feelings sensed and feelings held alone is a matter of learning to shift your attention from the individual to your internal experience. This idea was originally suggested by Theodore Reik and supported by research (Zanger 1967). In short, good empathy skill requires that we pay attention to the other person but also easily shift our attention to our own feelings and responses and back.

Empathy in the strictest sense ends in the third phase of the skill. However, to use the skill in relationships to build and secure those relationships, something more seems required. That something more is our *fourth phase*, which was originally suggested by Rogers (1957). This fourth phase is communicating our empathy experience of another to that person as accurately as possible.

ACCURATE EMPATHY AND ACTIVE LISTENING. Our own verbal and nonverbal communications will convey our inner experience of empathy just as the other person's thoughts and feelings were originally communicated to us. Learning to put our empathic feelings into descriptive words that reflect how we experience the other person extends the skill. Such communication should have a tentative quality so that we are able to adapt our sense of the other person moment by moment as his or her feelings change in the course of interaction. Sometimes this intentional communication of our sense of the other is called *active listening* (Egan 1975). This term suggests the involved attention to the other person that good empathy skill requires. Persons with low-empathy skill might simply ignore the feelings expressed by another. Persons with high-empathy skill will be able to express their experience of the nuances of the other person's feelings.

Empathy skill does several things in relationships to enhance them. The other person feels understood. Rogers (1975) believes that if a person feels understood, it helps him or her to have a better sense of themselves and to develop a growth-promoting attitude toward his or her self. This is because empathy helps people to better anticipate their own actions and feelings. Empathy also fosters the communication of feelings that in turn helps to place a relationship on a basis of openness and trust.

As we discussed in Chapter 2 on aggression, violence, and empathy, empathy is a precursor to compassion when we recognize the separateness of another person, yet sense and understand him or her as another expression of consciousness and human experience like ourselves. You will recall that we saw compassion as a mode of living that extends empathy as a value guiding action both day-to-day and in extreme situations. This kind of compassion or empathy in action is best illustrated by the examples of peace workers who draw upon empathy and compassion to develop communities of people working for peace and peaceful goals.

EMPATHY IN ACTION: CONSCIOUSNESS AND COMMUNITY. It appears to us that all the successful peacemakers in history have developed this skill of empathy to a high degree. Remember, we are not born with empathy—it develops or does not develop through the process of learning to become human. We could cite many examples of the empathic skills carried to a high degree.

Most of us know to some extent the stories associated with M. K. Gandhi and his understanding of his people. There are, however, many others we can point to as exemplars of empathy. More currently, Dom Helder Camara, the Catholic archbishop of Recife, Brazil, has developed extensive empathic skill in peacemaking and nonviolent action seeking social justice. Camara's work with the poor in Brazil is based on his concept of "openness to suffering." To understand the violence in the life of the poor, Dom Helder persists in living a life of simplicity. Learning to struggle nonviolently for the poor means having an analysis of the reasons for the gap between the rich and poor. For Dom Helder it also means learning poverty by living in what he terms *Abrahamic Communities*. These communities mix the socially concerned educated and the poor. They are designed to produce real land reform for the Brazilian peasantry.

In 1973 several of Camara's followers were arrested in a demonstration and were tortured by the government. Dom Helder speaks of his pain in this situation.

> Yes, I am like a father who sees his children tortured. More than once I have gone to the police with my bags packed to say, "If I am the one you seek, let these go their own way," to no avail. They can only harm those whom I love. But I could not show my suffering—if they could have seen it, they would have succeeded (Hope and Young 1979, 123).

The Archbishop's struggle continues as the world takes notice of his activities for peace and justice. What is important for us to realize is that Dom Helder's empathy continues to be reborn and informed by his interaction with suffering people.

A more secular exemplar of a high degree of empathy is Danilo Dolci who has been called the "Gandhi of Sicily." Dolci was trained in philosophy and architecture, but he was deeply touched by the violence and grinding poverty of Sicily. In 1947 he took a walk in the countryside watching the leaves fall to the ground.

> I saw that in the act of wasting away, they become reborn. And continuously the seeds fall and become fruit ready for eating. I felt—I didn't reason it—that Nature, that everything was a tragedy where the living devoured the dead. And slowly I felt the need to be consumed, like the seeds, to become manure myself. And then I understood the value of communion, that everybody must be together (MacNeish 1966, 13).

Dolci had recently seen a baby die for want of food. That scene began to haunt him. He went on a fast to protest the death and wrote to the authorities for 30 million lire to help the peasants in the area. He proceeded to lay down in the bed where the child had died and refused to get up until help came from the government. This almost killed Dolci; in fact, he suffered a stroke.

When he recovered he began to organize the peasants of the area into active community groups to protest their exploitation and to provide mutual support. At this time it was well known that anyone on the island could be killed for less than $80. Dolci's later struggles against government neglect and Mafia domination have changed things for the better in Sicily (Dolci 1970). Dolci's method of creating communities is based upon a concept quite like empathy. He calls it his "maieutic method." What it amounts to is a socratic process by which people in the community bring forth, share, and become more aware of their own ideas and feelings. In this way both Camara's and Dolci's empathy is extended to a kind of *critical consciousness* (Freire 1973) in which people develop a sense of shared concern and fate sufficiently strong to begin to act collectively in their own self-interest (Keefe 1980, 1978).

This, in a practical way, is what we call learning the skill of empathy. We are most likely to learn in the place where we learn other important human skills—in communities.

Social Networking. Together with other skills, empathy can foster relationships among individuals. They can therefore be useful in developing a network of people to whom we can turn to offer or secure information, help, or emotional support (Whittaker and Garbarino 1983). Most individuals have such networks formed naturally as a part of participating in life with family, friends, and co-workers.

These so called *social networks* are also fostered by each of us when we *reciprocate* in our interactions with others. That is, when someone does something helpful or useful for us, we usually find the opportunity and time to do something helpful or useful for them. Such reciprocity is part of the social fabric that holds all societies together (Keefe and Roberts 1984; Levi-Strauss 1969; Goldner 1960).

Empathy and reciprocity each help to build and secure social networks. Social networks are mechanisms or tools we use to cope with problems that may cause us emotional and physical stress. The help, information, and emotional support we derive from social networks of supportive others is called *social support*. Persons lacking social support are more vulnerable to stress and suffer from stress-induced physical illness (Gore 1978). Moreover, they are more likely to be depressed and suffer other psychological difficulties (Ferman and Gordus 1979).

Those who are able to build strong relationships with a set of supportive other people have more at their disposal to enable them to cope with the problems and stresses involved in achieving their goals. Peace workers can use the skills discussed so far to build supportive networks with like-minded people working toward the same goals and working on the same peace issues. Such networks can extend beyond the immediate family and encompass members of organized peace groups and even to coalitions of peace activists and groups.

To this point we have focused upon skills that foster collaborative relationships between individuals. However, the reality of human relationships insists that we address skills that deal with problematic communication and conflict that develops both in relationships between individuals and those between groups.

Observation and Intervention Skills for Improving Communication and Conflict Resolution.

Several of the skills involved in improving communication and conflict resolution are *observational skills*. Skillful observation of communication or conflict strategies can contribute to successful intervention to improve communication between individuals or groups to help resolve conflicts. Other skills are more active and are employed in actual *intervention*. What we wish to do here is introduce observational and intervention skills that are easily developed and readily applicable to conflictual situations between individuals or between groups, and are therefore of interest to peace activists. Like other skills we have discussed, these are presented only as an introduction; like all skills, they will require further exploration and practice before proficiency or expertise can be attained.

Ways of Responding to Communication.

The students of communication theory are concerned with the message, the unit in the transfer of meaning. How a person or group responds to a message can tell us a great deal about the prospects for continued communication and can suggest alternative responses that we might propose to parties attempting to communicate.

When a person or group (sender) addresses another (receiver), there are four possible responses (Watzlawick, et al. 1967):

1. *Accept.* The receiver can accept the communication and respond appropriately to the meaning of the message. "John, I like your new coat!" "Oh, thanks, I just got it yesterday," or "May I sit down?" "No, this seat is saved."
2. *Reject.* The receiver may reject the sender's message with a complete lack of direct response, ignoring the sender or turning away. This is not a negative response, as in the second example above.
3. *Disqualify.* The receiver may disqualify—that is, communicate a response that invalidates the sender's message as a relevant communication. The receiver may radically change the subject, digress, or obscure the response in strange mannerisms or behaviors that distract from the sender's message and to some extent existence of the sender. "Why does he do such things to me?" "I think we had better talk about where you are going to live." or "The policies of this agency are racist!" "We cannot conduct our business in this atmosphere."
4. *Symptom utilization.* The receiver claims not to hear or comprehend the messages because of hearing defect, language deficit, insanity, or other defect or malady that interferes with communication.

The product of repeated rejection or disqualification of messages is repeated stifling of communication. Sometimes these responses are completely unintentional. Whether intentional or unintentional, the effect on the sender is usually a subtle frustration or even depreciated sense of self. Such responses introduce problematic variables into relationships and serve as barriers to communication between parties trying to work out conflicts.

When in the role of mediator, or third party, recognizing and pointing out the nature of responses when they occur or before they are sent may facilitate continued communication when acceptance of a message is accomplished. Acceptance does not imply agreement, but it does foster continued communication.

Nonviolent Communication. Marshall B. Rosenberg (1983) suggests some communication skills that empower communicators to nurture and educate rather than influencing people to act on the basis of fear and guilt. First, we can separate what we observe from our *evaluation* of another's behavior. For example, rather than saying, "You're so slow!" we would say, "You turned your essay in late." Rather than, "Mary can't compete at the college level," we would say, "Mary's 10,000 meter time is over an hour. I think that is too slow to compete in college."

Second, sharing feelings encourages others to cooperate. Separating feelings from thinking and being specific is helpful. So instead of, "I think you misunderstood again," we would say, "I feel frustrated because I have not gotten my point across to you yet."

Third, it helps to communicate what we are valuing in our statements. To do this the use of the phrase, "Because I . . ." is useful. So is "Let's try this again, because I believe what we are doing is important."

Rosenberg believes using positive language is a valuable skill. This includes avoiding telling people how you think they think and feel. It also includes telling others what we want from them, not just what we don't want as in, "I would like you to use the walk," rather than, "Don't walk on the grass." Furthermore, it is useful to restate what another person says to us so we may check our own interpretation. This is very much like the skill of accurate empathy discussed above.

Such language skills can enhance people's sharing and agreeing. About his nonviolent language skills Rosenberg says, "nonviolent exchanges of resources and resolutions of differences are made possible when others believe our intentions are to nurture, educate, and protect and not to blame, punish, or dominate" (1983, 25).

The relationship and communication skills identified so far are useful not only in securing personal relationships and building supportive networks but also when in the role of a third party intervening to help resolve conflict.

Third-Party Conflict Resolution Skills. Pruitt and Rubin (1986) identify several aspects of what they call third-party intervention that help to delineate the scope of possible roles. We can be a formal mediator or arbitrator or we may be asked to function informally behind the scenes as a intermediary or special envoy. Peace worker Terry Wait filled this latter role when he attempted to attain the release of hostages in the Middle East; unfortunately he ended up a hostage himself. We may be invited or uninvited, acting as an individual or as a representative of an agency, group, or government. Also, a third party may have authority to advise only or to direct solutions. We might be acting from a position of impartiality or out of an acknowledged bias or be acting to resolve conflict interpersonally or between groups.

Kenneth Boulding, initiator of the term conflict resolution and a leader in the field of peace studies, saw resolution as but one way to end conflicts, which he spelled out in his book *Conflict and Defense* (Boulding 1962, 305–28). Later Boulding suggested the *Journal of Conflict Resolution* might better have been named the Journal of Conflict Management as "frequently conflicts are not and perhaps should not be resolved, but should be managed, at least to maximize the total gain to both parties, no matter what the distributional outcome" (1985a, 493). Conflict management might be a better and more realistic term. If we are to be successful in management or even resolution of conflict, however, the sanction of the parties to the conflict is usually needed.

SANCTION. Whether we are intervening with individuals or groups to improve communication or to resolve conflict, a very important element should be present. This is the *sanction* of the disputants, that is, the recognition and permission of the parties to the relationship or conflict. In modern industrial societies, sanction is usually attained through a formal role a person occupies that is widely and formally recognized in society. Clinicians usually must be licensed to practice. Lay people are sometimes appointed by a court to help resolve minor financial disputes to relieve the work load on the court. Social workers and lawyers will mediate disputes within families to avoid legal action and derive their sanction through their professional credentials as well as through agreement of the disputing parties. Professional mediators are hired to resolve labor disputes. Diplomats are appointed by the leaders of their respective countries and accepted by the host countries.

To become active in conflict resolution in modern society, both education and some kind of formal sanction is usually required. Conflict resolution is often a part of a professional's role that requires years of education. There are opportunities to engage in conflict resolution on an informal basis such as in conflicts between friends, family members, peace group members, or even between peace groups contending for roles in a collective effort. But most often, becoming involved in helping to improve communications and to resolve conflicts is a part of daily life. Thus it is a very momentary and informal activity.

Consequently, what we will identify in the way of communication and conflict-resolution skills are but a few tools in a very large body of expertise we would have to learn in the process of becoming a professional—including a professional peace worker. These skills and their description will serve to provide the flavor of conflict resolution and inspire the reader to further pursuits.

Strategies of Conflict. A first step toward conflict resolution is to identify the strategies of conflict that currently exist between the parties. Pruitt and Rubin (1986, 4), in their study of social conflict, defined conflict in a way that is applicable to conflict between individuals, groups, or even nations. They defined *conflict* as *"perceived divergence of interest, or a belief that the parties' current aspirations cannot be achieved simultaneously."* They point out that conflict per se is not necessarily bad. Conflict brings tensions within people and social systems into opposition and its resolution promotes change that can resolve ongoing inequalities or domination.

Pruitt and Rubin (1986) believe conflict manifests itself in five forms or strategies. First is *contending,* in which one party tries to impose its solution on another. Such might characterize lockouts and strikes in contentious labor disputes. Second is *yielding,* in which one party lowers its aspirations and settles for less. Such a strategy characterizes agreements arrived at through collective bargaining that does not reach the point of strike or lockout. Third is *problem solving,* in which a *win-win* solution is found and both parties get what they want. This might be an ideal strategy if it is possible to attain. A student wants to live off campus while at college. His parents want to insure he remains well-nourished by regular, balanced meals and fear he will not have the opportunity living in an apartment by himself. The parents and son agree to his living in a boarding house off campus in which regular meals are served. Fourth is *withdrawing,* in which one party leaves the scene of contention either physically or psychologically. In marriage and in combat this is a common strategy in which one is "free to fight another day." The last strategy is a working *combination* of two or more of the other strategies. Pruitt and Rubin observe that a single strategy is rarely used alone (1986).

To be able to recognize the strategy being employed by contending parties, whether they be individuals, groups, or even nations, enables us to suggest or work for alternative strategies that may have more peaceful outcomes. Such recognition can structure the nature of intervention, conflict resolution efforts, or even long-term peace efforts. Below are some examples of skills that can be used as a part of conflict resolution between individuals or groups.

Role Rehearsal and Reversal. The social roles we occupy, such as wife, husband, son, doctor, mediator, etc., carry with them rights and obligations that prescribe certain appropriate behaviors. These behaviors can be rehearsed much like rehearsing from a script for a play. Clinicians have encouraged role rehearsal for clients and patients so they may better perform their day-to-day social roles.

Sometimes, when two people are having difficulty communicating, rehearsing the communication situation in advance facilitates the process. When two parties can be brought together to focus on the communication between them, they may be encouraged to "take the role" or perspective and arguments of each other. Hence, a husband argues an issue from the wife's perspective and the wife argues the issue from the husband's.

We need not be trained clinicians to invite disputants to try to take and argue from the opposition's viewpoint in the interest of conflict resolution. Pointing out ways parties typically respond to messages can allow more authentic role taking. Careful control of the situation in which the mediator forbids insincere positions, etc., can result in improved appreciation of the partner's or opponent's position and improve communication.

Other Skills. Pruitt and Rubin (1986) have identified a set of third-party interventions based on social science research. Briefly summarized, these include modification of the physical and social structure of the conflict such as encouraging communication, as in role reversal, when parties can still profitably communicate. It also includes acting as an intermediary when communication is accusatory and otherwise unproductive. Moreover, setting time limits, finding neutral sites, and using sites that are open or closed to public view can variously affect problem solving between parties.

Interventions also can include identifying and separating the issues so they may be handled in sequence with those issues likely to provide a basis for further success if addressed first. One technique of conflict resolution called *logrolling* consists of one party conceding on issues that are of low priority to itself but of high priority to the other party thus gaining what it wants and fostering problem solving (Pruitt and Rubin 1986, 145, 147). Introducing new issues and alternatives can include the technique of *bridging*. This is simply the invention of an option that meets the underlying needs of both parties but does not reflect the initial demands of each.

International Conflict Resolution. Some of the third-party conflict-resolution skills are applicable in international disputes. In a study of conflict over territory, boundaries, and borders, political scientists Kratochwil, Rohrlich, and Mahajan (1985) used responses from national members of the United Nations to identify such disputes in the world. After in-depth study of eight cases of conflict and dispute—including the Falkland/Malvinas dispute, the Soviet-Japanese territorial dispute, and others—they drew some conclusions about the nature of international disputes and suggested procedures for third-party intervention that are quite similar to those useful in work with individuals and groups.

The authors believe that the degree of *congruence* or *incongruence* between each party's *perception of the situation* and *principles of resolution* play a role in the nature and outcome of the disputes. Disputes that have congruence between disputants as to perception and principles tend to yield peace and tight legal agreements. Disputes in which there is incongruence in both cases hold the least prospect for legal third-party intervention.

Third parties must work to bring congruence in perception and principles to achieve a resolution. Skills for achieving congruent perception include: fostering information gathering by all parties to clarify perceptions, having both sides explain and document their perceptions, generating options that fit the perceptions of both sides, achieving partial and interim agreements when complete settlement is not possible, changing the context in which the dispute is seen, and enhancing trust of both parties by using multinational third- party mediators (Kratochwil et al. 1985).

The authors believe legal reasoning and process mechanisms comprise ways of generating congruent principles for the resolution of international disputes. Such skills include: raising doubts about the applicability of principles in rigid confrontations over principles, reaching agreement on some small issues before moving on the larger principles involved, "untying the bundle of sovereign rights" generating overlapping or shared jurisdiction, including agreements that cannot be immediately implemented (Kratochwil et al. 1985).

The best hope of peace studies and international law and diplomacy is that such skills as these can be put to use. Certainly there is the need. The development of professionals acting as third-party interveners for conflict resolution is a goal for those deciding on careers in peace work. Whether international disputes will find third parties more interested in conflict resolution or in selling arms for profit to both sides is an open question. Certainly the development of professionals experienced in employing the skills identified here can only help the prospects for peace.

Summary Conclusions. Each skill identified in this chapter fosters and secures relationships among individuals, groups, and potentially among nations. Empathy, networking, and communication skills are most immediately applicable in our personal lives. Conflict-resolution skills have limited application in everyday life unless you are invited to help resolve disputes informally as a third party. Most conflict-resolution skills are a part of the tools various professionals—from counselors to diplomats—employ in their formal social roles. So some of the skills briefly presented here may inspire you to cultivate them further for use in your personal life and peace work. The others may invite you to explore careers in fields where conflict resolution and realizing peace are a product of your life's work.

In nearly every endeavor that involves the cooperation of people, small groups are the context, the medium. In working for peace, small groups—be they groups for planning, action, education, political organization and advocacy, or discussion of mutual support—are ubiquitous and important. The skills necessary for understanding and working with small groups of people, therefore, become valuable tools. We will identify and show the application of these useful skills in Chapter 14.

Chapter 14

Small Group Understanding and Facilitation

The importance of the small group to peace work stems from its importance in social life. The small human group has been the ubiquitous environment for most of human evolution. George Homans (1950), the pioneer social scientist who studied the small group, noted that forces of modern civilization such as centralized bureaucracy tear at the *small group,* but it remains at the core of social experience. It is an association of two or more individuals who are in communication with each other, take each other into account, and identify with each other to some degree (Olmsted 1959, 21).

The small group is the primary formal or informal unit of social organization. Entities as diverse as families and corporate boards can be seen as small groups. Individuals working for peace goals might be involved with community peace activist groups, student peace organizations, church social action committees, formal or informal networks of people working for peace goals, corporate boards, professional organizations, or staffs of political organizations. Understanding small group structure, processes, and development and having some beginning skills in facilitating them toward their goals can be valuable for members or leaders working for peace through the auspices of such small groups. In addition, knowing ways groups can influence social decisions of communities can lead to meaningful group social action.

In this chapter we will provide a brief introduction to understanding and skills for working with small groups and influencing social decisions in the communities to which groups belong. Social scientists, psychologists, group psychotherapists, group social workers, managers, coaches, and political activists are among the contributors to the vast base of knowledge and skills related to work with small groups. What we present here is not a comprehensive survey of knowledge and skills but what we hope is a useful distillation for beginning work with groups with which you find yourself associated. We hope this discussion will serve as a catalyst to further reading and learning about small groups and the skills useful in facilitating them.

Because one of the skills facilitating groups is understanding their structure and processes, we will begin with insights into the general shape and workings of small groups. *Groups* are usually changing, developing entities with leadership providing direction. Thus after presenting our version of the stages of growth and development small groups pass through, we will examine some principles of group leadership.

Small Group Structure and Process. One of the characteristic of small human groups is that they tend to organize themselves into particular structures. Both clinicians and scientists have noted the propensity of small groups to structure themselves in member hierarchies. Bales (1950), in his scientific observation of small group interaction, noted one dimension of group social structure is the relative status of group members. Much of what happens in small groups is conditioned by the stratification of its membership.

Consequently, skillful work with groups requires the understanding of the dynamic of *hierarchical ordering* in the group's life. At first the notion of human groups naturally stratifying into hierarchies may seem alien to persons who hold values of equality and democratic governance. Yet if we look closely at the determinants of group hierarchy formation, we find in this natural propensity the source of these very values.

Hierarchy and Interaction. Two members of a peace activist group may continually argue. The topic or "bone of contention" may be any of a thousand things. But behind the literal content of their argument may be an interpersonal dynamic. This is the jockeying for position in the status ordering of the group. Sometimes the decision of the group to go with one person may help to determine the interpersonal outcome for the relative status of the two members. Sometimes the leader of the group will choose whose point will prevail and at the same time determine the relative status of the two members. Much of the process or interaction that takes place in small groups can be seen as motivated by the quest for position in the hierarchy of the group.

Our experience suggests that the hierarchical ordering is fluid and seldom a rigid ladder or pecking order. But we must be conscious of this phenomenon if we are to fully understand much of what is taking place in the groups we work in and with. Leaders tend to hold positions at the top of the status order. Sometimes there are coalitions of individuals who constitute the higher status members. Adherence to group norms and working toward group goals help to insure a member's place in the groups hierarchy. The talents and resources that a member has which assist the group in meeting the environmental demands also seem to contribute to a member's relative status. New members are checked out by old members to determine if their characteristics will be compatible with the group's norms and goals. They also may constitute a threat to the ordering of the membership.

Leaders usually have a vested interest in maintaining the status quo in their group. A radical reordering of the group hierarchy may bring a reordering of leadership as well. Hence, leaders are seen to resolve disputes and act in ways that help to maintain group order. This characteristic of small groups to order themselves in hierarchies is often not a conscious endeavor or process by the membership. One member may find another unlikable and a constant rival and attribute these things to personality traits while nearly equal status may be an element in the friction he or she feels with that person. Another may constantly feel like the "low person on the ladder" but not define the feeling in direct relation to his or her status in the group.

The advantage to the group of this structuring of the membership is the efficient ordering of group tasks, responsibilities, and rewards. Basketball coaches had better know their starting lineup before the season is well underway so that they may put the best players on the court to face the opponents. Coaches must also know the virtue of some stability in the lineup to allow players to learn each other's capabilities and shortcomings.

Hierarchy, Equality, and Democratic Functioning. But where in this hierarchical view of the small group is there room for egalitarian and democratic values? Are such values really useful to the functioning of small groups? Let us return to the example of the basketball team. Sometimes the team will face opponents of very diverse talents. One night they may face a tall skilled team that will play slowly and deliberately. On another night they may face a shorter quicker team that will run the length of the court on most plays. If the team can change its lineup and put players most likely to cope with the different opponents on the court, they may stand a better chance of winning than if they simply started the same players each night. In short, the team has to *adapt* to its changing environment.

Each small group usually faces a variety of different tasks or environments that force it to draw upon different skills in its membership. If a group remained rigidly devoted to a membership hierarchy that did not allow members of lower rank in relation to one set of tasks or environment to rise when their particular skills were of greater value in another environment, the group would not be able to adapt. It may be unable to survive.

Consequently, it becomes important in the life of some small groups that their members achieve a level of awareness of the group's hierarchial ordering. It also becomes important for the membership to learn to allow changes in its membership hierarchy when environmental conditions demand responses or abilities of persons not high in the status hierarchy in a previous environment. Such awareness and conscious functioning is facilitated by groups that value the intrinsic equality of its membership in light of ever-changing environmental demands. Democratic processes help to prevent the subordination of talent and ability to rigid authoritarian processes. The rights of group members who rank low in one situation can be more easily realized when situations change if democratic processes give them a chance to participate and have a voice in the life of the group.

Skillful participation or leadership in a small group will be conscious of the hierarchical ordering and facilitating its flexibility and adaptation in the interests of the group.

Internal and External Systems. In his observations of groups George Homans detected two overlapping systems at work. The first is an *external system* of sentiment, activity, and interaction aimed primarily at the environment of the group that enables the group to survive. The second is an *internal system* of sentiment that group members develop toward one another in the process of the group's interactions (Homans 1950). Crudely stated, the external system is concerned with the tasks of the group, and the internal system is concerned with the social and emotional factors among group members. These systems interact and mutually influence each other. Groups working for peace ignore these realities at their own peril. Individuals in peace groups sometimes act as if they should not worry about external resources or individual feelings in the group. A higher rate of failure among such groups may be based on such lack of understandings.

Leaders can develop within each of the two systems. A task leader may set goals and keep the members on task or the group focused. A socioemotional leader may provide a model for sentiment and abet the group's morale. Sometimes task leadership and socioemotional leadership can come from the same person. Sensitivity to the two systems within a small group can facilitate both understanding what is going on and helping the group work toward its goals.

Group Norms. Small groups develop certain patterns and expectations of behavior for their members. Homans observed that industrial work groups developed expectations about the level of output of manufactured product expected from each worker. When a worker exceeded this level of output he was open to group censure for violating the group's norms. Homans (1950, 123) observed, "A norm, then, is an idea in the minds of the members of a group, an idea that can be put in the form of a statement specifying what the members or other men should do, ought to do, are expected to do, under given circumstances." Homans saw norms as affecting the member's social ranking. Group norms and an individual member's needs and desires to match the behavior, attitudes, and perceptions of the group are powerful determinants of human behavior (for a review of classic studies see Olmsted 1959, 65–81). For this reason, sensitivity to the processes of small groups enriches our understanding and effectiveness when working in and with small groups.

Group Responses. Scientists and clinicians who have studied and worked with small groups have observed a variety of behaviors of individual group members and membership of groups as a whole that seem to auger for stability and maintenance of the group. These are called *g-responses* (Kadis et al. 1963). The g-responses occur repeatedly throughout the life of the group. They seem to have the effect of restoring the group to a kind of *homeostasis* or stability. When the group members develop more anxiety than they can sustain, g-responses serve to reduce the anxiety to tolerable levels so that the group can continue to function. The most common g-response is the collective laughter that comes after and relieves a moment of tension. Another example of a g-response is the not unusual collective late arrival at a meeting. If the culture is one in which punctuality is valued, this g-response may signify members' resistance to the group.

TRANSFERENCE. Psychotherapists have long observed the phenomenon of *transference*. Originally Sigmund Freud identified transference neurosis as the regressive behavior observed in his patients in which they would hold intense feelings about him as the therapist that they originally experienced toward their parents (Freud 1920/1975). Clinicians have observed that members of therapy groups sometimes react to one another in distorted ways. This is called *parataxic distortion* (Kadis et al. 1963). They see traits in another member that other members do not see. Or they react with intense feelings that are partly based upon similarities between group members and important persons in their past. To some extent transference and parataxic distortion are present in all small groups. While it is all too convenient to attribute otherwise unexplainable feelings or behaviors among group members to transference, it is worth keeping in mind as a possible dynamic in group interaction. Sometimes such feelings can get in the way of the group's functioning and success. When this occurs, it is not recommended that you try to play therapist to the group. But as an equal member concerned for the group's effectiveness and well-being, helping a member or members to check out their perceptions with others in a deliberate way can alleviate problems or problematic feelings born of past relationships and carried into the group.

SCAPEGOATING AND OUTGROUPS. It is frequently observed that political leaders can consolidate the support of their followers if they can direct attention toward an enemy. An enemy constitutes a threat to the nation, the team, or the group. Patriots rally to protect while persons seen to undermine the status quo, especially in threatening times, are subversives.

As we have seen, the membership hierarchy in a small group can serve the group's processes. An external threat can cause the group to rally as individual members subordinate their own agendas to help meet the needs of the group. When this consolidates the current status quo the leader's position, as well as the positions of other group members, is secured.

Scapegoating within a group can have a similar function. A scapegoat bears the brunt of the group's rage, hostility, or teasing. Often the characteristics that group members do not find attractive in themselves are projected upon the scapegoat who is then persecuted by the group for harboring them. But behind the convenient psychological payoff to group members scapegoating a member is a deeper social function for the group's response.

A scapegoat is not always the most inept member. Sometimes it is a person who has considerable ability or resources relative to other group members but who also violates or flaunts the group's norms. Such people may constitute a threat to each member's status in that they could displace any member should they suddenly conform to the norms of the group. They also may be a threat to the group leadership were they not a scapegoat. So in an ironic way the scapegoat threatens the group's pecking order but also forces it to consolidate and support the leader. If a small group that behaves in a way that scapegoats a member can come to an understanding of its behavior, it will develop a conscious understanding of its own structure and dynamics. We can postulate that a small group, which is more tolerant and less inclined to scapegoat a member, is one with a flexible structure.

ACTING OUT. Behavior characterized as being destructive, repetitive, and not under the conscious control or will of the person carrying it out often occurs in small groups. When it does occur, it is a problem for the group. Such annoying or even antisocial behavior is called *acting out* because it is seen as springing from conflictual psychological tensions (Harriman 1963). Hence when a group member repeatedly is late to meetings and enters in a disruptive way, or when a member persistently fails to carry out tasks vital to the group's goals after promising to do so, it may be acting out.

Because the behavior is not under rational control, the person acting out cannot usually respond to reasoned arguments or suggestions. Unless the small group in which the behavior is taking place is a psychotherapy group, the person engaged in it should be referred for professional counseling. If this is not possible, reassignment to tasks unrelated to the person's conflicts or a new role for the person in the group may be in order. Acting out behavior is nettlesome and may prevent the group from achieving its goals. Sometimes small groups will ostracize or isolate individuals whose behavior is so destructive that it harms the group's purposes. So while tolerance is the sign of a group with a flexible, adaptive structure, there are limits to tolerance—especially when the existence and major goals of the group are defeated by acting-out behavior.

An example that occurs to us comes from the frustration of student groups in the 1960s. They had opposed U.S. involvement in the war in Vietnam for a number of years. By 1969 several of the more radical factions of Students for a Democratic Society (SDS) reacted to the situation with a kind of impotent rage. At one point a faction of the group vented its anger by participating in the "Days of Rage" in Chicago. This consisted of marching downtown and smashing storefront windows until confrontations with the police ended the spasm of violence.

Looking back on the situation, we can see that students were involved in a temporary lessening of their frustration by a random attack on what they saw as the status quo. It is nearly always true that violence in a social movement pushes the middle-of-the-road public into opposition to the movement. In this case the temporary "therapy" of doing violence clearly outweighed the long-term attitudinal changes and political changes the students sought. The temptation to fulfill personal psychological needs by acting out is always a threat to political goals that require difficult long-term efforts.

NEW MEMBERS AND STATUS CHANGES. As we briefly mentioned above, the addition of a new member to a group requires some adaptation by old members. They have to size up the new member as to their relative status and other characteristics. Perhaps just as important, the old members have to insure themselves that the new member can and will make similar investments in the group to those that they have made. Will the new member share sensitive feelings and keep sensitive information within the group? Will the new person make the same investments of time, money, or effort as older members have made? Will the new member conform to the group's norms? Is this new person as dedicated to our cause as we are? The testing and answering of these questions and similar ones that groups have of new members will take time.

Groups sometimes seem to reach a plateau relative to the pursuit of their stated purposes and goals. They sometimes seem to go nowhere. The addition of a new member or new members will cause a period of seeming stagnation while the new member is checked out. Actually, the group is engaged in a very important process of monitoring its boundaries of membership. For members and leaders who are conscious of this process, it may present an opportunity to move things along. New members can be described before they arrive, introduced, invited to talk or to participate, and given tasks that will demonstrate competence and involvement.

Open and Closed Groups. A group whose membership constantly changes is called an *open group.* An open group has the disadvantage of not progressing to levels of trust and involvement that it might if the membership was relatively *closed*. A *closed* group is one in which the membership does not turn over very rapidly. Indeed, some groups have the same membership for the life of the group and in rare cases for the lives of the group members. Sometimes, especially with community action groups and other citizen groups of the variety that might be involved with peace work, it may be beneficial for a group to ask whether it should not at some point limit its membership to allow the trust and involvement to develop beyond that which is allowed by an open membership.

Changes in the status of a group member, such as losing a job or getting married, can affect the other members of a group. It may change the configuration of the group or affect the level of anxiety as members identify with the affected person. Thus status change may also lead to a period of apparent stagnation or sorting out. This we hasten to say can be shortened with good open communication.

Stages of Group Development.

Observers of small groups sometimes develop their version of how the small group passes through stages or phases in the course of their existence. Our rendition of the stages of group development is not meant to apply universally. Some groups may depart from the stages we suggest. Groups intentionally formed to last a specified length of time or which have their structure and development controlled may differ, especially in the later stages, from the pattern we suggest. Some groups will never achieve the later stages. But being able to recognize typical stages of group development will enable members or leaders to help move the group to a more mature stage and thus closer to the goals of the group.

Orientation Stage. In the initial gathering of people they do not constitute a group. They are a collection of individuals. They do not identify with one another, they do not take one another into account. They do not share a significant commonality.

A collection of people on an elevator will become a group if they become stuck between floors for an extended period. This is because the ingredients and experiences for them to become a group can develop from their enforced proximity, shared experience, and communication.

Usually, when people get together for the first time they begin to question one another about their respective backgrounds and interests. The unspoken interpersonal agenda is to determine each other's relative status and to discover mutual interests. Prospective group members are determining if they can identify with one another. If during this *orientation stage* there is sufficient affinity and mutual interest, a group may develop, which is signified by the start of the second stage.

Mutuality Stage. In the *mutuality stage* the group consolidates its identity and aligns it member hierarchy with the group's requirements. Members of the group will recognize and identify with each other as members of the group even at times when the group is not formally meeting. Members begin to show their respective abilities and resources. This begets a status hierarchy and the development of group leadership. Later, group relations inevitably become more complex.

Drama Stage. Each member of a group brings to the group his or her experiences, ways of perceiving and relating. Seldom is there total harmony among members from start to finish. Because of different personal needs, agendas, or hang-ups, conflict, squabbles, emotional intensity, status hunger, jealousy, and other human proclivities emerge. As these complexities emerge in the group's life, they can be seen, if one develops some distance, as dramatic interactions. Hence this stage of small group development is seen as the *drama stage.* Much of what takes place in this stage is a testing of old patterns of behavior in the context of the group. Ideals about the goals of the group and the nature or character of the members meet the realities and are not always easily accepted. In some groups, even nontherapy groups, feelings and conflict can become intense and may involve competition for status and the acting out of deep transference problems. Because the purpose of most groups concerning peace work are not of a therapeutic or counseling nature, such dramatic problems must cool out on their own through continuing communication and work toward overall goals.

Love Ties. Successful marriages weather an initial romantic period of intense positive and negative feelings related to the collision of ideal images and the daily reality of a human partner. This survival leads to a conjugal affection between the partners in which the other is accepted with their shortcomings, foibles, and warts and valued for the real person he or she is. A similar process occurs among members of a small group as it weathers the drama stage and develops affectionate ties, *love ties,* with each other. A group may not reach this stage of development having been torn apart during the drama stage or simply never having grown to this level of development.

This stage of a group is usually marked by a good adaptation to the environment. Sometimes such groups persist for the lifetimes of the members. In small town rural America farmers still gather at the diner on Saturday morning to discuss the market, the weather, and other news. Their ties are strong, their manner is mellow, and their group will persist while they farm their land. Such groups are rare in mass industrial urban society, but they can be found. Some sports teams reach this stage as well as some business elites or churches. We see no reason why groups must automatically disband when such a stage of homeostasis is achieved. But sometimes changes in members or the environment causes the group members to move on.

Blossoming. In some groups that have achieved a stage of love ties, members continue to grow and change through other influences in their lives, such as continuing education or occupational development. For such members this change and growth may bring a decline in interest and involvement in the group as activities beyond the group compete for the member's time or meet the member's needs better than the group. Indeed, the experiences of the members in the group may precipitate such growth and give rise to new goals beyond the group and the confidence to pursue them. If substantial numbers of the group begin to change and grow in other directions, the group may come to an end, not so much through stagnation of the group but through *blossoming* that scatters the seeds of new involvements as members move on.

At this point we must sound a cautionary note in our discussion of small groups as emotionally bonded groups of people seeking, let us say, social justice or some aspect of peace. Michael Harrington, a laborer in those fields all of his adult life, talks about the creation of small groups in the 1960s seeking social change. To Harrington's mind (1973, 263), communities of people seeking social justice in that decade were destroyed after the death of Martin Luther King. "The movement," he says, "also died because the dream of a beloved community was and had to be an illusion. In a country profoundly suffused with economic, social, and psychological racism, it is possible to build a little island of love for a while; then the exigencies of struggle intervene, and one must choose from among competing bills, decide between politicians, deal with egos—and the community turns on itself."

In other words, small groups can be enormous sources of personal satisfaction and can give the emotional lift needed to work on issues such as justice or peace. Nevertheless, the real business of politics is compromise, tactics, partial victories, and defeats. This is the way progress is made, but it is also the way in which tightly knit groups are torn apart.

Group Leadership and Facilitation Skills.

From the advice of Niccolo Machiavelli to Lorenzo de Medici to modern research, much has been made of the skills for leadership. We will share a few of the more useful insights into the nature of small group leadership and facilitation skills after making the important distinction between leadership and group facilitation.

Early social workers used small groups to effect social goals in the settlement houses of our larger cities. These groups, working for the mutual benefit of their members, cooperated to improve their lot and the quality of their communities. Such groups developed their own leadership from among their members. Social workers working with such groups consciously cultivated the group's leadership without becoming leaders of each group themselves. They facilitated the groups and their leaders who were seen collectively as their clients. This basic notion of professionals facilitating a group's development, goals, and leadership is now a part of many approaches to work with small groups. Some psychotherapists, counselors, community organizers, and other professionals see themselves as group facilitators rather than as group leaders. For many such professionals, especially social workers, the group itself is their "client."

Some of the skills of facilitators and of group leaders are the same. We will review a few of these.

Skills for Group Leaders and Facilitators. A classic study of group leadership discovered that group members respond in different but roughly predictable ways to different leadership styles (Lippitt and White 1952). An *authoritarian* leader, strongly directive, aloof from the membership, who assigned tasks and arbitrarily praised or condemned, evoked either rebellion, apathy, or lack of involvement of members. A *democratic* leader, who used group discussion and decision making, turned responsibility over to the group, and talked and joked with members evoked friendly relations among members, better work toward tasks, and less scapegoating. A *laissez-faire* leader, who was passive and gave total responsibility to the group, evoked poor group achievement and development of skills for cooperation and planning.

George Homans (1950) enunciated some behaviors for leaders based on studies of small groups. These seem somewhat authoritarian today, but they were based on an industrial management model. A brief summary of Homans' suggestions follows:

1. A leader will maintain his or her position. His or her orders will be carried out. In every group there is a "zone of indifference" (Bernard 1938), that is, a certain latitude a group will allow a leader to give orders without consciously challenging them.
2. A leader will abide by the norms of the group and look out for the interests of the members.
3. A leader will lead—initiate interaction, take initiative.

4. A leader will not give orders that will not be obeyed.
5. A leader will use established channels—that is, the hierarchical ordering—to give orders.
6. A leader will not impose on members socially.
7. A leader will not praise or blame a member in front of other members.
8. A leader will consider the total situation, including the group's environment, the internal and external system, the tools and techniques the group needs to control the environment, and the group norms in his or her decisions.
9. A leader will facilitate group sanctions rather than inflict punishment.
10. A leader will listen. This enables him or her to gather feedback concerning the various aspects of the group and its environment as well as its reactions to leadership.

This classical advice has not been superceded but supplemented by modern guidelines for group leadership.

In summarizing characteristics of effective group leadership, one contemporary text's recommendations, which come very close to group facilitation as we have defined it, include: (1) Having a conceptualization of group process; (2) Self-knowledge, courage, willingness to model, presence, caring, a belief in group process, nondefensiveness, personal power, endurance, a sense of humor, and imagination; (3) Skills in group leading (after Corey and Corey 1987).

Generally, both leaders and facilitators want a group to develop an identity and a group feeling of affinity. They want the group to develop through the early stages into an effective entity. Both can make use of pragmatic procedural skills.

Procedural Skills. If the group is to conduct most of its business in a face-to-face setting, as in a planning group, setting up the physical meeting place is important. A *circular arrangement* of chairs in a manner that allows each member to have easy eye contact with each other member facilitates group interaction. This is especially true if the group is between five and ten members. Groups of larger membership than ten tend to break up into small subgroups if the topic of discussion does not command full attention. A room that prevents frequent interruption and has a door that can be closed signifying the start of business is best.

Often in groups that meet face to face and require discussion the simple technique of *going around* can be helpful in insuring participation of each member and in giving each a voice. With the group arranged in a circle, with each member on the circle as opposed to "hiding out" behind other members, the leader or facilitator can suggest that each person comment on the issue or topic. Such a procedure can help new members to get into the habit of talking. It can allow opinions and feelings that might otherwise go unexpressed to be expressed. Sometimes it can get things started at a first meeting, especially if prospective members are asked to share why they have come to the group's meeting and what they *expect or hope* to gain from membership in the prospective group.

If the group has specific external tasks and is divisive, as citizen action groups can be, *parliamentary rules* are advised when appropriate to the group's purpose. This would include the taking of minutes of the meeting. Minutes can allow members to refer to past meetings to check decisions or group policy.

If one is in a facilitator role and wishes to help the group develop its own leadership, it is best to be quite active at first. This activity can involve getting discussion started, keeping the group focused on tasks relative to its goals, inviting participation from quiet people, demonstrating appropriate participation, and so on. As the group begins to take on an identity and enter a mutuality stage, the facilitator can *withdraw* and gradually allow the natural leadership of the group to develop.

Some techniques that come from group therapy may be appropriate and useful in other kinds of groups likely to be encountered by peace workers. *Relating to masked feelings* of other group members sometimes opens up communication at critical moments. For instance, if you sense that a member is dissatisfied with a plan of action, encouraging that member to share his or her concerns could give voice to feelings other members have as well. Judicious use of such a skill may help the members work more in concert with the group's goals.

Keeping in mind the motivation power of the group's structure and the competition that can develop for position in the group's order, a leader or facilitator may wish to stop destructive disputes. This may entail supporting the existing hierarchy. Or it may be better managed by changing the group environment sufficiently to force the group to have to rely on the talents or resources of low-ranking members. Eventually a more flexible view of the group's order and a more egalitarian mode of functioning may develop. As we indicated above, these attributes of a mature group allow it to function in a variety of environments.

Sometimes a member or several members will repeatedly drift into topics or activities that are tangential to the goals of the group. If the group is still agreed on the goals, *gatekeeping* may be in order. This skill is manifest by leaders, facilitators, and other group members alike. Essentially, it is any action or communication that serves to limit the group's divergence from the goals and tasks and returns the group to its purposes. For example, communications proceeded by such phrases as, "Let's get back to the subject . . ." or "Can we deal with that later and get on with business?" or "I think we should be focusing on . . ." are examples of gatekeeping. Rounding up group members, enlisting the aid of high-status members to enforce the group's norms, calling members specially to come to meetings, gently cutting off or blocking communications from members who are disruptive are activities that also serve a gatekeeping function.

In the initial meetings of a group when a facilitator wishes to encourage group identity and participation prior to the development of a group leader, *summarizing* the events of the meeting and *anticipating* the next and future meeting coupled with sharing sincerely felt positive feelings about the group and its prospects are all helpful skills.

Small Groups, Social Decisions, and Action.

Many efforts to realize peace involve influencing *social decisions*. In democratic society these decisions may be of a political or economic nature that involve differing opinions and wills (Arrow 1963). Small groups of people can influence the social decisions of a community or larger social system through activities skillfully directed toward sources of power and appropriate strategies and tactics for change.

POWER. Peter Rossi (1969) identified five *sources of power* in a community that can critically affect social decisions. *Wealth* and *resources* are usually the most important. As Saint-Simon pointed out, those who control economic production in society are in the most powerful position. Hence they are in positions to influence social decisions disproportionately to their number.

Large numbers of people can become aware of social issues and begin to participate in social decisions by use of the *media*. Often the influence of persons with *prestige* and relationships with such persons can be sources of power and influence. A wealthy industrialist, a renown clergyman, academic, or movie star have influence with some constituents in a community.

A community's shared *values* are a source of power. Consensual values can rally support for a cause—like peace—when the relationship of values to the decisions at hand are articulated. Finally, solidarity groups such as ethnic groups, churches, and unions can generate enormous power and influence over social decisions as their number and activism allow.

Creative activities that can enlist these sources of power in a community to influence peace-related decisions can become meaningful and fruitful activities for groups working for peace.

STRATEGIES AND TACTICS. Usually sources of power are enlisted to influence social decisions through cooperative or conflictual *strategies*. Activist groups must learn to employ strategies and tactics that match the character of the issues or decisions to be made.

Specht (1969) provided a format for achieving this appropriate and therefore effective match (see Table 14.1). Much of what we share below stems from his important ideas.

Rearrangement of priorities or administration such as giving a peace studies course a prominent place in a curriculum or involving citizens in planning a defense project in a community are usually *consensual* decisions that require *collaboration* as a strategy and education and joint activity to achieve. *Redistribution* of resources usually results in differences of opinion, which can be met by a *consensus* arrived at through *negotiation*.

Table 14.1. Community Issues, Strategies, and Tactics

Issue or Decision	Response	Strategy	Tactics
Rearrangement	Consensus	Collaborative	Education
Redistribution	Difference	Campaign	Negotiation
Status and Power	Dissension	Contest	Violation of Norms (Nonviolence)
Reconstruction	Insurrection	Violence	Direct Harm, Force
Realignment	Disassociation	Autonomy	Individuation

Source: Adapted from Specht 1969.

However, when *status* and *power* are at stake in the decision, *dissension* results. *Campaign* strategies and tactics must be employed that may *violate norms* of the community. For example, nonviolent protest or illegal occupation of work sites and buildings may generate conflict rather than collaboration. Nonviolent conflict is not necessarily counterproductive. With conflict, issues may become clearer and more people may become aware and participate in the decision process.

If a radical *reconstruction* of an organization or community is underway, citizens may engage in insurrection against the current order. Harm or force may be employed by one or all sides. Such tactics seldom fit the values of persons concerned with peace and peace issues or even most citizens, unless their very survival is at stake.

What is important to bear in mind is that the strategies for influencing decisions must *fit the issue* to be effective. Hence, educational strategies alone will be unlikely to cause a redistribution of power and wealth from arms manufacturing sectors to job-generating civilian sectors of the economy. Similarly, nonviolent protest would probably alienate potential supporters if it were employed where simple education or negotiation would suffice.

Groups that have decided to form peaceful communities separate from the rest of society, such as the Amish or counterculture groups of the 1960s, add a dimension to the Specht format (Table 14.1). Such groups realign the values and behaviors of their own communities disassociating from the larger society to varying degrees. They attempt to develop autonomy and separate identity in keeping with their group's values. Conflict and even persecution by the larger society may follow. But their example may educate others about the value of decisions for peace and peaceful life-styles.

Summary Conclusions. Those interested in working for peace may find some form of small group as their medium. Understanding small group structure, process, and development, coupled with pragmatic leader and facilitator skills will enhance effectiveness. Much of what is effective in work with small groups of people must come from practical experience. Such experiences can be gained only through being involved with other people and influencing social decisions in the larger community toward such common and important a goal as realizing peace.

In Chapter 15 we will leave the domain of skills and look at the future through the changes and trends we see underway that will affect the course of our study of peace and the prospects for peace.

Chapter 15

Changes, Trends, and Prospects

Changes in technology and economic and social trends certainly affect the prospects for peace. We will examine technological changes first and follow with an overview of economic and social trends, although we will inevitably miss crucial changes or trends not yet apparent or underway. The serendipitous discovery or event may well alter much of what we see now. Also, in our analysis we knowingly enter the realm of prognostication and hope. Our sense of the future is wrapped in the desire for a peaceful and nuclear-free world.

Technological Change. At its most basic level of meaning, the word *technology* refers to the creation and use of tools. The use of complex tools is one thing which separates us from most animals. The tools we create, of course, are designed to change the world (or a part of it) to fit our desires. Whether they be designed for farming, manufacturing, the creation of medicine, or the destruction of war, our technologies change our environment and not always in ways we have come to expect.

Our use of tools not only shapes the world of nature, it also shapes our nature. That is another way of saying that as we change the world with our tools, we change ourselves as well. Again, we cannot always predict what course these changes will take.

The tools we have used for defending ourselves have evolved into the technology of modern weaponry—one of the important sorts of technology we examine in this chapter.

Basic Questions about Technology, Defense, and Human Values.

One of the slogans of some hunters and gun lovers in the United States in the 1970s was stated in this way: "Guns don't kill people, people kill people." Who can resist the logic here. Weapons do not kill by themselves.

We might however rephrase the question of who kills, people or guns, to another more practical question. Who is more likely to kill, an angry person with only his or her hands, a person with a knife, or a person with a loaded automatic weapon? We have structured our question to reflect the idea that all three of the potentially violent individuals share the same intense anger. All that has changed is the technology.

What is most obvious about technological change and warfare is that weapons have become much more deadly than those of our ancestors. It may not be so evident, however, how the new technology of warfare has changed other aspects of war and peace.

With the advent of firearms and gunpowder, individual skills such as were needed by medieval troops using the longbow, were no longer essential. With the increasing use of muskets and other guns, masses of soldiers with these weapons fired upon each other in close-range volleys.

Prior to the nineteenth century wars had been played out in Europe as "the sport of kings." There were generally accepted (though often broken) rules about exempting civilians from the violence of war. Rules of combat were held in esteem, and in theory you paid respect to your enemy on the field of combat.

All of this changed with the development of smokeless powder rifles and breechloaded cannon. The citizen armies of Europe began to slaughter each other in unheard of numbers in the nineteenth century. Nearly half a million Americans killed each other during the Civil War. While there was hand-to-hand combat, it was more likely that the enemy would be killed in a line of fire one thousand yards away. Warfare, like other modern institutions, was becoming impersonal.

During the nineteenth century diseases killed more soldiers than enemy troops. Before 1870 five troops died of disease for every one who died of wounds. By World War I that ratio had reversed itself (Howard 1976).

Nevertheless, the industrialization of war had only begun in the nineteenth century. The twentieth was to bring forth the new horrors of machine guns, tanks, submarines, aerial warfare, poison gas, and nuclear weapons. As we write, the United States and doubtless other countries are developing concepts of weapons that nearly eliminate personal experience in combat. This is the concept of the automated battlefield. We could also cite the example of a single Trident submarine capable of launching 16 missiles, each armed with ten 40-kiloton warheads. The far-off effects of this technological miracle would be the death of perhaps 18 million people, none of whom would have had any personal contact with their attacker (Morrison and Walker 1978).

As the enemy in war becomes more abstract and less of a diabolical human enemy, a new system of values arises for the combatants in high-technology war. As Sam Keen (1988, 72) tells us:

> The Ancient Warrior needed massive physical strength and agility, a passionate hatred and an ability to relish killing. . . . The modern warrior by contrast must be a specialist. Coolheaded and emotionally detached. He prevails only if his calculations are accurate and his mind uncluttered by any passion save the love of efficiency.

We have charted the new values of the participant in the high technological war and contrasted them to the military virtues of past times in Table 15.1.

It may be that the new destructive capacity of technological warfare exceeds our wildest imagination. It also may be the case that new forms of warfare will excite the imagination of the young even

Table 15.1. Values of Combatant

Values of the Low-Technology Combatant	Values of the High-Technology Combatant
1. Heroism	1. Ability to calculate
2. Loyalty	2. Bureaucracy
3. Heated emotions	3. Perfect control of emotions
4. Physical bravery	4. Mental rationality
5. Hatred of the enemy	5. Viewing the enemy as an abstraction

more than the earlier varieties of heroic warfare. We are still left with the question as to what we can do to find the moral equivalent of old fashioned warfare. Perhaps even more importantly, we must solve the problem of what to do with the killing technology we have already created.

Growing Case for Defense. As you recall from Chapter 11 dealing with thermonuclear war, a step-by-step path to disarmament was proposed by Randall Forsberg (1984). A key feature of this plan was an eventual reliance on defensive weapons for each nation. Indeed, it is ironic that nuclear weapons, those ultimate offensive instruments of power, should provide a large part of the motivation to move down the path Forsberg proposed.

The debate still rages over whether nuclear weapons have stabilized the world or made it less safe (see for example Fischman 1988). When asked if they would feel more or less safe should nuclear weapons magically be destroyed, the majority of a group of scientists at an international meeting said they would feel less safe (Dyson 1988). Nuclear weapons are seen to reduce the likelihood of war because the consequences for the aggressor are as terrible as for those attacked. This has held for some thirty years for the nuclear powers. But the numerous "client-state" wars that continue to take place suggest that were nuclear weapons to be abolished, the current nuclear powers could be drawn into conventional war with each other. However, the advent of nuclear "first-strike" weapons designed to take out the enemy's capacity to retaliate have introduced new instability into the world.

It is becoming increasingly apparent that nuclear weapons no longer provide the deterrence or pseudostability of a mutual suicide pact. Their number and variety are too great, too difficult to control, and too likely to eventually reach the arsenals of too many countries. Another form of stability must be found.

EUROPE. The signing of the Intermediate Nuclear Forces Treaty (INF) in 1988 gave the world a new burst of hope. It called upon Soviet and American governments to destroy about 4 percent of the nuclear weapons in their respective stockpiles. But with the signing of the treaty, new fears and prospects were voiced and new plans were made. Elements with political and economic interests in further nuclear weapons development and deployment saw the INF as a reason to push for a whole variety of new nuclear weapons. Such weapons included new air- and sea-launched Cruise Missiles, nuclear-tipped, Multiple-Launch Rocket Systems, nuclear-tipped artillery shells for eight-inch guns with greater range and power (Plesch 1988). Such a push would keep the nuclear option alive in Europe and would constitute a test of U.S. resolve to continue our defense of Europe. But these interests were countered by a new vision of defense both in Europe and worldwide.

In Europe a new approach to military preparedness seemed to be emerging that emphasized defense. So-called "deep-strike" weapons would be cut and other offensive weapons would be gradually reduced (Muller and Karkoszka 1988). Under such a plan the number of tanks would be limited to a prescribed density per square mile. The range and number of artillery shells, rockets, strike-aircraft would have agreed upon limits. New technologies such as networks of monitored seismic sensors and mobile mines would provide much cheaper defense by separating the intelligent components from the explosive ones (Muller and Karkoszka 1988).

Emphasis on defense would reduce the attractiveness and probable success of launching an attack in much the same way the presence of nuclear arms did for a period of their history. In effect, the costs would be too great to the aggressor. The Warsaw Treaty Organization and the North Atlantic Treaty Organization have begun to discuss such strategies. Such new terms as "nonoffensive defense," "stability/reduction talks," and the "cult of the offensive" are now heard (Conetta 1988). As technologies for secure defense develop, the prospects for their replacing nuclear arms and securing a stable peace may be enhanced.

STRATEGIC DEFENSE AND A STABLE PEACE. Discussion of *strategic defense* took what may have been an unfortunate turn with President Reagan's famous 1983 Strategic Defense Initiative (SDI) or "Star Wars" speech in which he advocated the development of a shield comprised of orbital weapons that could theoretically destroy offensive missiles after launching. The speech and subsequent Reagan administration argument suggested a way the nuclear terror could be eliminated while the military-industrial complex could keep rolling right along. A nuclear-arms freeze would be unnecessary. The debate over the plausibility of such a system of technologies raged during the latter part of the Reagan administration. While money for research was quite appealing, some reputable scientists refused to work on SDI projects because of the improbable effectiveness of the plan and their reluctance to see it substituted for real measures to reduce the arms race (Power 1987; Moberg 1985).

Criticisms of the SDI include: (1) the futility of attempting to stop large percentages of enemy missiles when even small percentages getting through a shield would destroy the country, (2) enormous costs of development and of getting the systems into orbit, (3) the doubtful likelihood that the system would in fact be scientifically possible or militarily effective, (4) the ease of destroying SDI weapons in orbit should the Soviets decide to do so, (5) the argument that the testing and deployment of weapons in space is prohibited by the ABM Treaty, and finally, (6) the argument that weapons such as the orbital laser have potential for use as an offensive weapon (see for example La Rocque 1988; Pike 1985; Rothschild and Peck 1985).

Physicist Freeman Dyson advocates abandonment of the more grandiose schemes emphasizing "boost-phase" defenses that would shoot enemy missiles on their way up. He advocates continued sober development of interceptor rockets and other "terminal defenses" that have no offensive potential and that would find more political acceptance (Dyson 1988). Dyson's qualified criticism is in keeping with the growing notion of defense as a military posture. Dyson sees the capacity to gather and process information as important to defense and projects the hope more sophisticated sensors, microcomputers, and data processors will help develop strategic defense that in concert with arms control will provide a safer and more peaceful world. Dyson asserts (1988, 229):

> The purpose of strategic defense is not to save our skins in case we get into a nuclear war. That is why the arguments which prove that defense is imperfect and uncertain do not prove that it is useless or undesirable. The purpose of defense is to create a state of mind. The purpose is to persuade political and military leaders all over the world that nuclear weapons are not a good buy. The purpose is to make nuclear weapons unnecessary and unattractive.

Like other comments on Strategic Defense Initiative, Dyson's may have a naive faith in technology as a solution to the problem of nuclear arms. Yet it is a possible path toward a safer world.

Strategic defense can lead to the condition that Kenneth Boulding calls a *stable peace* which is qualitatively different from deterrence, especially nuclear deterrence (Boulding 1985b). Stable peace, according to Boulding, began about the end of the Napoleonic Wars in 1815. In such a situation independent countries coexist without the preparation or intention of going to war. Boulding saw nuclear deterrence as ultimately unstable, otherwise it would not exist because nuclear arms would not threaten. In this light, traditional "national defense" is the enemy of "national security" and "can only lead to national destruction, and perhaps the destruction of the whole human race or even the whole evolutionary experiment on earth" (Boulding 1985b, 126).

While technology for defensive postures develop, those that enhance offense and the plausibility of nuclear war also develop. Smart missiles, ever more powerful and accurate warheads and guidance systems, and other new systems contribute to mistrust and instability. For example, the Ground Wave Emergency Network (GWEN) of 127 three-hundred-foot towers under deployment around the United States is intended to provide a means of communication after a nuclear war is underway (Barber 1987). Such a system could become an inviting target for a first strike and implies a policy of preparation to fight a protracted nuclear war. All of which suggests that there are those who believe such an endeavor is within the realm of reason.

New technologies can make a new path toward a more stable and peaceful world, but clearly the potential for greater endangerment is present as well. Nevertheless, the combination of development of the technologies of defense and the reduction and elimination of nuclear and eventually other offensive weapons is one facet of technological innovation that can lead to a more peaceful world, a stable peace. The major changes and developments beyond weaponry also hold much promise.

New Technologies and New Hopes. Dyson identified molecular biology, neurophysiology, and space physics as three areas of scientific knowledge not yet fully exploited that would give rise to a revolution in technology. The related technologies of genetic engineering, artificial intelligence, and space colonization hold much promise for change. Such discoveries or inventions suggested by Dyson as nitrogen-fixing and water-fixing plants, computers more closely resembling human intelligence, and the exploration and colonization of asteroids hold projects and hopes for a future in which war becomes less necessary (1988). If most cultures recognize the need to develop ways of using their excess energy or human labor, these new technologies may provide conquests of disease, ecological problems, and exploration beyond the earth as alternatives to war.

COMMUNICATION. In our discussion of the causes of war we identified communication technology as a vital force for peace. Little that happens in the way of mass violence now escapes the attention of the media. Some wars and some institutional violence receive wider coverage than other instances, such as the relatively wide coverage of conflict in Central America versus the relatively mute coverage of armed conflict in Sub-Saharan Africa. It is likely that policymakers must be increasingly aware of, and even accountable to, world opinion as it is informed and shaped by television and print news.

Communication between potential adversaries is also being shaped by new technologies. The "hotline" established in 1963 was the first communications link set up to reduce the possibility of nuclear war. The United States Nuclear Risk Reduction Center and the USSR counterpart were opened in March 1988. The new centers will exchange information and notifications required by treaty and agreements (U.S. Institute for Peace 1988).

RESEARCH AND CHOICES. Meteorological, medical, pharmaceutical, and a host of other technologies hold the promise of furthering the elimination of hunger, disease, and other sources of suffering. If the research money and brain power now devoted to the development of weapons technology were allocated to socially redeeming technologies, much more could be accomplished. Ruth Sivard (1987, 14) observes that research into new technologies generates "its own momentum through irresistible pressures to explore the next horizon." Unfortunately, she is speaking primarily of military research as she estimates "the U.S. Government devotes well over twice as much research money to weapons as to all other research needs combined—including energy, health, education, and food—and the Soviet pattern is believed to be similar."

Ultimately there is an interaction between what technology makes possible and the economic, social, and political choices we make about its emphasis and use. Changes in technology, therefore, merely define limits and potentials. The prospects for peace are also shaped by such human choices.

Economic and Social Trends. As we pointed out in our discussion and analysis of Third World militarism, hunger and disease are not static but growing problems. They are a kind of violence caused by or exacerbated by militarism employed in the interest of social structures that perpetuate radically unequal distribution of land and resources.

Military institutions have a basic appeal to different levels of society. The lower classes may see the military as a means to escape poverty and to gain a better standard of living. Middle and upper classes may see the military as securing their country from invasion or securing their social position and the social arrangements in society that benefit them. Finally, fear of the power of the military or the military in combination with large scale industrial interests can compel support and mute criticisms from citizens.

If growing military expenditures in the First World and the growing numbers of governments dominated by the military in the

Third World are valid indicators, there is a global trend toward increasing militarism. Traditional notions of the historical dynamics of social class as a force in social trends may be inadequate in light of the growing power and prevalence of the military in both industrial societies of the First World as well as in the Third World. Given these tendencies, what are the prospects for continued civilian political control of the military?

Social Democracy. A partial answer to this last discomforting question may lie in a countertrend. Plato asserted that democracy could only exist so long as all citizens could gather together in the courtyard. The prospects of democracy were tied, therefore, to the possibility of dialogue and participation. However, mass industrial society has employed representative democracy, bureaucratic control, control by elite ownership classes, military dominance, and other means to govern.

While control of the means of economic production was observed to be the major source of power in society, it has seldom been in the hands of those who do the work and produce the wealth. The bringing together of democracy and control of production would create and be created by profound changes in society. But such a coalition may be beginning in a variety of ways.

The major communist or state capitalist countries are introducing certain free-market mechanisms into their economies to provide incentive. *Perestroika,* or reorganization, in the Soviet Union and individual entrepreneurship in China contain elements of this trend. These economies have suffered from too much central control, particularly in the agricultural sectors. Allowing individual producers some say and opportunity to work in their own behalf on their own time does not violate some versions of socialism so long as employees are not exploited and great capital is not passed along to children to perpetuate a privileged class.

In private capitalist countries innovations of worker participation in management decisions and modest worker input into the conditions of work are small steps toward workplace democracy.

Such innovations may begin a process in which Plato's democracy can begin to thrive in the workplace instead of the courtyard. If the economic power basis of society was democratically controlled in the interests of the working majority, would this be a condition that would favor peace or war? As we observed earlier, war is sometimes—at least partially—a means to secure the position of a dominant social class. The World War I aphorism comes to mind: "In war there is a working man on both ends of the bayonet." When there is both a vital and economic interest in the perpetuation of peace, and those interests have a democratic say over the issues, peace may have the upper hand.

War and Its Prohibition in Religion. The claims and grievances of religion are enormously complex. Almost any statement about religious differences as contributors to war will meet with strong opposition. Religion is so closely linked with other cultural and ethnic variables that to separate religion as a variable in the prospects for war or peace is wholly artificial. Yet the reality of religion as a force for war and as a force for peace exists in the world.

Jerusalem is a holy city for three of the world's great religions. It may be a city of peace or of strife. At least a part of the conflict between Iran and Iraq is linked to religion. Hindus and Islamic people in India have suffered years of conflict that Gandhi fasted to end. From the time of the Crusades through the mass starvation of the Catholic Irish and the genocide of European Jews until present day Lebanon, war and mass violence has been tied to religion.

As we have stressed earlier, religion can be a moral force that can propose ideal solutions and provide visions for peace. Two such attempts to provide moral and religious leadership toward peace through the abolition of nuclear weapons have emerged recently and may be a sign of a trend toward a religious and moral perspective on the nuclear arms race.

On May 3, 1983, the Catholic bishops approved a letter setting forth their perspective on war and peace. "The Challenge of Peace: God's Promise and Our Response," deals with several issues including conscientious objection to war (American Council of Catholic Bishops 1983). Most controversial was their stand regarding nuclear arms, which is in opposition to U.S. policy.

The bishops' letter bases its stand on moral principle. While a just war and a nation's right and duty to defend itself is upheld, using nuclear weapons against civilian populations and relying on nuclear weapons as a permanent means to deter aggression is morally wrong. The bishops maintain further that the arms race is a danger and an act of aggression against the poor. The bishops also condemn the initiation of nuclear war and the concept of a limited nuclear war. As a message to all Catholics in the United States the letter is a moral force pressing for U.S. Catholics to work to end the arms race and to influence U.S. policy away from nuclear weapons and toward a defensive military posture.

In April 1983 the Council of Bishops of the United Methodist Church unanimously adopted a letter to the over 9 million members of the church in the United States and fifteen other countries calling for a freeze on production and a dismantling of nuclear weapons (United Methodist Council of Bishops 1986).

The letters provide a moral imperative to do away with nuclear arms and a vision of an interdependent world in which nations can defend but do not attack each other.

One World Consciousness. The bishops' letter suggests an interdependent world. This vision was seen as a possibility by numerous leaders who tried to achieve unity through conquest, economic revolution, or religious conversion. One-world government has been a recurring theme from such thinkers as Alexander Hamilton and Albert Einstein (Dyson 1988). Jonathan Schell reported another vision of interdependence in the *Fate of the Earth* (1982), sociologist Kenneth Boulding described *The World as a Total System* (1985b), and biologists Ehrlich, Sagan, Kennedy, and Roberts warned our consciousness of "nuclear winter" (1984). The "Beyond War" movement in the United States adopted a one world or unity theme in its efforts for peace. (*Beyond War* 1984). Such visions were made concrete when the photographs of Earth taken from space began to appear in the world mass media.

Is this concept the product of a serious transnational discussion? Does it spring from a concern over a serious ecological problem? Or does it arise from opposition to nuclear weapons and fear of the consequences of their use. Whatever the case, a trend toward consciousness of our collective interest in the preservation and repair of the Earth is a trend of our era.

The powerful myths of the Earth as Mother Goddess, with human beings as her children, coalesces with the psychological development notion of children exploring first the bodies of their mothers and then the world about (Pearce 1977). As we have been created by Earth, as we have drawn sustenance and been nourished by Earth, as we have explored her, we now must repair the damage of youthful ignorance and greed and perhaps begin a tentative exploration beyond her grasp.

Shortly before his death Joseph Campbell, a lifelong student of myth and its effects on human consciousness, during a stunning interview with Bill Moyers spoke of the developing collective consciousness of the Earth. In a casual reference he said that he saw with the eyes of the Earth. He saw himself, each individual, as arising from the Earth. He saw human beings as the Earth's means of consciousness (Campbell 1988). Such a vision suggests that the end of the nuclear arms race and a peaceful world is a kind of rite of passage to responsibility as well as to survival.

Conclusion. The changes and trends we have identified will shape the direction and evolution of peace studies and our work for peace. We hope our technology will be employed toward peaceful goals and the trends we see will shape a possible future. Certainly the study of peace will enlarge our consciousness of prospects for peace as well as those conditions and changes that threaten it. We must conclude that the study of peace is fundamentally a study of necessity, a prerequisite for species adulthood if our mutual destiny is to be realized.

References

Abramovitz, Mimi. 1986. The Privatization of the Welfare State: A Review. *Social Work* 31 (4 July–August): 257–64.

Adams, Paul. 1977. Social Policy and War. *Journal of Sociology and Social Welfare* 4 (3–4 January/March): 419–38.

Adler, Alfred. 1969. *The Science of Living.* New York: Basic Books.

Adorno, Theodore W. 1972. *Aspects of Sociology.* Boston: Beacon Press.

Adorno, Theodore W., R. Nevitt Sandford, and Else Frankel Brunswik. 1950. *The Authoritarian Personality.* New York: Harper and Brothers.

American Council of Catholic Bishops. 1983. *The Challenge of Peace: God's Promise and Our Response.* United States: Catholic Conference.

Amundson, Ron. 1985. The Hundredth Monkey Phenomenon. *Skeptical Inquirer* 9: 348–56.

Anthony, Edward, editor. 1951. Survival at Home. *Woman's Home Companion* May, 21–27.

Arendt, Hannah. 1970. *On Violence.* New York: Harcourt, Brace, and World.

Aron, Elaine, and Arthur Aron. 1986. *The Maharishi Effect.* Walpole, New Hampshire: Stillpoint Publishing.

Arrow, Kenneth J. 1963. *Social Choice and Individual Values.* New York: Wiley.

Axelrod, Robert. 1984. *The Evolution of Cooperation.* New York: Basic Books.

Bainton, Roland. 1962. *Early and Medieval Christianity.* Boston: Beacon Press.

Bales, Robert F. 1950. *Interaction Process Analysis.* Cambridge, Massachusetts: Addison-Wesley.

Bandura, A. 1973. *Aggression: A Social Learning Analysis.* Englewood Cliffs, New Jersey: Prentice-Hall.

Barber, Lois. 1987. GWEN Across America: Preparing for Nuclear War. *Sane World* (Spring): 12–13.

Barrett-Lennard, G. T. 1981. The Empathy Cycle: Refinement of a Nuclear Concept. *Journal of Counseling Psychology* 28 (2): 91–100.

Bernard, Chester Irving. 1938. *The Functions of the Executive.* Cambridge, Massachusetts: Harvard University Press. As quoted in George C. Homans. 1950. *The Human Group.* New York: Harcourt, Brace, World.

Bernard, Viola, Perry Ottenberg, and Frity Redl. 1970. Dehumanization: A Composite Psychological Defense in Relation to Modern War. In *Behavioral Science and Human Survival,* edited by Milton Schevebel. Palo Alto: Science and Behavior Books.

Beyond War: A New Way of Thinking. 1984. Palo Alto, California: Creative Initiative.

Bloch, Donald. 1984. What Do We Tell the Children? *Family Therapy Networker* 8 (2 March–April): 28–31.

Bloom, Martin. 1980. Primary Prevention: Revolution in the Helping Professions. *Social Work in Health Care* 6 (2): 53–67.

Bok, Sissela. 1979. *Lying: Moral Choice in Public and Private Life.* New York: Vintage.

Boston Study Group. 1979. *The Price of Defense: A New Strategy for Military Spending.* New York: Times Books.

Boulding, Elise. 1988. Image and Action in Peace Building. *Journal of Social Issues* 44 (2): 17–37.

Boulding, Kenneth. 1985a. *Collected Papers.* Edited by Larry D. Singell. Boulder, Colorado: Colorado Associated University Press.

___. 1985b. *The World as a Total System.* Beverly Hills, California: Sage.

___. 1962. *Conflict and Defense.* New York: Harper Brothers.

Broom, Leonard, and Philip Selznick. 1963. *Sociology.* Third Edition. New York: Harper and Row.

Brown, Bruce. 1973. *Marx, Freud, and the Critique of Everyday Life: Toward a Permanent Cultural Revolution.* New York: Monthly Review Press.

Brown, Lester R. 1972. *World Without Borders.* New York: Harper and Row.

Burtt, E. A. 1955. *The Teachings of the Compassionate Buddha.* New York: New American Library.

Caldicott, Helen. 1983. Lecture given at the University of Northern Iowa.

Campbell, Joseph. 1988. Joseph Campbell and the Power of Myth, Part 1. Interview with Bill Moyers, *National Public Television*, June 5.

Camus, Albert. 1968. *Lyrical and Critical Essays*. New York: Knopf.

Cannon, W. B. 1953. *Bodily Changes in Pain, Hunger, Fear, and Rage*. Boston: Brantford.

Caplan, R. D. 1979. Social Support, Person-Environment Fit and Coping. In *Mental Health and the Economy*, edited by L. A. Ferman and J. F. Gordus, 144–58. Kalamazoo, Michigan: Upjohn.

Carrol, Lewis. 1956. *Through the Looking Glass*. New York: Golden Books.

Castelli, Jim. 1984. *The Bishops and the Bomb*. Garden City, New York: Image Books.

Center for Defense Information. 1989. The First Step: Halt Nuclear Weapons Testing. *Defense Monitor* 18 (1): 1–8.

___. 1988. After the INF Treaty: U.S. Nuclear Buildup in Europe. *Defense Monitor* 17 (2).

___. 1987. Soviet Compliance with Arms Agreements: The Positive Record. *Defense Monitor* 16 (2).

___. 1986. Accidental Nuclear War: A Rising Risk? *Defense Monitor* 15 (7).

___. 1974. U.S. Strategic Momentum. *Defense Monitor* 3 (4 May): 2.

Chagnon, Napoleon. 1974. *Studying the Yanomamo*. New York: Holt, Rinehart, and Winston.

Chant, Christopher, and Ian Hogg. 1983. *Nuclear War in the 1980's?* New York: Harper Row.

Clayton, James. 1977. A Comparison of Defense and Welfare Spending in the United States and the United Kingdom, 1946–1976. *Journal of Sociology and Social Welfare* 4 (3–4 January/March): 401–18.

Cockburn, Alexander. 1988. Oh, What a Lovely War. *Nation* 247 (4): 18, 120.

Cohn, Carol. 1987. Sex and Death in the Rational World of the Defense Intellectuals. *Signs: Journal of Women in Culture and Society* 12 (4): 687–718.

Conetta, Carl. 1988. *Perestroika* in Soviet Security Policy. *Defense and Disarmament Alternatives* 1 (2 April): 1, 7, 8.

Corey, Marianne Schneider, and Gerald Corey. 1987. *Groups: Process and Practice*. Belmont, California: Brooks/Cole.

Crum, Thomas. 1987. *The Magic of Conflict*. New York: Simon and Schuster.

David, Steven R. 1987. *Third World Coups d'Etat and International Security*. Baltimore, Maryland: Johns Hopkins University Press.

Deau, K., and L. S. Wrightsman. 1984. *Social Psychology in the 80's*. Fourth Edition. Monterey, California: Brooks Cole.

Des Moines Register. 1986. Reagan Carries Out Decision to Exceed SALT II Arms Limits. Associated Press (November 27): 6A.

Deutsch, Morton. 1985. *Distributive Justice: A Social Psychological Perspective*. New Haven: Yale University Press.

Divale, William. 1974. Migration, External Warfare and Matrilocal Residence. *Behavior Science Research* 9: 75–133.

Dolci, Danilo. 1970. *Report from Polermo*. New York: Viking Press.

Dollard, J., L. W. Dobb, N. E. Miller, O. H. Mowrer, and R. R. Sears. 1939. *Frustration and Aggression*. New Haven, Conn.: Yale University Press.

Dumas, Lloyd. 1986. Ending the Military Economy. *In These Times* (May 21–27): 17.

Dyer, Gwynne. 1986a. Don't Bet Arms Will Bankrupt Soviets. *Des Moines Register* (July 15): 7A.

___. 1986b. *War: A Commentary*. National Film Board of Canada.

Dyson, Freeman. 1988. *Infinite in All Directions*. New York: Harper Row.

Earle, Ralph II. 1980. *World Military Expenditures and Arms Transfers. 1969–1979*. Washington, D.C.: U.S. Arms Control and Disarmament Agency.

Edelman, Marian Wright (President). 1985. *A Children's Defense Budget: 1986*. Washington, D.C.: Children's Defense Fund.

Edwards, Paul. 1967. Wilhelm Reich, in *The Encyclopedia of Philosophy*, edited by Paul Edwards. New York: Macmillan.

Egan, Gerard. 1975. *The Skilled Helper*. 69. Monterrey, California: Brooks/Cole.

Ehrlich, Paul R., Carl Sagan, Donald Kennedy, and Walter O. Roberts. 1984.

The Cold and the Dark: The World After Nuclear War. New York: Norton.

Encyclopaedia Britannica, 15th ed. s.v. Economic History Since 1500.

___. s.v. Ideology. Signed article by Maurice Cranston.

___. s.v. Thorstein Veblen. Signed entry by Francis S. Pierce.

___. s.v. The State. Signed entry by D. D. Raphael.

Escalona, Sibylle K. 1982. Growing Up with the Threat of Nuclear War: Some Indirect Effects on Personality Development. *American Journal of Orthopsychiatry* 52 (4 October): 600–607.

Estes, Richard J. 1985. Toward the Year 2000: A Social Agenda for Mankind. *Social Development Issues* 9 (1): 54–63.

Evlanoff, Michael. 1943. *Nobel-prize Donor: Inventor of Dynamite.* Philadelphia: Blakiston.

Fanon, Franz. 1965. *The Wretched of the Earth.* New York: Grove Press.

Ferman, Louis, and Jeanne Gordus, editors. 1979. *Mental Health and the Economy.* Kalamazoo, Michigan: Upjohn Institute.

Fischman, Joshua. 1988. The Security of Uncertainty. *Psychology Today* 22 (6 June): 28–33.

Forest, James. 1976. Nhat Hanh: Seeing with the Eyes of Compassion in Nhat Hanh. *The Miracle of Mindfulness! A Manual on Meditation.* Boston: Beacon Press.

Forsberg, Randall. 1988. INF: A First Step Toward What? *Defense and Disarmament News* 3 (2 February).

___. 1984. The Freeze and Beyond: Confining the Military to Defense as a Route to Disarmament. *World Policy* I (2): 285–318.

Freire, Paulo. 1973. *Education for Critical Consciousness.* New York: Seabury Press.

___. 1970. *Education for Critical Consciousness.* New York: Seabury Press.

Frenkel-Brunswik, Else, and R. Nevitt Sandford. 1949. Some Personality Factors in Anti Semitism. *Journal of Psychology* 18: 271–91.

Freud, Sigmund. 1920/1975. *A General Introduction to Psychoanalysis.* New York: Pocket Book, Simon and Schuster; originally published by Liveright Publishing Co.

Fromm, Erich. 1966. *You Shall Be As Gods*. New York: Holt, Rinehart, and Winston.

___. 1955. *The Sane Society*. New York: Harper and Row.

Geismar, Peter. 1969. Franz Fanon: Evolution of a Revolutionary. *Monthly Review* 37 (5 May): 116–37.

Gellen, M. 1970. Finger Blood Volume Responses of Counselors, Counselor Trainees, and Non-counselors to Stimuli from an Empathy Test. *Counselor Education and Supervision* 10 (1): 64–74.

Gervasi, Thomas. 1984. *Arsenal of Democracy. Vol 3. America's War Machine: The Pursuit of Global Dominance*. New York: Grove.

Gilbert, Neil. 1986. The Welfare State Adrift. *Social Work* 31 (4 July–August): 251–56.

Ginsberg, Eli. 1965. *One Hundred Years of Lynching in America*. New York: Bantam Books.

Gleitman, H. 1981. *Psychology*. New York: W. W. Norton.

Goldner, A. W. 1960. The Norm of Reciprocity: A Preliminary Statement. *American Sociological Review* 25: 161–79.

Goldstein, Jeffrey H. 1986. *Aggression and Crimes of Violence*. Second edition. Oxford: Oxford University Press.

Gore, Susan. 1978. The Effects of Social Support in Moderating the Health Consequences of Unemployment. *Journal of Health and Social Behavior* 19: 157–65.

Gorney, Roderic. 1980. Cultural Determinations of Achievement, Aggression, and Psychological Distress. *Archives of General Psychiatry* 37: 452–59.

Grant, James P. 1988. *The State of the World's Children*. New York: UNICEF.

Gray, Colon, and Keith Payne. 1980. Victory Is Possible. *Foreign Affairs* 39: 14–17.

Halperin, Morton. 1984. *Beyond War: A New Way of Thinking*. Palo Alto, California: Creative Initiative.

Hampden-Turner, Charles. 1971. *Radical Man*. Garden City, New York: Doubleday.

___. 1970. *Radical Man: The Process of Psycho-Social Development*. Cambridge: Schenkman Publishing.

Harriman, Philip L. 1963. *Handbook of Psychological Terms*. Paterson, New Jersey: Littlefield, Adams.

Harrington, Michael. 1977. *The Vast Majority: A Journey to the World's Poor*. New York: Simon and Schuster.

Harris, Marvin. 1974. *Cows, Pigs, Wars, and Witches: The Riddles of Culture*. New York: Vintage.

Hashimi, Rasool M. 1985. Welfare Versus Warfare in the Third World. *Social Development Issues* 9 (1): 64–73.

Hass, Eric. 1958. CBS-TV Interview. In *The Great Thoughts*, 1985, edited by George Seldes. New York: Ballantine.

Helgartner, Stephen, Richard Bell, and Rory O'Connor. 1982. *Nukespeak: Nuclear Language Visions, and Mindset*. San Francisco: Sierra Club Books.

Herkin, Gregg. 1987. The Earthly Origins of Star Wars. *Bulletin of the Atomic Scientists* 43 (8 October): 20–30.

Hiatt, Howard, as quoted in "The Threat of Nuclear War." 1981. *Union of Concerned Scientists*. Cambridge, Massachusetts.

Homans, George C. 1950. *The Human Group*. New York: Harcourt, Brace, and World.

Hoogvelt, Ankie M. M. 1977. *The Sociology of Developing Societies*. Atlantic Highlands, New Jersey: Humanities Press.

Hope, Marjorie, and James Young. 1979. *The Struggle for Humanity*. Maryknoll, New York: Orbis Books.

Horney, Karen. 1973. *Theories of Psychopathology and Personality*, edited by Theodore Millon. Philadelphia: W. B. Saunders.

Howard, Michael. 1976. *War in European History*. London: Oxford University Press.

Isbister, Claude. 1987. Third World Debt: IMF and the World Bank. *Behind the Headlines* 4 (4 March).

Jansen, G. H. 1979. *Militant Islam*. New York: Harper and Row.

Johnson, David, and Roger Johnson. 1984. Cross-Ethnic Relationships: The Impact of Intergroup Cooperation and Intergroup Competition. *Journal of Experimental Education* 78: 75–79.

Jourard, Sidney. 1966. Psychology of Transcendent Perception. In *Explorations in Human Potential,* edited by Herbert Otto. Springfield, Illinois: Thomas.

Kadis, Asya L., Jack D. Krasner, and Charles Winick. 1963. *A Practicum of Group Psychotherapy.* New York: Hoeber Medical Division, Harper and Row.

Kahn, Herman. 1960. *On Nuclear War.* Princeton, New Jersey: Princeton University Press.

Kapleau, Philip. 1967. *The Three Pillars of Zen.* Boston: Beacon Press.

Keefe, Thomas. 1986. Meditation and Social Work Treatment. In *Social Work Treatment: Interlocking Theoretical Approaches,* edited by Francis J. Turner. New York: Free Press.

_____. 1984. The Stresses of Unemployment: A Challenge for Social Work Practice. *Social Work* 29 (3): 264–68.

_____. 1983. *Relationships in Social Service Practice.* Monterey, California: Brooks/Cole.

_____. 1980. Empathy Skill and Critical Consciousness. *Social Casework* 61 (7 September): 387–93.

_____. 1978. The Economic Context of Empathy. *Social Work* 23 (6 November): 460–67.

_____. 1976. Empathy: The Critical Skill. *Social Work* 21 (1 January): 10–15.

_____. 1975. Empathy and Social Work Education. *Journal of Education for Social Work* 11 (3): 69–75.

Keefe, Thomas, and Donald A. Maypole. 1983. *Relationships in Social Service Practice.* Monterey, California: Brooks/Cole.

Keefe, Thomas, and Ron E. Roberts. 1984. Reciprocity, Social Support, and Unemployment. *Social Development Issues* 8 (3): 116–26.

Keen, Sam. 1988. *Faces of the Energy: Reflections of the Hostile Imagination.* New York: Harper and Row.

Keyes, Ken. 1982. *The Hundredth Monkey.* Coos Bay, Oregon: Vision Books.

Kim, Hyung Shik. 1985. Social Welfare and the Development Process. In *Social Welfare in Asia,* edited by John Dixon and Hyung Shik Kim. London: Croom Helm.

Klausser, Joseph. 1956. *The Messianic Idea in Israel.* Boston: Beacon Press.

Kohn, Alfie. 1988. Make Love, Not War. *Psychology Today* 22 (6 June): 35–38.

___. 1986. *No Contest: The Case Against Competition.* Boston: Houghton Mifflin.

Korotkin, Arnold. 1985. Impact of Military Spending on the Nation's Quality of Life. *Social Work* (July–August).

Kramer, J. C. 1977. Heroin in the Treatment of Morphine Addiction. *Journal of Psychedelic Drugs* 9 (3): 193–97.

Kratochwil, Friedrich, Paul Rohrlich, and Harpreet Mahajan. 1985. *Peace and Disputed Sovereignty: Reflections on Conflict over Territory.* New York: University Press of America.

La Rocque, Gene R., director. 1988. Star Wars Reality: The Emperor Has No Clothes. *Defense Monitor* 27 (1): 1–8.

Lazarus, R. S. 1977. Cognitive and Coping Processes in Emotion. In *Stress and Coping,* edited by A. Monet and R. S. Lazarus. New York: Columbia University Press.

Lesser, Alexander. 1968. War and the State. In *War: The Anthropology of Armed Conflict and Aggression,* edited by Milton Fried et al., 92–96. Garden City, New York: Natural History Press.

Levi-Strauss, Claude. 1969. *The Elementary Structure of Kinship.* Boston: Beacon Press.

Levitan, Sar A. 1986. The Evolving Welfare System. *Society* 23 (2 January/February): 4–9.

Lifton, Robert J. 1979. *The Broken Connection.* New York: Simon and Schuster.

Lippitt, Ronald, and Ralph K. White. 1952. An Experimental Study of Leadership and Group Life. In *Readings in Social Psychology,* revised edition, edited by Guy Swanson, Theodore Newcomb, and Eugene Hartley. New York: Henry Holt. As quoted in Olmsted, 1959.

Lorenz, Konrad Z. 1966. *On Aggression.* London: Methuen.

Machiavelli, Niccolo. 1532/1980. *The Prince.* New York: New American Library.

Mack, John E. 1984. Resistances to Knowing in the Nuclear Age. *Harvard Educational Review* 54, no. 3, 11–12.

___. 1982. The Perception of U.S.-Soviet Intentions and Other Psychological

Dimensions of the Nuclear Arms Race. *American Journal of Orthopsychiatry* 52 (4 October): 590–99.

McGinnis, Kathleen, and James McGinnis. 1983. *Parenting for Peace and Justice.* Maryknoll, New York: Orbis Books.

MacLaine, Shirley. 1987. *It's All in the Playing.* New York: Bantam Book.

MacLeish, Kenneth. 1972. The Tasadays: The Stoneage Cavemen of Mindanao. *National Geographic* 142: 219–48.

McNeish, James. 1966. *Fire Under the Ashes.* Boston: Beacon Press.

Mader, Eric. 1986. Bombs Away. *Progressive* (February): 50.

Magaia, Lina. 1988. *Dumba Nengue: Peasant Tales of Tragedy in Mozambique.* Trenton, New Jersey: Africa World Press.

Maier, S. F., and M. E. P. Seligman. 1976. Learned Helplessness: Theory and Evidence. *Journal of Experimental Psychology* 105: 3–46.

Marcuse, H. 1955. *Eros and Civilization.* Boston: Beacon.

Marx, Karl. 1867/1974. *Capital: A Critique of Political Economy.* New York: International Publishers.

Mason, J. W. 1971. A Reevaluation of the Concept of 'Non-Specificity' in Stress Theory. *Journal of Psychiatric Research* 8: 323–33.

Masserman, Jules H. 1961. *Principles of Dynamic Psychiatry.* New York: Saunders.

May, Rollo. 1977. *The Meaning of Anxiety.* New York: Norton.

___. 1972. *Power and Innocence,* as quoted in *The Great Thoughts,* 1985, edited by George Seldes. New York: Ballantine.

Mead, Margaret. 1961. *Cooperation and Competition Among Primitive Peoples.* Boston: Beacon Press.

Melman, Seymour. 1974/1985. *The Permanent War Economy: American Capitalism in Decline.* New York: Simon and Schuster.

Melville, Herman. 1851/1943. *Moby Dick or The Whale.* New York: Heritage Press.

Merton, Thomas. 1965. *The Way of Chuang Tzu.* New York: New Directions.

Milgram, Stanley. 1974. *Obedience to Authority.* New York: Harper and Row.

___. 1964. Group Pressure and Action Against a Person. *Journal of Abnormal and Social Psychology* 69: 137–43.

Miller, N. E. 1941. The Frustration-Aggression Hypothesis. *Psychological Review* 48: 337–42.

Mills, C. Wright. 1959. *The Causes of World War III.* New York: Ballantine Books.

Moberg, David. 1985. Scientists Say No to Star Wars. *In These Times* 10 (1) (November 6–12): 2.

Montgomery, M. R. 1987. Forgotten Days of the First A-Bombs. *Des Moines Register / Boston Globe.* (August 11): 6A.

Moore, G. E. 1904. *Principia Ethica.* Cambridge: Cambridge University Press.

Morgenthau, Hans J. 1948, 1978. *Politics Among Nations: The Struggle for Power and Peace,* Fifth Edition, Revised. New York: Alfred A. Knopf.

Morris, D. 1967. *The Naked Ape.* New York: McGraw-Hill.

Morrison, Phillip, and Paul Walker. 1978. A New Strategy for Military Spending. *Scientific American* 239 (4 October): 52.

Müller, Albrecht, and Andrzej Karkoszka. 1988. A Modified Approach to Conventional Arms Control. *Defense and Disarmament Alternatives* 1 (3): 1.

Myrdal, Gunner. 1970. *The Challenge of World Poverty: A World Antipoverty Program in Outline.* New York: Vintage Books.

Neumann, Franz. 1942/1944. *Behemoth: The Structure and Practice of National Socialism, 1933–1944.* New York: Harper and Row.

Northwood, L. K. 1977. Warfare-Welfare as a Serious Social Problem for Study and Action. *Journal of Sociology and Social Welfare* 4 (3–4 January/March): 305–22.

O'Brien, Conor Cruise. 1970. *Albert Camus of Europe and Africa.* New York: Viking Press.

Olmsted, Michael S. 1959. *The Small Group.* New York: Random House.

One by One, the Terror Victims are Being Cleared. 1988. *Moscow News* (July): 12.

Orlick, Terry. 1978. *Winning Through Cooperation: Competitive Insanity, Cooperative Alternatives.* Washington, D.C.: Acropolis Books.

Orwell, George. 1956. Politics and the English Language. In *The Orwell Reader,* 355–67. New York: Harcourt Brace.

Owens, D. J., and M. A. Straus. 1975. The Social Structure of Violence in Childhood and Approval of Violence as an Adult. *Aggressive Behavior* 1: 193–211. Cited in Deau and Wrightsman, 1984.

Oxford Dictionary of English Etynology, edited by D. A. Onais. 1966. Oxford University Press.

Parker, Dewitt H. 1968. *The Philosophy of Value.* New York: Greenwood Press.

Pearce, Joseph C. 1977. *Magical Child.* New York: E. P. Dutton.

Pentagon New Speak. 1983. *Village Voice* (May 9).

Peters, F. E. 1973. *Allah's Commonwealth.* New York: Simon and Schuster.

Pike, John. 1985. "Strategic Defense" Will End Hope of Nuclear Arms Control. *In These Times* 10 (1): 3–5.

Pinson, Koppel S. 1966. *Modern Germany: Its History and Civilization.* Second edition. New York: Macmillian.

Plesch, Dan. NATO's New Nuclear Weapons. *Defense and Disarmament Alternatives* 1 (3 May): 2.

Power, Jane, editor. 1987. Star Wars: Faculty Push to Change Foreign Policy, *Higher Education Advocate* 4 (9 April): 1.

Prabhupada, A. C., and Bhaktivedanta Swami. 1972. *Bhagavad-gita: As It Is.* Los Angeles, California: Bhaktivedanta Book Trust.

President Calls Soviets "focus on evil." 1983. *New York Times* (March 9).

Pruitt, Dean G., and Jeffrey Z. Rubin. 1986. *Social Conflict: Escalation, Stalemate, and Settlement.* New York: Random House.

Randi, James. 1982. *Flim Flam!* Buffalo: Prometheus Books.

Raths, Louis, Merrill Harmin, and Sidney Simon. 1966. *Values and Teaching.* Columbus, Ohio: Charles E. Merrill.

Ray, Oakley. 1983. *Drugs, Society, and Human Behavior.* St. Louis: C. V. Mosby.

Roberts, Ron E., and Douglas Brintnall. 1982. *Reinventing Inequality.* Cambridge: Schenkman Publishing.

Roberts, Ron E., and Robert M. Kloss. 1979. *Social Movements: Between the Balcony and the Barricades.* St. Louis: C. V. Mosby-Times Mirror.

Roberts, Ron E., and Thomas Keefe. 1986. Homelessness: Residual, Institutional and Communal Solutions. *Journal of Sociology and Social Welfare* 13 (2 June): 400–18.

Roethke, Theodore. 1966. *The Collected Poems of Theodore Roethke.* New York: Doubleday.

Rogers, Carl R. 1975. Empathic: An Unappreciated Way of Being. *Counseling Psychologist* 5 (2): 8–9.

———. 1957. The Necessary and Sufficient Conditions for Therapeutic Personality Changes. *Journal of Consulting Psychology* 21, no. 2, 95–103.

Romanyshyn, John M. 1971. *Social Welfare: Charity to Justice.* New York: Random House.

Rosenberg, Marshall B. 1983. *A Model for Nonviolent Communication.* Sherman, Texas: New Society Publishers.

Rossi, Peter H. 1969. Theory, Research, and Practice in Community Organization. In *Readings in Community Organization Practice,* edited by Ralph M. Kramer and Harry Specht, 49–61. New Jersey: Prentice-Hall.

Rothschild, Matthew, and Keenen Peck. 1985. Star Wars: The Final Solution. *Progressive* 49 (7 July): 20–26.

Russell, Bertrand. 1964. *Political Ideals.* New York: Simon and Schuster.

———. 1963. *Freedom Versus Obligation.* New York: W. W. Norton.

———. 1930. *The Conquest of Happiness.* New York: Liverright.

Sagan, Carl. 1986. Mars: A Chance for Soviet-American Cooperation. *Parade Magazine* (August 8): 13–14.

Sagan, Carl et al. 1983. The Nuclear Winter: Global Consequences of Multiple Nuclear Explosions. *Science* (December): 1283–92.

Sane. 1985. *Do You Know What Your Defense Dollar Buys?* Washington, D.C.: Committee for a Sane Nuclear Policy.

Scheer, Robert. 1986. Laser Weapons Could Burn Cities in Minutes. *Des Moines Register* January 12: 7A.

———. 1983. *With Enough Shovels.* New York: Random House.

Schell, Jonathan. 1982. *The Fate of the Earth.* New York: Avon Books.

Schwebel, Milton. 1982. Effects of the Nuclear War Threat on Children and Teenagers: Implications for Professionals. *American Journal of Orthopsychiatry* 52 (4 October): 608–18.

Selye, H. 1956/1978. *The Stress of Life.* New York: McGraw-Hill.

Shapiro, Deane H., and Roger Walsh, editors. 1984. *Meditation: Classic and Contemporary Perspectives.* New York: Aldine.

Sherif, Muzafer. 1961. *Intergroup Conflict and Cooperation: The Robbers Cave Experiment.* Norman, Oklahoma: University Book Exchange.

Shipley, Joseph T. 1945. *Dictionary of Work Origins.* New York: Philosophical Library.

Simon, Sidney, Leland W. Howe, and Howard Kirschenbaum. 1972. *Values Clarification: A Handbook of Practical Strategies for Teachers and Students.* New York: Hart Publishing.

Sivard, Ruth Leger. 1987. *World Military and Social Expenditures 1987–88.* Washington, D.C.: World Priorities.

Sivard, Ruth Leger, editor. 1985. *World Military and Social Expenditures, 1985.* Tenth edition. Washington, D.C.: World Priorities.

Skinner, B. F. 1971. *Beyond Freedom and Dignity.* New York: Knopf.

Smith, Maury. 1977. *A Practical Guide to Value Clarification.* La Jolla, California: University Associates.

Sommer, Mark. 1985. *Beyond the Bomb: Living Without Nuclear Weapons.* Boston: Expro Press.

Sorel, G. 1972. Reflections sur la Violence, Paris, 1908. As reviewed in N. McInnes, "Georges Sorel. *Encyclopedia of Philosophy* 7: 496–99. New York: Macmillian.

Soviet Appeal to Congress: O.K. Arms Plan. 1986. *Des Moines Register* (January 20): 1.

Specht, Harry. 1969. Disruptive Tactics. In *Readings in Community Organization Practice,* edited by Ralph M. Kramer and Harry Specht, 372–86. New Jersey: Prentice-Hall.

Staub, Irwin. 1988. The Evolution of Caring and Nonaggressive Persons and Societies. *Journal of Social Issues* 44 (2): 81–100.

___. 1979. *Positive Social Behavior and Morality.* Vol. 2. New York: Academic Press.

Stoessinger, John G. 1974. *Why Nations Go to War.* New York: St. Martin's Press.

Stouffer, Samuel, and Paul Lazarsfield. 1949. *The American Soldier.* New York: Social Science Research Council.

Straus, M. A., J. R. Gelles, and S. K. Steinmetz. 1979/1980. *Behind Closed Doors: Violence in the American Family.* New York: Doubleday.

Strick, Anne. 1978. *Injustice for All.* New York: Penguin.

Sunseri, Alvin R. 1985. *From Medieval Madness to the Mitlamp: War and Society in the Modern World.* Dubuque, Iowa: Kendall/Hunt.

Thomas, Gwyn. 1976. "The Teacher" in *The Penguin Book of Welsh Short Stories,* edited by Alun Richards, 134. Middlesex, England: Penguin Books.

Thurlow, Setsuko. 1982. Nuclear War in Human Perspective: A Survivor's Report. *American Journal of Orthopsychiatry* 52 (4 October): 638–45.

Tinbergen, N. 1952. The Curious Behavior of the Stickleback. *Scientific American* 187: 22–38.

___. 1951. *The Study of Instinct.* Oxford: Clarendon.

Tirman, John. 1985. The World's Nuclear Cop. *Nucleus, Union of Concerned Scientists* 7 (2): 3.

Titmuss, Richard M. 1969. *Essays on the Welfare State.* Boston: Beacon Press.

Tolstoy, Leo. 1948. *The Law of Love and the Law of Violence.* New York: Rudolph Field.

Torture in the Eighties: An Amnesty International Report. 1984. London: Amnesty International Publications.

Townsend, Peter. 1971. Quoted in Hyung Shik Kim, Social Welfare and the Development Process, in *Social Welfare in Asia,* edited by John Dixon and Hyung Shik Kim. London: Croom Helm, 1985.

Tuchman, Barbara. 1984. *The Pursuit of Folly.* New York: Ballantine Books.

Turnbull, Colin. 1972. *The Mountain People.* New York: Simon and Schuster.

UNICEF, The State of the World's Children. 1981. *Associated Press* December 18.

Union of Concerned Scientists. 1981. *The Threat of Nuclear War*. Boston, Massachusetts: Union of Concerned Scientists.

United Methodist Church. 1987. *In Defense of Creation*. The Methodist Bishops' Statement on Nuclear War.

United Methodist Council of Bishops. 1986. *In Defense of Creation: The Nuclear Crisis and a Just Peace*. Nashville: Graded Press.

United States Institute for Peace. 1988. *USIP Journal* 1 (2 April): 12.

von Muller, Albrecht, and Andrzej Karkoszka. 1988. A Modified Approach to Conventional Arms Control. *Defense and Disarmament Alternatives* 1 (3 May): 1, 8.

Wallace, R. K. 1970. Physiological Effects of Transcendental Meditation. *Science* 167: 1751-54.

Walsh, Roger. 1984. *Staying Alive: The Psychology of Human Survival*. Boulder: Shambhala Publications.

Watson, Lyle. 1979. *Lifetides*. New York: Simon and Schuster.

Watzlawick, Paul, Janet Helmick Beavin, and Don D. Jackson. 1967. *Pragmatics of Human Communication*. New York: Norton.

Weinberg, Authur. 1963. *Instead of Violence*. Boston: Beacon Press.

Whittaker, James K., and James Garbarino. 1983. *Social Support Networks: Informal Helping in the Human Services*. New York: Aldine.

Wilensky, Harold L., and Charles N. Lebeaux. 1965. *Industrial Society and Social Welfare*. New York: Free Press.

Willens, Harold. 1984. *The Trimtab Factor: How Business Executives Can Help Solve the Nuclear Weapons Crisis*. New York: William Morrow.

Wilson, E. O. 1978. *On Human Nature*. Cambridge, Mass.: Harvard University Press.

Wilson, E. O. 1975. *Sociobiology: The New Synthesis*. Cambridge, Massachusetts: Harvard University Press.

Wismar, Adolf. 1927. *A Study in Tolerance*. New York: Columbia University Press.

Yudkin, Marcia. 1984. When Kids Think the Unthinkable. *Psychology Today* (April): 18–25.

Zanger, A. 1966/1967. Clinical Empathy as a Function of Attentional

Patterns and Identification Tendencies. Smith College School of Social Work Order No. 67-4156. *Dissertation Abstracts International* 27:4347B–4348B.

Zietlin, Steve. 1984. What Do We Tell Mom and Dad? *The Family Therapy Networker* 8 (2): 32.

Zillmann, D. 1979. *Hostility and Aggression.* Hillsdale, New Jersey: Erlbaum.

Zimbardo, P. G. 1984. *The Human Choice: Individuation, Reason, and Order versus Deindividuation, Impulse and Chaos.* In *Nebraska Symposium on Motivation,* 1969, edited by W. J. Arnold and D. Levine. Lincoln: University of Nebraska Press, 1970. As cited in Deau and Wrightsman, 1984.

Index